Britain Explained
Understanding British Identity

Britain Explained

Understanding British Identity

Martin Upham

JOHN HARPER PUBLISHING

Britain Explained: Understanding British Identity

John Harper Publishing, London
www.johnharperpublishing.co.uk

ISBN 978-0-9934549-7-4

Text font, Palatino; covers, Johnston Underground

Printed and bound by Gutenberg Press Ltd, Malta

Table of Contents

About the author

Martin Upham was a prominent figure in the 'study abroad' world for a quarter of a century, also teaching at Birkbeck College and the Open University. He has degrees from Manchester, Bristol and Hull universities and was formerly research officer of the Iron and Steel Trades Confederation.

He has always combined teaching with writing. His publications include *Trade Unions and Employers' Organizations of the World* (1993), *Tempered – Not Quenched: the history of the ISTC 1951-1997*, and *A Visitor's Britain* (2000) as well as reviews and articles for diverse publications including the Industrial Relations Journal, the Bulletin of the Society for the Study of Labour History and the London Literary Review.

He lives in London.

Preface

This book arose from faculty conversations during my directorship (2004-2014) at AHA International (now GEO) London Centre, which provides 'study abroad' courses for American students. My colleague Susie Thomas had long lamented the absence of a single-volume treatment of British Life and Culture. Yet 'BLC' is a core course on many study abroad programmes. AHA's 'Britain Today' was one such, evolving from political science to embrace UK history and the country's socio-cultural aspects: it gave a context to our many educational excursions.

I wrote *Britain Explained* for the same reason I taught 'Britain Today'. First, to offer a digest of UK particulars. What are Oxbridge, the NHS, a public school or the BBC? Why is the UK a monarchy, multicultural, urbanised yet green? Second, to illuminate a managed society: many enjoy free visits to art galleries, obtain subsidised theatre tickets or receive free health care without asking why.

I wanted to probe identity too. What kind of country is this? Those who once thought they knew are now less sure. While I was writing most political parties changed leaders, 17 million voted to leave the European Union, Tate Modern opened a giant extension and tiny Iceland knocked England out of the European football championships. The old clichés about UK stability now seem inadequate. As author I felt like an unfit marathon runner, struggling to catch up. Study abroad students must feel breathless too.

The methodology is simple. Twenty-one freestanding chapters address individual topics chosen to illustrate the country's character. Each is packed with information, commonly from a primary source – a government agency's description of its role or that of an industry association, court of inquiry or profession. If primary sources were unavailable I used authoritative reportage, often from the BBC, the Financial Times or the House of Commons. Footnotes are deliberately excluded. Of course *Britain Explained* is no substitute for specialised texts or actual experience. Students should still visit the Science Museum, watch a Shakespeare play, attend a Commons debate and read *Mrs Dalloway*. But if they do, they will find it a helpful companion to their explorations.

I am indebted to John Harper, Joan Pegram and Sumitra Upham for their close reading of chapters 9, 12 and 15, and to Susie Thomas for her invaluable scrutiny of early drafts of the first five chapters. I also gratefully acknowledge the positive encouragement of John Harper and Susie Thomas throughout. Opinions, where they intrude, and mistakes – which I hope are few – are entirely mine.

My biggest debt is to the thousands of young Americans from the University of Notre Dame, the University of Oregon, St Lawrence University and many others whose gatekeeper to British culture I was for 22 years. While writing, I was talking to them. *Britain Explained* is written for those following their UK footsteps, and other curious travellers wondering 'what the hell is going on over there?' And – I should add, in the wake of the Brexit vote – it is also very much for my fellow British citizens wondering 'what the hell is going on over here?'

Martin Upham
London
March 2017

1. The United Kingdom of Great Britain and Northern Ireland

What is the right name of the British state? Its correct title (and the name of this chapter) conflates the territorial and the constitutional. Parse it and you start with 'United', a positive adjective but one that implies the possibility of disunity. Next we learn it is a kingdom (more correctly a monarchy), which is a literal truth but also a misleading one. Then follow references to the territorial reach of the state. Great Britain is an island, the biggest in an archipelago off the coast of the European mainland, and the third most populous island in the world behind Java (Indonesia) and Honshu (Japan); added to this, to make the United Kingdom, is part of the island of Ireland – Northern Ireland. Thus what is called the British state comprises the island of Britain (and many smaller islands) to which is added a part of the island of Ireland. 'Britain' and 'the UK' are not therefore strictly speaking coterminous though (as is general usage) it will at times in the following chapters be convenient to treat them as such.

The archipelago contains further complications. There are 'Crown dependencies': the Bailiwicks of Jersey and Guernsey (and its dependencies Alderney, Sark and Herm), known as the Channel Islands; and the Isle of Man. Crown dependencies have their own directly-elected legislative assemblies, administrative, fiscal and legal systems and courts of law. They are self-governing so not part of the UK though the queen is their head of state.

The 20th century was largely an era of nation states, especially after the collapse of empires. It is immediately obvious that the UK does not properly belong. Britain is peopled not only by the English but also by the Scots and the Welsh as well as a growing number of immigrants. That part of Ireland still within the UK brings a fourth, conflicted nationality as we shall see. The English, however, or more correctly those dwelling in the territory of England, greatly outnumber residents in the three minority territories and always have. Historically, English numerical preponderance has propelled expansionism. Wales, by virtue of early conquest, was never a real threat to England after a united English kingdom emerged in the 10th century. Scotland by contrast was a source of chronic strategic insecurity to England until the mid-18th century. Ireland, a separate island, also threatened (English) national security. Always the least malleable domestic conquest, it (or rather the greater part of it) became the first to break away. Only rarely has a genuinely unitary state run the entire archipelago. Most of the time national identities have been expressed within the political system.

The possibility of a disunited kingdom runs through the UK's history

The possibility of a *disunited* kingdom runs through the UK's history.

During the 2014 Scottish independence and 2016 EU referendum campaigns (see chapters 7 and 9) the UK was vaunted as one of the most successful states in the world. If this implied stability and a relatively peaceful society it was persuasive enough: the UK remained an elective (if at first limited) democracy throughout the turbulent 20th century. If it implied longevity, it was highly misleading since the most recent territorial adjustment was the loss of most of Ireland, less than a century ago. Many 2014 referendum observers were shocked to discover that only panicky last-minute concessions averted a Scottish breakaway; the 2016 result caused a global shock. Preserving a United Kingdom of Great Britain and Northern Ireland seems to require constant attention. This chapter considers factors that bind it – the symbolism of flag and crown, constitutional stability and a consensus on civic rights and obligations.

Symbolism

United States visitors to the UK, accustomed to seeing the Stars and Stripes on private land, sometimes remark on the absence of national flags. The flag in question is the union flag (popularly if incorrectly called the union jack) that overlays the English, Scots and Irish flags. While its visibility is increasing it is generally re-served for government buildings and state occasions. Territorially, it is most likely to be found in Northern Ireland where it acts as a vehicle for the beliefs of a majority 'loyalist' population defined partly by a UK identity. There were more flags on show in 2014, the centenary of the Great War and its still-potent memory of loss. The last three decades have again seen frequent actions by British troops, giving the chance for more flag-flying, even though the mil-itary these days fights as part of a multilateral force.

But the union flag is not the only one on display in the UK. In Scotland public displays of the cross of St Andrew (the saltire) out-numbered it long ago, a harbinger – for those with eyes to see – of a recrystallised Scottish iden-tity. In Wales official build-ings may occasionally fly the cross of St David but they are more likely to run up a red dragon on a green back-ground for much the same reason as Scots fly the saltire. In England, least flag-in-clined of the home nations, private flying of the flag of St

Saltire (left) and Union flag, Scottish and the United Kingdom standards (flags)

George increased from about 2000. Flags are always in evidence on sporting occasions but St George is also favoured by parties and factions on the extreme political right: the English Defence League (EDL) and its many predecessors. They are exploiting a certain kind of nostalgia for an imagined England. In 2014 a Labour politician was forced to resign her position after tweeting a picture of a private house draped in the emblem during a by-election. She was under-stood to be sneering at the values of the white working class: her party lost. In Scotland and Wales, sometimes even in Northern Ire-land, the chosen national flag may be found fluttering next to the many-starred emblem of the European Union (EU). This is rarer in England, and indeed a more uncommon sight across the UK than elsewhere in the EU. It will soon be rarer still.

Queen Elizabeth II is UK head of state. For all intents and purposes she has no power despite the definition of the state as a kingdom. The next chapter discusses the distinction between crown and
monarch that lubricates the motor of executive power; here the subject is symbolism. Thus in Northern Ireland, the region least sure of
its future in the UK, a majority identifies with the monarchy in the
most exaggerated way as well as waving the most union flags. It is
not alone. Few Scottish independence campaigners during the 2014
referendum called for a Scottish republic. While they rejected the UK,
they dreamed of a return to the 17th century Union of Crowns under
which one reigning family united separate English and Scottish
states. As for Wales and England republicanism rarely bobs above
10 per cent and is not assertive. Monarchy seems to have an attraction for all classes and regions regardless of political affiliation. The
present queen – the longest-reigning monarch – may not rouse mass
enthusiasm but she does command universal respect.

As head of state, the queen is nominal commander-in-chief of
the armed forces, focusing loyalty. Ships and regiments are named
for her or her family. Many institutions and even some commercial
organisations which enjoy royal sponsorship are permitted to display the royal coat of arms. Crossrail, London's new east-west
rapid transit, has been re-christened 'the Elizabeth Line'. A large
number of arts and scientific organisations flaunt the prefix 'royal'
as do numerous sporting and musical venues and even whole
towns or units of local government. The first new royal park in a
century (built on the 2012 Olympics site) is called the Queen Elizabeth II park. These examples are sectional or local but do indicate
that monarchical values diffuse British society. Given the fame and
longevity of parliament as a democratic symbol, thoughts sometimes turn to who an alternative head of state might be. The speaker
of the House of Commons has been suggested, but he is an elected
politician. Neither he nor any other MP attracts a small fraction of
the respectful approbation given to the queen.

In April 2016 Queen Elizabeth II lit the first of more than 900 beacons across the UK and overseas to mark her 90th birthday. She has
already reigned longer than Queen Victoria (1837-1901) and the line
of succession is secure via her eldest son (Prince Charles, the Prince

of Wales), eldest grandson (Prince William) and now her great-grandson (Prince George). Recent legislation has erased primogeniture, the relic of Norman practice whereby succession passed only through eldest males but this may not be relevant for some time. Court insiders avow that the queen's abdication is out of the question despite her advancing years, but she is mortal and identified with the institution itself. No-one under 70 remembers another monarch, but none has ever been more visible.

Expectations of the head of state in our time have been shaped by this queen. Her coronation in 1953 was the first to be televised and was watched by over 20 million people in the UK. Citizens see her touring the entire country opening schools and hospitals, launching ships and cutting inaugural ribbons. The media regularly project her reading speeches, welcoming visiting heads of state to Buckingham Palace (her London home) and 'showing the flag' – making state visits to other countries (often as part of an export drive). Her reign spans 12 prime ministers and seven archbishops of Canterbury. She has made state visits to 117 countries, travelling more than a million miles. She is universally praised for her dedication to duty and service. Longevity and a certain deceptive familiarity, fed by more than 130 official portrait paintings, have projected her into novels, film, stage and TV. Playing the queen has become a rite of passage for English actresses of a certain age. At the 2012 London Olympics Her Majesty was even persuaded, briefly, to play herself.

It was not always so. A generation ago it was more common to perceive her as the frowsty mother-in-law of the glamorous Princess Diana, estranged wife of Prince Charles. Compared to

Queen Elizabeth II at her coronation in 1953

the touchy-feely Diana the queen seemed stiff, aloof, buttoned-up and incapable of showing emotion even when her daughter-in law died in a Paris car crash. This

A generation ago it was more common to perceive her as the frowsty mother-in-law of the glamorous Princess Diana

negative impression was gleefully played on by the media which was not short of stories: the dubious business dealings of her second son (Prince Andrew), the collapsed marriages of three of her four children, the politically incorrect views of Prince Philip (her consort throughout her reign and five years her senior). The queen, with her many homes, 'posh' accent, tweedy couture, addiction to horses and pet corgis clearly belongs to the landed aristocracy. Yet her very remoteness compounded with the sheer glamour of medieval pretence has made it almost impossible to imagine the country without her.

Yet imagine it eventually must, and so must the rest of the world. The former Princess Elizabeth was crowned at 25 without a trace of political opinion attributed to her and has avoided controversy ever since. Prince Charles is already in his late 60s and has spoken out publicly on architecture (traditionalist), hunting (favourable), GM crops (opposed) and alternative medicines (in favour). Butts of his criticism dislike undemocratic interference from his privileged position. Meanwhile, government ministers hear from him at length, via 'black spider' memos (a cruel reference to the prince's handwriting), responses to the cabinet papers he receives in preparation for his eventual succession. When this occurs his views, unlike hers, will be a known quantity, feeding suspicion of monarchical interference for the first time since the reign of Queen Victoria. Against this it could be argued that the prince has contributed to the modernisation of the royal family not only by entering public controversies but also via the Prince's Trust which has helped three quarters of a million young disadvantaged people to gain work experience and forge careers. The 'royal family' – a Victorian PR invention – may have been little help to the queen in the eyes of

Elizabeth was crowned at 25 without a trace of political opinion attributed to her and has avoided controversy ever since

the public, which tends to approve her but condemn ill-defined 'hangers-on': in fact, the monarchy would be a lot less visible without the princes, dukes and various minor royals.

Constitutional stability

The UK in 1945 had considerable reason to congratulate itself. Leaving aside neutral Ireland, Sweden and Switzerland, no other European country had avoided totalitarian rule or occupation through six years of total war. It had defied Hitler without becoming a police state, retaining much civil liberty, a free press, even holding wartime elections. Perhaps this was evidence of a peculiar constitutional robustness? The UK had after all avoided revolution in the 19th century, extending the pale of the constitution to ever more layers of the population while retaining tried and tested political institutions. It even felt confident enough to export them to many newly-independent nations as it decolonised. This self-confidence was one strand in British reluctance to join the emerging European Economic Community (EEC): what, after all, did it have to learn from such recently failed states? By the 1960s, however, this certainty was faltering. Entry to the EEC in 1973 led over the decades to major constitutional and cultural change. For some it meant lost sovereignty and in 2016 this forced a referendum on membership and a decision to withdraw (see chapter 9).

For almost three centuries, political energy was directed towards unifying the UK under a single system of laws made by a sovereign Westminster parliament. Acts of Union for Scotland (1707) and Ireland (1800) eliminated rival Edinburgh and Dublin legislatures, though a chief secretary for Ireland was thought necessary. Today it seems remarkable for how short a time Westminster sovereignty lasted. Social revolt convulsed Ireland until the 1880s, after which the British government thrice attempted, unsuccessfully, to introduce home rule. Scotland was peaceful after 1745; even so its national identity was acknowledged by setting up a new cabinet office of secretary of state as early as 1885. When most of Ireland was lost in 1921, government gave complete devolution to what remained: Ulster's Stormont parliament was unhindered as it punished nationalists still within its borders. Wales finally received a secretary of state in 1964. Powerful Scottish and Welsh secretaries in a British cabinet might be said to serve to reinforce Westminster sovereignty; a Northern Ireland secretary finally joined them after Stormont lost control of Ulster in the 1960s. But this 'direct rule' now confronted rebellious nationalists with UK state power and the British army, precipitating 30 years of violent conflict.

Late 20th century Westminster went into reverse. 1979's feeble devolution attempts in Wales and Scotland (explored in chapters 6 and 7) bequeathed a sense of thwarted destiny. In 1998 however, the pattern of reinforcing central sovereignty was finally broken. National elective and representative bodies – a parliament with tax-varying powers for Scotland, an assembly for Wales – received powers delegated (devolved) from Westminster. The ripening Northern Ireland peace process allowed a power-sharing assembly to join them: unionists regained a shadow of what they had lost to direct rule and republican Sinn Fein came in from the cold. A sovereign parliament in a unitary state had yielded self-government to its nationalities. While it retained those powers defining the UK – economic and welfare, migration and the control of borders, defence and foreign affairs – it had changed radically in order to stay the same.

But this was not federalism. Each minority nation had a different arrangement and attempts to devolve within England were a fiasco (see chapter 4). Nor did the new dispensation last. The Welsh assembly, by unanimous agreement, will become a parliament in 2021. Northern Ireland power-sharing (which initially required the participation of all parties) is giving way to an experiment with opposition. Above all, Scotland's UK future depends on significant further devolution. Between the Act of Union and the Scottish secretary 178 years passed; between the Scottish secretary and the first attempt to restore a Scottish parliament, 94 years; between this and full fiscal devolution, 37 years. Each shift has a shorter lifetime. The UK constitution stretches back three centuries and more: can it still be said to unite the country?

Civic consensus

If symbolism and constitutional stability bind the Union so too does a consensus about common values. For decades a 'British' way of life was assumed as cultural fact: public moderation in a rules-based society that respected domestic privacy. By 1993 Conservative prime minister John Major, under pressure from Euroscepticism, felt the need to make it explicit:

> 'long shadows on county [cricket] grounds, warm beer, invincible green suburbs, dog lovers and pools fillers and – as George Orwell said – "old maids bicycling to holy communion through the morning mist".'

This vision was more English than British, rather rural for a nation of townies, and male too. It was already obsolete in an England mostly now scornful of deference, newly unafraid of emotion and visibly – not just ancestrally – a land of immigrants. The popular mild addiction of 'doing the football pools'– having a modest bet on the outcome of the Saturday matches – had crumbled before the darker attractions of internet betting, bringing debt and despair to many. Even most of the beer now drunk was continental-style lager, served cold.

Keen minds saw that these and other changes meant that the implicit might now need spelling out. Every city and town of any size was now multicultural, home to a social pot-pourri that certainly included many of the unassimilated. English as a Second Language (ESL) programmes had been in place since the 1980s but beyond this the state had been officially content with celebrating 'multiculturalism': difference in other words. Perhaps 'British values' might be a way of binding Britain's large immigrant (or first generation) population to the British state? This notion gained renewed impetus from the discovery that all four perpetrators of the 7 July 2005 London bombings were British-born with good life chances. The UK,

John Major, Margaret Thatcher's successor: a sentimental vision of a lost England

which had once disdained citizenship in- ***The UK, which had once***
auguration ceremonies on the American ***disdained citizenship***
model, now intro- ***inauguration***
duced them along
with a loyal decla- ***ceremonies on the***
ration or oath. ***American model ... now***
But what were ***introduced them***
citizens to swear
loyalty to? Answering raised the question of
what – apart from the symbols specified
above – 'Britishness' might consist of.
Under the premiership of Tony Blair
(1997-2007) tentative definitional es-
says were undertaken; Gordon Brown,
who was to succeed him, had promul-

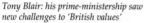

Tony Blair: his prime-ministership saw   gated an explicit list of 'British' values
new challenges to 'British values'   in 2004:

> '...this British belief in liberty has been matched by a British
> idea of duty as the virtue that reinforces neighbourliness
> and enshrines the idea of a public realm and public service.
> A belief in the duty of one to another is an essential element
> of nationhood in every country. But whether it arose from
> religious belief, from a noblesse oblige or from a sense of
> solidarity, duty in Britain has been, to most people, the
> foundation of rights rather than their consequence.'

He later added that 'Britishness has also meant a tradition of fair
play.'

Brown's formula rapidly encountered objections. It was thought
vague, populated by feel-good attributes other nations might also
claim as theirs; more narrowly, what was British as opposed to English about such values as 'fair play'? Was the emphasis on duty
overly coloured by Brown's own Scottish Presbyterian background?
He was not alone in finding 'Britain' an elusive cultural construct.
And with time, the easy economic progress of the early 2000s faltered, the international outlook darkened and confidence in the
'British way of life' weakened. Almost a decade after the July bombings, there were thought to be 730 British citizens fighting with

ISIL/DAESH. A number were making explicit threats on social media to the 'kaffir society' of the UK.

The second decade of the 21st century brought alarms about teaching in faith (usually Muslim) schools, where the arts and liberal values (always included in definitions of Britishness) were said either not to be promoted or to be disparaged while faith-based practices such as gender segregation were imposed. (The education system is discussed in chapter 14.) This led the Department for Education to seek greater precision in the definition of Britishness, specifying 'the fundamental British values of

Gordon Brown, Blair's successor as prime minister: a clergyman's son, he saw a sense of duty as the foundation of society

democracy, the rule of law, individual liberty, and mutual respect and tolerance of those with different faiths and beliefs'. Pupils should acquire:

> 'an understanding of how citizens can influence decision-making through the democratic process; an appreciation that living under the rule of law protects individual citizens and is essential for their wellbeing and safety; an understanding that there is a separation of power between the executive and the judiciary, and that while some public bodies such as the police and the army can be held to account through parliament, others such as the courts maintain independence; an understanding that the freedom to choose and hold other faiths and beliefs is protected in law; an acceptance that other people having different faiths or beliefs to oneself (or having none) should be accepted and tolerated, and should not be the cause of prejudicial or discriminatory behaviour; and an understanding of the importance of identifying and combatting discrimination.' (Department for Education: *Promoting fundamental British values as part of SMSC in schools*; departmental advice for maintained schools, November 2014)

This more sophisticated list encompasses both institutions and values, but it was formulated after centuries when it had not been thought necessary. Nor was multiculturalism the only challenge faced by the state. In both England and Scotland, willingness to self-identify as British was in secular decline. The 2014 pro-independence 'Yes Scotland' campaign cheerfully distinguished 'Scottish' (i.e. social-democratic) values, from what it perceived as the more market-oriented beliefs flourishing 'south of the border' (i.e. in England). Scotland's rejection of British political parties in 2015 and re-election of a nationalist government in 2016 seemed to underline the point. But across the UK four million general election voters had backed the United Kingdom Independence Party (UKIP), a populist party that explicitly rejected multiculturalism, pointedly dissenting from a key pillar in the official definition of Britishness. 'Vote Leave' campaigners in the 2016 EU referendum campaign would capture these and other scattered discontents in a single demand to withdraw and 'get our country back'.

2. Political parties, parliament and elections

The UK parliament is at least eight centuries old. Its origins lay in the need of medieval kings for counsel from the estates of the realm: the landed aristocracy, the hierarchy of the church and the merchant class (the 'commons').

This advisory function developed into a parliament, a combined assembly that eventually gained control of 'supply' – the

The 'Glorious Revolution' of 1688 was the final blow to the doctrine of divine right

funds monarchs needed to pursue foreign and dynastic policy. Its ranks teemed with individuals owing their presence to landed or mercantile wealth: lords and bishops in one house, the commons in another. When in the 17th century religious difference crystallised opposition to arbitrary power, parliament sought to regulate the monarchy, fighting two successful wars against the king. The 'English Revolution' that followed briefly interrupted but did not abolish parliament, and after the Restoration of the monarchy (1660), in the person of Charles II, supply disputes resumed. Three decades later these were finally resolved when parliament consolidated its power as the political vehicle of the English ruling class. This 'Glorious Revolution' of 1688 was the final blow to the doctrine of divine right, confirming that sovereignty (including the right to make law) rested not with the king but with parliament itself.

From this point on parliament would be the crucible of politics, the indispensable instrument of political control, despite being unrepresentative of most of the population and largely unelected. Only the prolonged (1832-1928) extension of the franchise – pressed by the vigorous social agitation of the excluded – changed it. This expanded elective base weakened the unelected House of Lords but

The Houses of Parliament: the crucible of politics since the 17th century. The buildings date mainly from the 19th century

strengthened the elected and therefore increasingly representative House of Commons. Early in the 20th century the Commons curbed the Lords and reserved all tax power to themselves. An ancient advisory institution had become a representative one, however slowly – though universal suffrage was still half a generation away. Votes for 18-year olds (1970) were the only recent franchise extension, though 16- and 17-year olds voted, uniquely, in the 2014 Scottish referendum. If, in the 21st century, parliament's paramount position has been eroded it has occurred through cultural change and shifting political practice.

The parties: history and belief

Within parliament recognisable parties can be traced back nearly four centuries. Tory ('Court') and Whig ('Country') factions formed under the Stuart (17th century) monarchy differed fundamentally over the legitimacy of royal power. In the 18th century this cleavage was replaced by support for the policies of the current monarch or opposition to them (often in cahoots with the heir to the throne). Thus when 1832 brought the first hesitant steps towards a truly representative parliament, political parties were already almost two centuries old. Instead of a new parliament and new parties the old bodies transformed themselves. A new requirement to communicate with – and therefore also to organise – the growing electorate, transformed Tories and Whigs into Conservatives and Liberals (though the word 'Tories' is to this day often used in connection with the Conservatives, especially by their opponents). By 1870 both were behaving like modern political parties. A generation later a new party did emerge outside parliament. Labour (originally the Labour Representation Committee) was formed to achieve working-class representation independent of the established parties. It took Labour only a quarter of a century to form its first government and less than half a century to achieve a parliamentary majority. In the second half of the 20th century it alternated in government with the Conservatives; the Liberals were marginalised. A new two-party system had replaced the old.

Today's party system closely resembles that of mainland Western Europe in its ideological span. Labour and Conservative are both to some degree coalitions of different interests and views; ideologically they overlap, though this does not lessen the strength of tribal identity, at least among the party activists and faithful. During its rise to major party status, Labour demanded state intervention in industrial policy and social welfare. Once this was achieved its radical impulse weakened. The Conservatives, patrician in origin, supplely accommodated themselves to Labour's post-war social-democratic settlement: the term 'Butskellism', combining the names of Conservative leading light R.A. Butler and Labour leader Hugh Gaitskell, came to define the convergence of the two ends of the party coalitions. This consensus about general direction, if not about pace or ultimate destination, lasted a generation; it ended in reaction to the economic shocks of the 1970s, and in 1979 Margaret Thatcher came to power, unceremoniously pushing aside the Butskellites (now disdained by Conservative hardliners as 'wets'). Her government in the 1980s sought to shrink the power of the state, pulling politics decisively to the right.

In almost two decades of rule, from 1979 to 1997, the Conservatives undermined the traditional acceptance of public ownership and state regulation among the public, and in so doing forced Labour to shift its ground too. It returned to office under Tony Blair

in 1997 but branded as 'New Labour', abandoning ideas of nation-
alisation of industries and putting an emphasis on its social agenda.
The two parties eventually found new common ground on the market economy and reformed social services, for all their fierce electoral rivalry. From 2007 recession undermined the Labour
government and it gave way to a Conservative-Liberal coalition
after the 2010 general election. In the 2015 general election Labour
was accused of tacking to the left, but it accepted the need for an
austerity programme, challenging only its undue haste. For their
part the Conservatives continued and extended the social welfare
reforms of New Labour: the new prime minister, David Cameron,
consciously sought to be a Conservative version of Tony Blair and
in some respects appeared more comfortable with his Liberal Democrat coalition partners than with the hardliners on his party's
own right-wing. Much social policy remains contested but with one
striking exception. In government, each party drastically reorgan-
ised the National Health Service but both go out of their way to endorse its principles (see chapter 18).

Unlike in America, issues of 'personal conscience' have usually been kept out of partisan politics

Unlike American political
parties, the mainstream of the
Labour and Conservative parties share a socially liberal outlook. This has had the effect of
preventing what British politi-
cians regard as 'issues of conscience' (abortion, the death penalty,
religious convictions, and the like) becoming partisan ones. In the
1960s and 1970s race relations and gender legislation was pioneered
by Labour, sometimes against Conservative resistance. Since the
Millennium however both parties have fashioned a permissive consensus, the most recent example being the coalition government's
2014 legislation enabling gay marriage (passed with Labour support). Social liberalism is also the bedrock of the traditional third
party, the Liberal Democrats, and if more shakily, of the Scottish
Nationalists, who are now the third largest party in Westminster.
However, the 2015 general election saw the UKIP surge noted in
the last chapter, while the 2016 EU referendum result suggested
popular opposition to the social liberal consensus at Westminster

lurked across the country. This may explain why the electoral ground – at least of the two big parties in parliament – has looked less secure.

Why the parties have declined

At the 1951 general election the Labour and Conservative parties garnered almost 97% of all votes cast. After this their combined share of the vote fell steadily if erratically; in 2015 it was 67% (see table).

1951	97%	
1955	96%	
1959	93%	
1964	86%	
1966	88%	
1970	88%	
1974 (Feb)	75%	
1974 (Oct)	75%	
1979	81%	
1983	70%	
1987	73%	
1992	76%	
1997	74%	
2001	72%	
2005	68%	
2010	65%	
2015	67%	

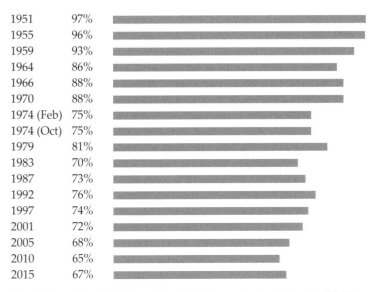

Combined share of the vote of the two main parties, Labour and Conservative, by general election

Over the same period the US Democratic and Republican parties, similarly dominant, were periodically challenged but always re-asserted their duopoly. The British electoral system of locally-counted pluralities ('First Past the Post', FPTP), like that of the USA, greatly favours two big parties but in Britain they are not thriving. Instead British election results increasingly resemble those of mainland Europe, where electoral systems often favour multi-party representation. How is this paradox to be explained?

1. *Failure to extinguish the third party.* US third parties and candidates have tended to be an affair of one presidential election. In the UK, the Liberals, displaced as one of the two main parties in the 1920s, neared extinction in the 1950s, but survived as a deep-rooted party, reinventing themselves as a vehicle for protest votes and social and 'conscience' issues considered secondary by the main parties. From a low point of five seats they rebuilt, gaining 20 per cent of votes (3-4 per cent of seats) by the early 1980s. They then allied with a right-wing Labour breakaway (the Social Democratic Party, SDP), afterwards merging. Thereafter the combined Liberal Democrats corralled about one in five of all votes at general elections until 2010, though the cruelties of the electoral system meant their biggest haul of seats, in 2005, was still only 62. In 2015 their share fell below 8 per cent, reducing their parliamentary representation to just eight. They still attracted nearly 2.5 million votes but these were inefficiently distributed.

    British elections increasingly resemble those of mainland Europe, with a decline of the two-party system

2. *Fragmentation of national identity.* The late 20th and early 21st centuries were marked by growing national consciousness in all three minority territories. Of course Northern Irish politics had never been about anything else, unlike Britain where economic questions have normally been paramount. For decades this was disguised, because an integrated 'Conservative and Unionist' party stood in all UK seats. This was ruptured when the Conservatives introduced direct rule from Westminster, leading Ulster Unionists to organise separately. Since the Catholic/nationalist/republican vote had always been separately organised, Northern Ireland evolved its own distinct party system with contrasting visions of the future of the province: no British parties were represented; no Northern Ireland party sought seats in Britain.

The Conservative, Labour and Liberal parties had always stood candidates in all Scottish and Welsh seats, necessarily so in order to have an arithmetical chance of forming a UK government. All three were unionist parties though after 1959 it was Labour rather than the Conservatives which expressed union-

At the 2015 UK general election an astonishing 56 of the 59 Scottish seats returned SNP MPs

ism better by being strongly represented in all three countries of Britain. Increasingly all three found themselves pitched against surging nationalism, both at general elections and, after 1999, at elections for new devolved bodies in the minority nations (see chapters 6 and 7). By 2007 the nationalist Plaid Cymru (PC, the 'Party of Wales') had been propelled into coalition with Labour in Wales; even more dramatically, the Scottish National Party (SNP) formed its first Scottish government (being re-elected in 2011 and 2016). At the 2015 UK general election an astonishing 56 of the 59 Scottish seats returned SNP MPs leaving the three 'British' parties with one apiece. FPTP did not hinder the SNP. With one million fewer votes, all from Scotland, it returned seven times as many MPs as the Liberals gained in the whole of Britain, replacing them as Westminster's third party.

3. *Proliferating elections.* EU membership, devolution, new elective positions and referenda on top of local elections have made voting an annual experience for most UK voters, providing ample opportunity for experimentation. There are assemblies in Wales and Northern Ireland, a parliament in Scotland, a growing number of directly elected mayors and police and crime commissioners (in England) – the last two attracting a large number of successful independent candidates.

4. *Varying voting systems.* The Greens gained over two million votes in the 1989 FPTP European parliament elections but electing no MEPs. The same elections a quarter of a century later were held on a proportional list system so UKIP, which topped the poll, gained 24 MEPs. The Scottish parliament and Welsh assembly both have mixed-member systems which align the

share of votes and seats more closely and favour smaller parties. Northern Ireland votes proportionally. Greater London has
an alternative vote system.

5. *Popular disaffection.* Scottish and Welsh nationalists have been
campaigning against the 'Westminster establishment' for
decades, attracting a large anti-establishment vote. English voters are also turning away from the three traditional main parties but the impact of their disenchantment on parliamentary
representation is muffled by FPTP. Nonetheless it is real. In
2015 one million Green Party voters and four million UKIP voters returned just one MP for each party. Above all the 2016 referendum disclosed vast disaffection with establishment
opinion, especially in England, much the largest of the three
countries, where millions voted for 'Brexit' (see chapter 9).

6. *Narrowing of choice.* From the 1990s ideological differences between the main parties narrowed. Tony Blair's New Labour
took power in 1997 pledged to observe the spending programme of the outgoing Conservatives. Before he led his party
back to office in 2010, the Conservative leader David Cameron
pronounced himself the 'heir to Blair'. Labour in 2015 was committed to the Conservatives' austerity programme, if not to its
severe timing. In the 1970s and 1980s there had been fears that
the big parties' partisan memberships were more ideologically-
inclined than potential voters; by the second decade of the 21st
century, the fear was that radically-inclined voters were turning
away from the parties! It had an impact. Labour responded to
its 2015 general election defeat by electing veteran left-winger
Jeremy Corbyn as its new leader; in 2016, Conservative Brexit
campaigners struck an increasingly populist note.

Declining civic engagement

The second half of the 20th century brought a sharp fall in electoral
participation. The first four general elections of the 21st century
recorded an average turnout of 63 per cent, 20 percentage points
below the levels of the early 1950s. The main parties reaped a dimin-

ishing share of this diminishing turnout. They also suffered increased difficulty in attracting and retaining members. A parliamentary report commented: 'Membership of the Conservatives, Labour and the Liberal Democrats is at a historic low. In 2015 1.0% of the electorate was a member of these three parties…this compares to 3.8% in 1983.' Labour and Conservatives had each boasted one million members at mid-20th century; by 2015 they and the Liberals were reduced to fewer than half a million. However, this is not the whole story. Other parties have become significant membership organisations: UKIP, the Greens and in Scotland the SNP, which quadrupled its membership after losing the 2014 referendum. Nor are past trends necessarily a guide to the future for the traditional main parties either: Corbyn's elevation from backbench obscurity to the Labour leadership electrified his party, dramatically propelling its own declining membership beyond half a million; the Liberal Democrats reported a surge in membership after the Brexit referendum as 'Remainers' sought a home.

> *There have been 451 women MPs in the nearly 100 years since 1918 – and 192 of them are in the current parliament*

Suffragette leader Emmeline Pankhurst being arrested in 1914. Women over 30 got the vote in 1918, with a property qualification, and all women over 21 had the vote from 1928

The parties have failed in other ways. Since 1918 there have been 451 women MPs. Remarkably this cumulative total is smaller than the number of men currently sitting in the House of Commons! There are 192 women MPs, just under 30 per cent of the House. Eight of 22 cabinet members are female (including the prime minister), as was a narrow majority of Corbyn's first shadow cabinet. The black and ethnic minority population is not accurately represented either, though 2015 brought the first Muslim cabinet minister and 2016 London's first Muslim mayor. Many occupational sectors are also poorly reflected in the House of Commons (agriculture, manual work and trade unions, medicine, engineering); many are over-represented (the law, education, the media). Self-exclusion might also be at work: many feel politics has ceased to be about political parties. Alternative forms of engagement exist, campaigning organisations with narrower aims such as the Campaign for Nuclear Disarmament (CND), the Countryside Alliance, the Council for the Protection of Rural England (CPRE), the Stop the War coalition and the People's Campaign against Austerity.

The electoral system at national and local levels

FPTP enjoyed great prestige in the two-party heyday. It produced clear outcomes – invariably a majority government – and an apparently clear choice of governing parties. The parties published a manifesto and, if elected, legislated key planks of it. Deriving executive power from domination of the House of Commons they could govern until the next election either endorsed or ejected them. Many credited it with underpinning the UK's political stability. FPTP also brought legitimacy to the electoral system by facilitating local representation. The UK electorate was, and remains, divided into local districts ('constituencies') with roughly equal numbers of voters (currently around 75,000). MPs were, and are, expected to speak up for their constituents and all crave the reputation of 'a good constituency MP'. Since the House of Commons is a very large chamber of 650 MPs there is a high ratio of representatives to the UK's 46 million electors. Any shift towards a more proportional system – many different kinds are in use in Germany, Ireland, Belgium or elsewhere – must dilute local representation, first by changing the mechanics of casting and counting votes, and second by reducing the number of locally-chosen MPs.

But as the main parties' voting share slipped, so did the reputation of FPTP and the House of Commons it produced. The Liberals' principled stance against a system which under-rewarded their share of the vote was spiced with self-interest, but over time they learned to win seats despite the odds. As their share rose, so that of the main parties fell. In the 1980s and 1990s governments were elected with large parliamentary majorities but only 43 per cent of votes cast (Thatcher) or 42 per cent (Blair). The alchemy that transmuted plurality into majority was dubbed the 'winner's bonus', its obverse being the loser's penalty suffered by the Liberal Democrats. Yet by 2010 even that did not work for the Conservatives who had to form a coalition with the Liberals. Five years later they narrowly won an overall majority but had attracted less than 37 per cent of the vote, while electing 331 MPs. UKIP, with over 12 per cent of the vote, had just one!

The whole of the United Kingdom elects local authorities to deliver environmental, housing and leisure services. In England not only central but also local government persists with FPTP and with similar results in the shape of single-party domination. Local government is the Cinderella of British politics. For a generation after 1945 it was central government's vehicle for delivering housing and welfare at a local

Local government is the Cinderella of British politics

level. Massive growth of staff and budgets followed, obscuring its reduction to branch office status. After political fashion changed it gradually shrank to become little more than a manager for the delivery of local services. These are partly funded by a 'council tax', a levying power it retains and shares only with the devolved bodies and parliament itself. Turnout in local elections is poor and in by-elections can struggle to pass ten per cent. In the 1990s local Scottish elections went proportional but English and Welsh local voters beyond Greater London only ever experience FPTP.

The legitimacy of parliament

In the 21st century events have confounded traditional observations about voting systems. Many Liberal Democrats had assumed that only electoral system reform would allow them significant representation in the Commons let alone enable them to enter government; the 2010 result contradicted this, making them kingmakers and propelling peacetime Liberals into the cabinet for the first time since the 1930s. While the Liberal star has waned, the SNP has also demonstrated how to win UK seats even under this system – if there is a local concentration. Mixed-member electoral systems for the devolved bodies were partly designed to prevent a nationalist majority. Yet when SNP opinion gained critical mass in 2011 they failed. These more proportional systems accurately represented smaller parties by matching seats won to share of votes cast, increasing their authority and visibility. The impact proved contagious when the SNP advanced from its Scottish dominance to capture nearly all the country's Westminster representation. On a single electoral roll, the chance of voter behaviour 'bleeding over' is strong. Not since the days of Parnell's Irish Party (the 1880s) has a nationalist party had such influence over British politics.

Not since the nineteenth century has a nationalist party had such influence over British politics

In Westminster-speak, 'parliament' is often used as a term specifically for the House of Commons. But parliament has two chambers. Growing doubts about the legitimacy of the Commons might have been offset by a more defensible upper house. But the House of Lords, roughly one-third larger, lacks a single elected member. Until 1911 it was non-elective as the political expression of property, comprising male hereditary peers alone – an apparently impregnable bastion of Conservative privilege. But that year's Parliament Act subordinated it to the elected Commons and also stripped its ability even to consider (let alone reject) money bills. A House of Lords Reform Act (1999) expelled seven-eighths of the hereditary peers but did not address the question of elected members. The chamber has been dominated by 'life appointments' to a title ever since.

In principle the Lords is a revising chamber, whose consent to legislation is needed, but in practice it usually acknowledges the electoral mandate of the Commons. In the Commons MPs ultimately remain loyal to the party leadership because they need their party's endorsement at the next election. The Lords are free of such electoral considerations and have become increasingly likely to defy the government of the day: one calculation lists 450 defeats of Labour in 1999-2010 and 99 of the 2010-15 Conservative-Liberal Democrat coalition. Without its former Liberal Democrat allies in the Lords the new Conservative government lost a large number of votes there after May 2015. No one party has overall control. The Lords have

> *The Lords have become an irritant to all governments but ... cannot be an effective counterweight*

become an irritant to all governments but, lacking the legitimacy an elective base would confer, they cannot be an effective counterweight. However the power of modern governments springs from majority control in the Commons, leaving little incentive to support giving the Lords a firmer base of legitimacy such as would be gained, for example, by election.

Keeping elections fair

The UK is broadly free from gerrymandering. Boundaries are set by the Electoral Commission, an independent elections watchdog and regulator of party and election finance. Its powers are broad, extending to responsibility for administering well-run elections and referenda and ensuring voter awareness. Its report on the 2015 general election found that nine in ten people believed the polls were well run. The Electoral Commission was sufficiently self-confident that it overruled the government on the wording of the 2016 EU referendum question. The government had wished to ask: 'Should the United Kingdom remain a member of the European Union?' but was forced to change to the more balanced 'Should the United Kingdom remain a member of the European Union or leave the European Union?'.

By parliamentary decision the Commission was instructed to produce new boundaries for a House of Commons with 600 members, a reduction of 50. Its 2016 recommendations suggested this could not be achieved without crossing many local government

> *The Electoral Commission overruled the government on the wording of the 2016 EU referendum question*

divisions. If implemented they will take effect in 2020, when the next general election is due.

In respect of party finance the Commission has had some success in preventing spending inflation – the 2015 general election, for example, was less expensive than that of 2005. In 2015 the Conservative Party spent over £15m to Labour's £12m and the Liberal Democrats' £3.5m. Such numbers seem modest in comparison to the stratospheric levels prevailing in US presidential elections. But UK general elections are brief, concentrated into about four weeks: these figures relate only to this official campaign period. Parties also receive some state subsidy for projecting their message: party election broadcasts, free post, access to the electoral register. All parties are of course ultimately constrained by how much money they can raise: there is a long-term pattern of business donations to the Conservatives and trade union donations to Labour. And the UK remains a parliamentary system with each constituency represented by a single MP. At this level there are strict controls over spending to promote an individual candidate: in 2015 the ceiling was about £15,000.

3. Monarchy, government and the constitution

The British monarchy is so adept at creating medieval royal fantasy that many believe it has real power. In fact, two centuries have passed since a king or queen shaped substantive political events; the monarchy as a political player has been in decline for more than three centuries. During that time parliament (and latterly the government that derives its legitimacy from it) has switched dynasties and enforced abdications. At the dawn of the 18th century, a prime minister managed the House of Commons on behalf of the monarch. But today, he or she is final arbiter if backed by a majority of members of parliament (MPs).

Confusion arises only because of the extraordinary effort put into pretending things are otherwise. Politicians speak of 'Her Majesty's government' and 'Her Majesty's loyal opposition'; the armed forces swear loyalty to Queen Elizabeth as commander-in-chief; the monarch in person reads out the legislative proposals of the government of the day to both houses of parliament assembled. But real executive power is now highly concentrated in the office of a prime minister furnished with almost all of the powers the medieval monarchy once jealously monopolised. There are constraints on prime ministers but these are informal and political and the monarchy is not one of them: it is entirely subordinate and cannot resist a prime minister who has parliament behind him or her. A hit West End play of the 2014 season was *Charles III* a neo-Shakespearean fantasy imagining the current Prince of Wales as activist monarch: it ends, literally, in tears.

> **There are constraints on prime ministers but ... the monarchy is not one of them**

The prime minister and elections

The study of true executive power in the UK thus begins with the prime minister. There is no constitutional description of this post: the powers and duties of the current prime minister might be summed up as those exercised by previous prime ministers. Similarly, there is no prescription of the route to office: in practice the prime minister is one who commands – or at least leads – a majority of MPs in the House of Commons. In modern times such a majority has normally been organised in a single political party. Given this backing a UK prime minister is one of the most powerful government leaders anywhere.

How did this combination of opaqueness and crude power come about? The explanation lies partly in the steady assumption by prime ministers of the powers of monarchs, a trend that accelerated once parliament itself became an elected body. All the defining powers – to make peace or war, to appoint to office, to call elections – were derived thus. Other powers like leading the executive, chairing cabinet and being a party leader followed necessarily from the emergence of representative government. Once prime ministers depended less on monarchs than on voters, the ability to manage an electoral majority (and therefore – probably – a parliamentary majority) was key.

The 21st century saw important shifts in the position of prime minister. First (in 2010) came the open combination of two parties – Conservatives and Liberal Democrats – to form a peacetime coalition government. Lack of a single party majority in the House of Commons forced this on them; they coalesced temporarily to form one. They rejected the other possible solution: a minority government with guarantees of support from the smaller party. Forming a coalition allowed leaders of both parties to take office (David Cameron, as leader of the larger Conservative Party became prime minister; Nick Clegg, Liberal Democrat leader, deputy prime minister) and pursue an agreed legislative programme. This coalition defied prophecies of doom and lasted a full five-year term. It also confounded forecasts of impotence by passing a great deal of legislation, some of it radical. Conservatives and Liberals fell out periodically, and sometimes thwarted each other over constitutional issues, but they gave the country five years of coherent government.

Each coalition partner needed to be able to count on the other not to walk out and force an early general election, likely to be disastrous for both. This political necessity led to

this clearly constitutional change was passed on a simple majority

a constitutional change: the Fixed-term Parliaments Act 2011 which provides that general elections will always take place on the first Thursday in May every fifth year. Despite its self-serving character this clearly constitutional change was passed on a simple, albeit two-party, majority.

Dispassionate constitutional consideration might of course well have produced fixed-term parliaments, though perhaps not at five-year intervals. Since the average life of post-war UK governments was then about four years, this neat device brought the parties mutual security without greatly disturbing current practice. An apparently considerable surrender of one of his traditional powers was a sacrifice David Cameron may have felt worthwhile in order to take office as prime minister. Predecessors had been able to pick the general election date, subject to parliament not lasting more than five years, but this power was a mirage. Governments in the 1992 and 2005 parliaments kept going until the last possible moment, but not to their advantage: they still crashed and burned.

Other powers of the prime minister

The heart of prime ministerial power is patronage, notably the power – without ratification – to appoint all members of their own government. This power is checked only by what is politically feasible and can be sold to the public, internal party factions and backbench MPs. In the 2010 coalition, Cameron was constrained by the need to provide positions for the Liberal Democrats. With the resumption of single-party government in 2015, he was nominally free to make all his own appointments and his heir presumptive, the chancellor of the exchequer George Osborne was elevated to first secretary. However, not all in his cabinet proved reliable when it came to the 2016 EU referendum and Cameron's position was not strong enough to exercise authority over his own appointees. He was obliged to allow six of 21 cabinet ministers to break collective responsibility and campaign against the new membership terms he himself had negotiated.

A prime minister's power to make peace or war, exercised with comparative freedom in the 19th and early 20th centuries, does seem to be in decline. In 2013 Cameron had sought Commons support to make a distinctly limited military intervention against President Assad's Syrian regime, engaged in a civil war against large numbers of his own people. History weighed heavily on the occasion. Many MPs rued their vote a decade earlier for war on Iraq at prime minister Tony Blair's request. But Blair's decision to submit to a parliamentary vote had been a political, not a constitutional necessity: the whole country had been bitterly and vociferously divided on whether to go to war and he needed parliamentary backing. This contingent decision created an inescapable precedent for Cameron. Forced to seek backing in his turn, he suffered the merits of his case being judged partly in the light of the earlier, by now near universally derided, decision. He lost.

Beyond the detail of coalition politics – and most Liberals backed Cameron on the Syrian issue – a new limit appeared to have been placed on the prime minister's freedom of action. He seemed constrained by public opinion mediated via MPs worried about and responsive to constituency opinion. Cameron made no secret of his disappointment, or of his wish to reverse the vote, but would not risk a second defeat. He authorised the assassination, probably by drone, of two British jihadis in Syria without suffering domestic political damage. In December 2015 he again presented the case for a Syrian aerial war to parliament, this time seeking to fight not Assad but Assad's

David Cameron: a confident and assured prime minister, he fatally underestimated the Eurosceptics in his own party

most lethal enemies ISIS/DAESH. Now he succeeded. However, it now seems inconceivable that a prime minister could take the country to war without parliamentary approval. This power has been curbed, but empirically and not through a constitutional process.

Cameron made no secret of his disappointment ... but would not risk a second defeat

The return to single-party government

Cameron used his other powers to the full. As party leader in the House of Commons and the country he was widely seen as a plausible incumbent: fluent, articulate, largely unruffled and very confident. This brought considerable electoral advantage to a Conservative Party less popular than he was, despite his negative image in some quarters as a member of an out of touch elite. Late in 2014 two Conservative MPs exasperated by his centrism defected to UKIP, resigned their seats and were triumphantly re-elected on their new party ticket. This increased the already considerable pressure on Cameron to curb immigration (which he had manifestly failed to reduce in line with 2010 commitments), to radically renegotiate the terms of Britain's EU membership and intensified any collateral damage to the Conservatives from their very tough austerity programme that had missed both debt- and deficit-reduction targets.

Nonetheless the Spring 2015 election campaign saw Cameron at his most plausible. He was confident enough to refuse to participate in a live TV debate with five other party leaders, remaining aloof and prime ministerial. Of course, these exchanges do not have the quasi-constitutional status they have acquired in the United States. Even without them, Cameron looked the part and the opposition leader did not. He may even have strengthened his standing by making it known that he did not intend to seek a third term of office, implying retirement before 2020. Perhaps he hoped to avoid the fate of Margaret Thatcher, who had outstayed her welcome and been ousted by her own MPs.

He was to be disappointed. Once the Conservatives returned to office, all their suppressed tensions re-surfaced. Free of the need to appease the Liberal Democrats, they expected to sip from the cup

Once the Conservatives returned to office, all their suppressed tensions re-surfaced

of conviction. Cameron had subdued the Eurosceptics with a 2013 promise to renegotiate Britain's EU membership terms and put them to a national referendum by 2017. As 2015 closed this date began to loom, illustrating the limits not only of prime ministerial, but of parliamentary power. Cameron was increasingly preoccupied with foreign affairs, a common trait of second term prime ministers. But domestically, where Osborne was the prime policy mover, he suffered rebuffs: dissenting cabinet ministers would be allowed to campaign against EU membership, his preferred wording of the referendum question was rejected, restive backbench Eurosceptics broadened their critique of government policy.

The story of the referendum campaign is told in chapter 9. Its impact on politics was colossal, disclosing the limits as well as the powers of prime ministers. Once the country had rejected his renegotiated terms Cameron had little political capital left. He appeared outside 10 Downing Street the following morning to announce his intention to step down. He proposed to serve until October before giving way to a new Conservative leader, but this leisurely plan was disrupted by a fractious fight to succeed him. As rival candidatures imploded one by one, only home secretary Theresa May remained. She was acclaimed new party leader barely two weeks after the Brexit vote. Cameron at once resigned (relinquishing his constituency seat later in the year), moved out of Downing Street and May took his place as the UK's second woman prime minister. It was not the most rapid exit of all time, but as an exercise in people power it had few equals.

Theresa May: adroitly positioned herself to take up the reins of power when Cameron stumbled

May's actions on taking office underlined that patronage was intact. Large numbers of Cameron loyalists were unsentimentally sacked, headed by the combative chancellor, George Osborne. Marginalised figures were brought into the heart of government. Many prominent positions were given to women. Above all, three prominent Leave campaigners were elevated to handle the EU withdrawal process: foreign affairs, international trade and Brexit itself. This last illustrated that prime ministers not only allocate personnel but remould the very shape of government in line with policy priorities: a new inelegantly named 'Department for Exiting the European Union' was but one of several departments reshaped or created as responsibilities were redistributed across Whitehall. In speed and execution, the transition from Cameron to May illustrated the risks and enduring powers of a prime minister. May had not faced election but was the undoubted choice of her party. Since that party retained its majority in the Commons she necessarily became prime minister. Nor had there been a general election, for the very good reason that the UK has a parliamentary and not a presidential system.

In speed and execution, the transition from Cameron to May illustrated the risks and enduring powers of a prime minister

The civil service

Politicians do not govern alone. From the mid-19th century the UK developed a core of high-calibre career public servants working to ministers. They would serve the government of the day but would have an overarching loyalty to the state. Political patronage would not extend to them.

Today 'Whitehall' (sobriquet for senior civil servants running the great departments of state) loyally helps the government of the day develop and implement policy as effectively as possible. While politically impartial and independent of government, it works to ministers in central government departments, agencies, and non-departmental government bodies. The boundaries of the civil service and politics are, inevitably, blurred. The head of the service doubles up as cabinet secretary and secretary to the prime minister; governments regularly seek to reform the service, thus gaining influence over the species if not over each individual.

Admirers of the civil service like to compare it to a smoothly-running and well-oiled Rolls-Royce engine, equal to all challenges; detractors deplore its conservative inclination to frustrate change. *Yes Minister*, the widely-admired and amusing BBC sit-com of the 1980s depicted an urbane permanent secretary (head of department, a 'mandarin' in Whitehall parlance) constantly outmanoeuvring his frus-

trated minister. This is a caricature: not all ministers are publicity-crazed and self-serving buffoons, nor is the civil service necessarily conservative. When transitions, necessarily, occur, 'queen's government' must be carried on. Traditional arrangements allow senior civil servants to brief opposition leaders on pressing policy matters during a general

Downing Street, off Whitehall, is home of the prime minister (No 10) and the chancellor of the exchequer (No 11)

election: today's opposition is tomorrow's government. A further value of this tradition is that wholesale sackings of senior civil servants do not occur after an election: only the politicians lose their jobs.

Altering the constitution

British politics is always enlivened by references to constitutional change, but it is often hard to pin down just what is being altered. Since the UK has no single basic law (a constitution) there can be no prescribed path for amending it.

We have already seen how a simple majority vote brought in fixed-term parliaments, unarguably a constitutional innovation. UK political institutions emerged from this kind of empirical adjustment, plus tradition and convention. Most adjustments at least take the form of law but they may simply arise from executive decision. In such cases it can be unclear whether the constitution has actually changed or not.

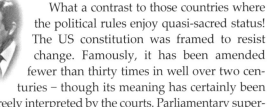

What a contrast to those countries where the political rules enjoy quasi-sacred status! The US constitution was framed to resist change. Famously, it has been amended fewer than thirty times in well over two centuries – though its meaning has certainly been freely interpreted by the courts. Parliamentary supermajorities are required for alterations to take place both in the United States and in Germany (where there is still awareness of how the pre-Nazi Weimar constitution was first subverted by decree). France has a constitutional court to prescrutinise possible constitutional changes. Such is the case wherever a new government system was devised from scratch: every newly-emerging state begins by promulgating a basic law.

Yes Minister: civil servants constantly outwitting their political masters

since the underlying principles of the constitution are a series of ad hoc arrangements ... it has been easy to adjust them

But, as explained in chapter 1, the 17th century foundations of British politics turned on whether king or parliament should exercise executive power. When parliament triumphed, it did not set down new governing principles all at once: there was no 'day one' of the new era. And since the underlying principles of the constitution are a series of ad hoc arrangements and laws disguising a brutal power snatch, it has been easy to adjust them. A majority in a sovereign parliament can do a great deal without admitting to changing the basic rules. The Thatcher and Major governments (1979-1997) scorned constitutional change and vaunted the sovereignty of parliament. The Blair and Brown governments (1997-2010) explicitly led and embraced constitutional change. Yet the first passed the Single European Act, entered the Exchange Rate Mechanism, curbed municipal powers and actually abolished an entire tier of local government. The second transferred significant parliamentary powers to elected bodies in all three UK territories, invented executive mayors, passed a Human Rights Act and attempted more. Both were constitutional reforming governments whether they said so or not. They moved the goalposts without a qualm.

The post-war UK was prestigious, the only European combatant to maintain its political institutions through six years of total war. Small wonder British lawyers drafted the European Declaration on Human Rights, founding document of today's European Court of Human Rights in Strasbourg. And its constitutional influence was not just continental but global: Britain exported its institutions to many former colonies as they gained independence, confident that political stability would follow. It had done the same when Australia, New Zealand, Canada and South Africa gained dominion status; traces of the British constitution survive even in the United States. This confidence was misplaced: these 1950s and 1960s constitutions of Asia and Africa mostly succumbed to ethnic, tribal or political strife.

Even at home, declining confidence in national institutions compounded fears over the fraying of consent. Former certainties vanished, causing the pace of constitutional reform to accelerate and increasing its frequency. The country that prided itself on possessing the secret of gradual change now obsessively tinkered with its public institutions. In barely two decades the UK established the Scottish parliament, Welsh assembly, Northern Ireland assembly (all in 1998); introduced a Human Rights Act, expelled hereditary peers from the House of Lords, switched to a regional list voting system for European Parliament elections (all in 1999); set up an elected Greater London Authority (2000); installed a Freedom of Information Act (2003); recast the historic office of lord chancellor (2003); created a Supreme Court (2009); inaugurated fixed-term parliaments (2011); held a Scottish independence referendum (2014), and a referendum on EU membership (2016). This is not an exhaustive list. It suggests there is great dynamism propelling UK constitutional change. Many further shifts must be expected as the process of EU-uncoupling unfolds.

The country that prided itself on possessing the secret of gradual change now obsessively tinkered with its public institutions

Legitimising constitutional change: the referendum

These constitutional changes were all achieved – at least in part – by legislation, often on a partisan (i.e. contested) vote. Other measures – government for the English regions, introduction of the alternative vote for House of Commons elections – were proposed to parliament but failed the test of popular opinion in a referendum. Yet the referendum was once unknown in UK politics, scorned as the chosen instrument of dictators. Few would take that line today, for Westminster has less and less confidence that its decisions can be made to stick without popular endorsement: the scope for referenda is widening all the time. But while the actual conduct of a referendum is largely determined by the non-partisan Electoral Commission, the decision when to hold a referendum and on what remains a political one.

The US constitution was explicitly designed to resist amendments, and this may have obstructed necessary change, as with Article Two on the right to bear arms. By contrast the UK constitution, a mere century older, might be thought too malleable. Parliamentary sovereignty, its founding principle, legitimises the power of governments to alter the rules of democracy itself: parties enjoying a majority are unlikely to surrender this power; parties hoping for a majority may mute their opposition. Every popular vote diminishes the authority of parliament, yet referenda are now the preferred instrument for resolving irreconcilable party difference and legitimising constitutional change.

It is instructive to compare the 'Europe' referenda of 1975 and 2016. In each case the subject was renegotiated terms of entry; in each case, an embattled prime minister sought to solve a party problem by a public vote; both referenda shattered party unity. But there the resemblance ends because the 2016 decision for the first time pitched popular opinion against Westminster sentiment, with consequences as yet incalculable. No basic law prevents future prime ministers from using a referendum to resolve internal party difficulties. The powerful UK central executive still sharply differs from states like Switzerland that regularly submit constitutional propositions to popular vote, but parliament's sovereignty seems to have passed to the people. The referendum genie cannot be put back in the bottle.

The genie more usefully works its magic as a legitimiser of constitutional change with all-party backing. Voters in Scotland, Wales, Northern Ireland and London were all asked – and agreed – to pre-legitimise new principles of local

The referendum genie cannot be put back in the bottle

government (chapters 4,5,6 and 7); the election of a majority Scottish government on an independence ticket clearly required a further vote there . Yet even here matters remain opaque. Establishment of a special parliamentary procedure for constitutional change has so far yielded only a speaker's ruling to debate it on the floor of the whole House of Commons; the track record of various expedients – a speaker's conference, a constitutional convention – is not encouraging. Who decides what is constitutional change and therefore worthy of a referendum? Some purely executive acts may in time prove more influential. What of yielding the Treasury's monetary powers to the Bank of England (1997), approval of select committee chairs by the House of Commons (2010), and the Succession to the Crown Act (2013)? The 2015 'ministerial code' (mandatory advice to government ministers) was simply issued without parliamentary vote but critics noted it replaced an explicit obligation to 'comply with the law including international law and treaty obligations' with 'comply with the law'.

4. England and the Union

English national identity can be elusive. It can be smothered by elision of terms: English for British is easily said when five-sixths of Britons live in its most populous country. Some visitors conflate England, Britain and the UK, irritating the Welsh, Scots and Irish. It is an understandable confusion given that to this day it is common in other countries to refer to 'the English' as a synonym for 'the British' and in the UK itself terminology such as 'the United Kingdom government', rather than the 'British government', is only erratically employed. Given England's numerical superiority, an aggressive English nationalism would be hard to ignore but for the time being has been largely monopolised by the fringe of the English Defence League (EDL) and the far right – though an echo may be found in elements at least of the United Kingdom Independence Party, notwithstanding the party's name.

The effervescence of London has further complicated – even obscured – England's identity. Whatever social characteristics the country as a whole may have, London – England's capital as well as that of the UK – possesses to the extreme. Many of those outside London worry

Many of those outside London worry that it embodies their unwanted future

that it embodies their unwanted future. The 2016 referendum vote for Brexit will bear many interpretations. One of them is certainly a rejection of so-called metropolitan elites, an assertion of a wider England's claims against its globalised capital.

England clearly rejected the European Union in the referendum, voting Leave in 8 of 9 regions (all except London), but how is it to be represented politically inside the UK? Federalism, never popular, has foundered on the unbalanced populations of its constituent nations. Regionalisation of England, reducing it to manageable components, might have offered a way out, but has died out after desultory experimentation; recent initiatives have focused more on the older structures of city and county.

Most English cities were chartered centuries ago: they are planted in a long-settled landscape. Modern transition to official city status is not on open access and is rather rarely granted. England's 51 cities outnumber the seven in Scotland, four in Wales and four in Northern Ireland. In the entire 20th century only 14 new UK cities were created. In the 21st, Brighton and Hove, Inverness and Wolverhampton were promoted to mark the Millennium; Preston, Newry, Lisburn and Newport to honour the Queen's Golden Jubilee; Chelmsford, Perth and St Asaph on the occasion of the 2012 Diamond Jubilee. This rather mixed list shows that size is no prerequisite for city status; nor is the possession of a cathedral. Meanwhile, most of England's ancient counties have like cities endured. But their boundaries have been rudely shifted for central administrative convenience and some (Rutland, Westmorland) even abolished. Now they face further erosion, this time from elected mayors. But since they remain in roughly the same place they, like cities, remain a convenient way to dissect England.

Who speaks for England?

It was the re-emergence of minority nations that first altered the political chemistry of the UK. England's large population at first suggested the creation of regions more comparable to the Welsh, Scots, and Northern Ireland populations: Yorkshire's population, for instance, was broadly comparable to Scotland's five million. These regions, jealously observing the accumulation of power by minority nations once seemed fertile destinations for political devolution. Labour's early 21st century government proposed to give them strategic assemblies promoting economic development, transport, planning, housing and culture and tourism. But it failed to commit more than minimal resources and could not dispel misgivings about a new and bureaucratic level of administration. When in 2004 the

North East was invited to vote for such a body, it rejected it by almost 4:1 with nearly half the electorate voting in a postal-only ballot. An embarrassed government abandoned plans for similar referenda elsewhere. There was strong local political opposition but there were cultural objections too. Regional boundaries (see below) seemed ill-defined and offended local identities. Many doubted the validity of regional government in England's small geographical area. No further initiatives were undertaken, and after 2010 a successor government swept away all lingering traces of regional administration.

In 2015 the House of Commons adopted standing orders implementing 'English votes for English laws'

For many this was a triumph over balkanisation. Yet among the resisters some sought a vehicle for a strong single English voice. In a reaction to the greater devolved powers promised by an anxious UK government to Scotland in the referendum campaign, in 2015 the House of Commons adopted standing orders implementing 'English votes for English laws' (EVEL). This was a defensive counterweight to wider devolution but not one that passed power from the centre to different points of the English compass. Under EVEL only MPs for English constituencies consider matters deemed by the speaker to concern England alone – effectively a veto. The change strengthened England's political voice, just as devolution had strengthened that of Scotland, Wales and Northern Ireland, but it did not address the imbalance of power and influence between the regions of England or the overweening presence of London.

Government now settled on directly-elected mayors, proposing referenda to establish them in the 12 most populous English cities. Both Leicester and Liverpool subsequently established mayors by council vote and Bristol voted 'yes' by referendum, electing its first mayor in 2012. The other nine cities rejected the mayoral system leaving only 16 local authorities with elected mayors. Government's response was to increase the incentive: more devolved powers and budgets, but only after agreement on a directly-elected mayor. Six established and combined authorities – Greater Manchester, Sheffield, North East (without Gateshead), Tees Valley, West Midlands and Liverpool – agreed to establish a directly-elected mayor model. Three other areas – Greater Lincolnshire, West of England, and East Anglia – are set to follow. The 'Northern powerhouse', of which more below, began as an ill-defined project to redress under-development and, during the remainder of the Cameron premier-ship, grew into an omnibus project embracing devolution all round. An early critique focused on its indifference to local identity, ele-vating the centre's need for a single and convenient point of contact above the distinct (and often rivalrous) identities of towns and an-cient counties.

The parameters of the devolution debate in England are Lon-don's millennium-old predominance; the obduracy of local loyalties – some of them of narrow span; and the absence of an English re-gional government tradition. While administrative devolution to the North has some historical pedigree, it is exceptional. No coun-try-wide framework has endured though it has been tried twice. The seven distinct Anglo-Saxon kingdoms were competing polities mostly dominated by one: the hegemony of Northumbria was eclipsed by that of Mercia which in turn gave way to that of Wessex, which absorbed the others and established England. After despair-ing of parliamentary rule in the 1650s Oliver Cromwell turned to his major-generals to administer regions of England. This turned out to be a very brief experiment, foundering on their varying abil-ities. Each experience preceded the democratic age; both yielded to autocracy. And yet, while the English regions are political pyg-mies they have some cultural reality in their own eyes and the eyes of those that behold them.

That is not to say their borders are fixed in people's perceptions: the nine official English regions are used for some purposes, includ-ing statistics and European parlia-ment elections, but are blunt instruments: those in Kent, the county furthest to the south-east, scarcely see themselves as neigh-bours of those in areas abutting the West Midlands; and not a few in Cornwall, the far south-western tip, with a Celtic heritage, see themselves as inhabiting a land on its own. Such examples could

The nine official English regions ... are blunt instruments

be multiplied. For the purposes of this chapter, therefore, we shall use a simpler formula: East, West, South, North and – the land between all of these four – the Midlands. London of necessity demands a chapter of its own.

East

Of all the English regions the East has the weakest identity. Eastern England certainly includes: 'East Anglia' (Norfolk, Suffolk, and northern Essex) and the Fenlands (Cambridgeshire; the southern part of Lincolnshire, known as Holland). Some national organisations divided regionally add Hertfordshire and Bedfordshire. This, however, dilutes any sense of regional solidarity, while the redrawing of some county boundaries affronted older identities.

This East has an extensive coastline, large rivers and estuaries and comparatively sparse population. In the absence of metropolitan areas, the largest cities are Peterbor-

The nine official regions of England: (1) North East, (2) Yorkshire and the Humber, (3) East Midlands, (4) East of England, (5) London, (6) South East, (7) South West, (8) West Midlands, (9) North West.

ough (200,000), Norwich (under 150,000), Ipswich (130,000) and Cambridge (125,000); no other town exceeds 100,000. The coastline is peppered with modest or declining seaside resorts; at the southern edge Harwich and Felixstowe enjoy significant maritime trade. Rail access to London and the North is good but less so across country. Roads are relatively poor since the nearest motorway travels north along the westward edge of the region. There are universities in Norwich, Bury and Peterborough while Cambridge regularly features as among the top three universities in the world.

The Iceni tribe gave a strong British identity to East Anglia and beyond, though this was expunged after the Romans suppressed the Boudican revolt. The Anglo-Saxon kingdom of the East Angles flourished until the 8th century in roughly the same area and the Fens were the site of the most enduring resistance to Norman occupation. After this the medieval East was distinguished by an intense piety: it is still home to England's most famous Christian shrine (Walsingham). Norwich, long the second city of the English kingdom, had more churches than any other. The region strongly backed the Pilgrimage of Grace, that most dangerous challenge to the Henrician Reformation. Norfolk retains the largest concentration of medieval churches in the world. From the 17th century onwards the region was home to a strong nonconformist element.

The great 17th century work of draining the Fens reclaimed a vast fertile plain from inundation by the Wash but was socially and physically disruptive. The East was the mainstay of parliament in the English Civil War of the 1640s. Oliver Cromwell, MP for Huntingdon, first drilled the New Model Army there. After this the East entered into relative decline. While trading opportunities were plentiful, raw materials were not: it was marginal to the industrial revolution and many enterprising citizens emigrated to the New World. But it was and is the most fertile area of England and source of much home-grown produce. Ethnic diversity in the Eastern counties is relatively low, with the exception of Peterborough, its largest city. However, the region's farms are worked by significant numbers of seasonal labourers from other parts of the European Union. A vast science park housing over 100 companies has grown around Cambridge University. A strong Norfolk accent may be heard across the county and, in diluted form, beyond.

The glory of Cambridge, King's College chapel, begun in 1446

The region has little administrative coherence following the demise of regional health authorities. The East of England Tourist Board embraces only Norfolk, Suffolk, Essex and Cambridgeshire. Yet common concerns do seem to bind the East. The 2016 EU referendum returned an emphatic majority for Leave of almost 400,000. Leave support in Boston, a coastal town, exceeded three-quarters of all votes cast; even Peterborough, the largest city, returned a Leave total above 60 per cent. As elsewhere in England, Leave strength tended to move inversely with prosperity: proximity to Cambridge or London increased support for Remain.

The 2016 EU referendum returned an emphatic majority for Leave

The West

The West certainly contains the counties of Devon, Cornwall, Somerset and Dorset. Arguably Wiltshire, Gloucestershire, and even west Oxfordshire also belong: the Cotswolds (spanning the last two) share something of the 'West Country'. Like the East, the West has an extensive coastline – the two sides of a long peninsula stretching to aptly-named Land's End. The Tamar and, especially, the Severn, are impressive and dramatic estuaries. Also like the East, the West has few large cities though Bristol, with just under half a million is one of England's largest and sometimes functions as a (poorly-located) regional capital. Like Bristol, Plymouth (250,000) and Exeter (125,000) suffered massive bomb damage and lost population after World War II. However the former rail town of Swindon (over 200,000) is enjoying resurgence partly due to rapid access to London. Bournemouth, one of England's boom towns, approaches 200,000. The motorway system reaches as far as Exeter but not beyond, leaving Plymouth and the western (i.e. Cornish) peninsula poorly served. Rail links beyond Exeter are also poor, focusing on one spinal route with occasional branch lines. Their vulnerability was exposed when a coastal section of the main line was destroyed by a 2014 storm: no trains ran for weeks.

Cornwall (Kernow) is perceived to share a Celtic past with Wales, Ireland and Western Scotland though its language (Kernewek) barely survives, kept alive by some enthusiasts but largely ignored by the county's half-million residents. Cornwall exported tin from its own mines in the Iron Age; in the industrial revolution its china clay trade flourished. Fishing, once a mainstay, is much reduced but the establishment in 2012 of the University of Falmouth has made higher education local for the first time. Today Cornwall's main business is tourism, the benefits of which divide opinion: the north coast town of St Ives, famed among painters for its light, has banned property sales to second-home buyers. Devon, also popular with tourists, shares some of Cornwall's sense of apartness but has a more robust economy. Further east, Dorset and Somerset project little sense of regional solidarity even if outsiders ('grockles') detect a unifying West Country accent. There are universities in Plymouth, Exeter, Bath and Bournemouth. The University of Bristol is one of England's most prestigious universities, the elder of the two in the city.

In the 1st century AD the region was easily pacified by the Romans. Though it contains the core territory of the Saxon kingdom of Wessex (from which the English kingdom first grew) it offered

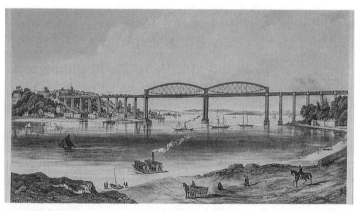

Isambard Kingdom Brunel's 1859 bridge across the Tamar. The bridge still links Cornwall with the wider South West by rail, though to Cornish traditionalists the land beyond the bridge is virtually 'another country'

no prolonged resistance to the Norman occupation or to the Reformation. Bristol was a strongly parliamentary city in the Civil War but elsewhere loyalties were mixed: there was brutal fighting the length of the peninsula. Though not without mineral resources, the West lacked the strategic materials whose extraction powered the industrial revolution elsewhere and so, like the East, it did not share in the explosive population growth of the 18th and 19th centuries. Bristol, and to some extent Plymouth, waxed on the Atlantic trade in slaves, founding important industries like tobacco processing in return. Later they thrived on trade in manufactures and passengers but expanding air travel and the maritime shift towards Europe of the later 20th century disadvantaged them as ports.

After World War II the whole region derived considerable economic benefit as a playground for the holidaying masses, boosting the regional economy and giving the West an identity in visitors' eyes. Some residents are ambivalent, lamenting the extinction of traditional industry and fishing. The 2016 referendum saw a regional majority for Leave of more than 150,000. At first sight there was a strong urban bias to Remain with Bristol and Exeter returning majorities nearing three-quarters. Yet Bournemouth, for all its language schools, voted 5:4 for Leave, as did Swindon; the Leave majority in Cornwall was greater still and even higher in Plymouth.

The South

The South of England eludes exact definition. Longitudinally, where does it end and West or East begin? Latitudinally, where does it yield to the Midlands? And how is it to be considered separately from the giant metropolis it encloses? Administratively and in the 2016 referendum it has been convenient to demarcate a 'South East', meaning the bottom right-hand side of the country minus London. The wider South certainly includes the southern coastal counties of Hampshire, Sussex, Kent and the Isle of Wight. Moving northwards, Berkshire, Surrey, Buckinghamshire, much of Northamptonshire and Oxfordshire also seem to belong (though Oxfordshire has at times been allocated to the Midlands); on cultural grounds Essex, Hertfordshire and Bedfordshire should be included too. Thanks to neighbouring London, the region's transport links are good, for the principal routes by road or rail all radiate through these counties: Southern Railways was the first in England to electrify. Rivers, even the Thames at a distance upstream from London, are modest and there is little visual drama.

The pattern of settlement of the South contrasts especially with the North. It is not a region of large conurbations: instead modest but busy towns and well-peopled villages are sprinkled liberally across the landscape. The principal cities are relatively small and all of them are distinct places rather than part of conurbations: Southampton (250,000), Brighton (285,000) Milton Keynes (a new post-war town, 250,000), Northampton (above 200,000), Portsmouth (200,000), Reading (150,000) and Oxford (125,000).

However, most towns in the South – in contrast with those in the North – have grown substantially in recent decades, once sleepy market towns becoming bustling urban centres in a web with London at its heart.

Whether broadly or narrowly defined the South has been more prosperous than the North at least since the Norman Conquest of 1066.

The Royal Pavillion, built for the Prince Regent (later George IV) in the early nineteenth century at the heart of the newly fashionable seaside resort of Brighton

For a millennium it has benefited from proximity to London, though contemporary complaints abound that its towns and cities are becoming dormitories for the capital. Over the same period it has been richly-resourced: abbeys and churches in medieval times; handsome coaching towns thereafter. Its principal natural resources – Purbeck marble and

the South has been more prosperous than the North at least since the Norman Conquest

Cotswold stone – are building materials, leaving a pre-industrial legacy that in post-industrial England easily converts to wealth. Wool was the main economic product of these shires before the industrial revolution but its ancient woollen products industry remained small-scale when that of the North took off; of the industrial revolution itself there is little enduring sign. There are major universities in Southampton, Brighton (Sussex), Canterbury (Kent), and Reading. Oxford is regularly one of the top three performing universities globally (and No.1 in 2016): its adjacent science park houses over 60 companies. Much of picture-postcard England may be found in the South: thatched cottages, gentle streams, manageable hills, and pleasant villages grouped around a green overlooked by church and pub.

The prosperity of the South appears to have driven a strong Remain vote in the 2016 EU referendum but it was insufficient to carry the region. The pro-Remain preferences of Oxford and Reading might be unsurprising, but coastal Southampton, as well as Portsmouth, voted Leave. A thick band of rural areas stretching north-west from Sussex to Oxfordshire backed Remain, but were almost the only ones in England to do so. To the east of London, Kent and Essex were solid Leave territory as were the other rural areas and smaller cities and towns.

The Midlands

The Midlands is a region that is hard to pin down. It is, seemingly, defined less by what it is than by what it is not – it is what lies south of the North and north of the South. This amorphousness regularly stimulates other attempts to give this large and populous region coherence, principally a division into East (Derbyshire, Leicestershire, Nottinghamshire, possibly Lincolnshire) and West Midlands (Warwickshire, Worcestershire, Staffordshire, possibly Shropshire). Between the two lie not only considerable distances but a sharp contrast of accents. There are large rivers: the Avon, the Ouse, the Trent. Birmingham (1.1 million) lays claim to be England's second city, as it once did to being the 'second city of the empire' (a claim robustly disputed by Glasgow). Stretching north-west from Birmingham as far as Wolverhampton (population 250,000) is the 'Black Country', whose name testifies to its urbanisation in the age of smoke and grime of the industrial revolution. The Birmingham-Black Country conurbation has a population comfortably in excess of two million.

Other large centres are Coventry (350,000), Leicester (325,000), Nottingham (over 300,000), Derby (250,000) and Stoke-on-Trent (250,000). Midlands cities generally have highly concentrated immigration and ethnic diversity, a high birth rate and relatively young population. Residents are less likely to define themselves as being from the Midlands than to self-identify locally: as a 'Brummie' (from Birmingham), from the Black Country, or from the Potteries (the clay-products producing area around Stoke-on-Trent). Few in the West Midlands feel an affinity with those in the East Midlands, and vice-versa. When elected mayors were first on offer, Coventry (straddling the East and West Midlands and 22 miles from Birmingham, centre to centre) was reluctant to throw in its lot with a West Midlands metropolitan mayor.

Important Roman roads crossed the Midlands. At the intersections were fortified camps, the origins of many of today's cities. Mercia, a powerful Saxon state, stretched from the Welsh border to East Anglia and even included London. Its eventual fusion with Wessex led to the first English kingdom. Medieval times saw the Midlands endowed with rich abbeys and cathedrals; many key battles of the 17th century Civil War were fought here. The Midlands is considerably more industrial than the South, though its mineral wealth (coal, iron, china clay) is no longer exploited. Sophisticated transport systems facilitated fast coastal access for its products: in the 18th century, canals; in the 19th coal-powered locomotives; today motorways and electric rail. In the 18th and 19th centuries the West Midlands was home to a vast network of smaller, craft-based workshops and factories; in the 19th and 20th textiles output thrived in the East Midlands. After World War II the UK car industry made its home here, introducing mass production for the first time. Despite this it remains a region primarily of workshops and crafts, not heavy industry. There are major universities at Birmingham, Coventry (Warwick), Nottingham and Leicester.

Residents are less likely to define themselves as being from the Midlands than to self-identify locally

Though at the heart of England, the Midlands, perhaps because of the very lack of a distinct regional identity have tended to be overshadowed not just by the South but by the North. Birmingham is England's second city by population but it is Manchester that is generally seen as England's second city – the BBC's second home, the location of the biggest airport outside the London area, the home of the biggest university population outside London and dwarfing Birmingham in sporting prestige. The Midlands have much pleasant pastoral scenery but this is rarely a destination: it is more commonly seen by travellers through the window of a car hurrying elsewhere along the motorways that crisscross the region.

A motorway sign: the Midlands can seem a sort of no man's land uneasily poised between the two strong identities of North and South

The North

From 2014 an assortment of infrastructural notions and political reforms sponsored by then chancellor of the exchequer, George Osborne, acquired the label 'Northern powerhouse'. It was a political response to a gathering sense that the UK economy was regionally unbalanced with the South – and especially London – generating and enjoying too much of the national income. The 2011 census figures revealed that the North's share of England's population has fallen to its lowest point since 1821. The concept of the Northern powerhouse calls for coherent agglomerations of local authorities, doing some violence to rival local identities across this vast region.

the North's share of England's population has fallen to its lowest point since 1821

Though counties have swapped territory here and there, the boundaries of the North are not disputed. The region comprises Lancashire, Yorkshire, north Cheshire, Cumbria, Durham, north Derbyshire and Northumberland and stretches to the Scottish border. However, it contains three component identities, each separately acknowledged in the 2016 referendum: the North West (including the major cities and towns of southern Lancashire); Yorkshire and Humberside; and the North East of Northumberland and Durham, of all regions the one least marked by multi-ethnicity and the one whose population is growing most slowly. Cumbria (an amalgam of ancient Cumberland and Westmorland) is uneasily north-western but has much in common with the North East.

The North contains England's most dramatic scenery, much of it in national parks (see chapter 21). It is cleaved by great rivers: the Humber (confluence of the Ouse and Trent), Tees, Tyne and Tweed to the east; the Mersey, Ribble, Lune and the Solway estuary to the west. The Pennine chain runs like a spine through the North, a rugged natural boundary dividing Lancashire from Yorkshire, Cumbria from Northumberland; Cumbria's Lake District is home to England's highest mountains. The geophysical picture is completed by the complicated coastline of the west coast, the empty and endless littoral of the east coast. Until modern times it was the most turbulent English territory, with a rich tradition of armed resistance.

Roman imperial rule centred on York (Eboracum) near to the location of one of the last great revolts against them by the Brigantes, a British tribe. In the 5th and 6th centuries the Northumbrian Anglo-Saxon kingdom was England's strongest. It was a cradle of European Christian culture, at first distinctively Gaelic rather than Roman. Its famous monasteries produced the Lindisfarne Gospels and the first English history. This great age was ended by the Viking invasions that in the 10th century culminated in a new kingdom ruling half of England from York (Jorvik). Resistance to the Norman invasion of William the Conqueror led in 1070 to the 'Harrying of the North', a ruthless devastation of the whole territory and its people. Despite this brutality a distinct Northern identity survived and found new expression via the bishops-palatine of Durham, the Archdiocese of York (see chapter 13) and – later –

The industrial revolution indelibly etched the image of the North

the medieval Council of the North with its own lord president. In the 16th century successive Northern adherents of the 'Old Faith' rose against Protestant Tudor rule; in the English Civil War, the king initially held the North but the towns mainly held for parliament.

The industrial revolution indelibly etched the image of the North. This is the classic region of big English cities such as Leeds (750,000), Sheffield (550,000), Manchester (500,000), Liverpool

(475,000) and Newcastle (275,000). It is also the region of conurbations: Manchester is at the heart of a sprawling area of suburbs and semi-distinct towns which together have in excess of 2.5 million people; one and a quarter million live in the Leeds-Bradford conurbation; between Newcastle and the coast is a continuous necklace of towns along the river Tyne – a conurbation of 800,000; over a million live in Liverpool and its hinterland, on both sides of the Mersey.

Many Northern cities are centuries old but were small until the industrial revolution. Their transformation to major urban centres arose either from their proximity to raw materials or their emergence as transit points for the manufactures made from them. In the course of barely a century each city passed from unplanned chaotic growth to urban development and civic pride, building city halls, libraries, art galleries, concert halls and – eventually – universities. From 1750 onwards, English coal-mining, iron & steel, engineering, textiles and shipbuilding were all concentrated in the North: the 19th century empire provided it with a vast global market.

Through the first half of the 20th century the North remained a stronghold of industry, albeit with times of slump and unemployment, especially between the wars. The 1930s, however, showed the first signs of a future trend: while traditional industries in the North stagnated – 'the thirties' becoming a synonym for unemployment in the North – in London and the South new light industries sprang up along arterial roads, with a housing boom in their wake. North and South were diverging and the process slowly gathered pace after World War II as industries such as cotton (Lancashire), coalmining (widely in the North), shipbuilding (especially in the North East) and engineering (especially in Lancashire and Yorkshire) subsided in the face of foreign competition in former export markets and imports to the UK of cheaper foreign substitutes. The shops of once thriving Northern towns became filled with imported goods that they had once made themselves; the oceans of the world were no longer ploughed by ships made on Tyneside fuelled by Northern or Welsh coal. Even those imported goods no longer arrived by ship in Liverpool but came in containers by air or sea to ports in the South.

In the decades after World War II the Northern cities lost population and became subordinated to central government policy and increasingly took on the character of branch offices delivering the welfare state. While local government grew exponentially, its scope for political initiative shrank. Services replaced manufacturing as the main source of employment. The expansion of higher education from the 1990s provided another major source of employment and income as thousands of students poured into cities all over the North. Today a reliance on public sector employment and the student economy is a feature of many towns. Among the most prominent universities are Durham, Leeds, Liverpool, Manchester, Newcastle, Sheffield and York. The pattern of immigration has been mixed with large Asian communities in some towns: likewise the pattern of assimilation has also been mixed and in some declining industrial towns there is a sharp spatial separation between the Asian and white populations.

Blackpool's half-size replica of the Eiffel tower. The North's premier resort once rivalled the South's Brighton, but while today's Brighton booms, Blackpool has become dilapidated, a symbol of Northern decline

Manchester has been the most successful of the Northern cities in raising its national profile and also the greatest beneficiary of administrative devolution from London. The Northern powerhouse emerged first as a set of plans to boost Manchester. The broader Northern powerhouse concept requires directly-elected mayors to rule vast metropolitan areas, subordinating major towns (for instance: Bolton population 275,000, is part of the Manchester Metropolitan Area). Such steps may offend local identities, but the Cameron government was willing to devolve considerable planning and transport powers to city regions such as this. Devolved taxation is also promised. Meanwhile, Blackpool, Bradford, Newcastle-Gateshead and Sheffield have been shortlisted to host a two-month

Great Exhibition of the North in 2018 to showcase the region's creative, cultural and design sectors.

North and South

The North cradles strong local identities. Those from Newcastle ('Geordies') or from Liverpool ('Scousers') speak distinctively and have a fierce pride in their cities – more particularly, perhaps, when in other parts of the country. Natives of Yorkshire, the largest county (big enough to be divided into thirds – 'ridings' – until the late 20th century), also assert a strong identity. Yorkshire simply assumes itself to be England's premier cricketing county; the formerly Lancastrian cities of Liverpool and Manchester each house two of the Premiership's leading football clubs. Such local loyalties thrive independently but are also swept up in a broad Northern identity which contrasts itself most specifically with that of the South. Stereotypes abound either side of this division, which would probably push the boundary thirty miles south of the administrative North. (The South, on this approach is the not-North, and emphatically includes London, the Midlands being ignored.)

As seen from the North, Southerners are caricatured as limp-wristed, effete, evasive, hypocritical and posh, the kind of people Macbeth probably had in mind when he learned of Malcolm's flight to England: 'let him dine amid the English epicures'. Northerners suffer their own caricature in the South: uncouth, uncultured, gruff, moody and without finesse. There is no Southern equivalent of *Coronation Street*, Manchester-based Granada TV's Channel 3 evening soap now well into its sixth decade: *EastEnders*, BBC's younger rival product, projects a London rather than a Southern identity (though viewers from Mars, observing the plain-speaking, pub-frequenting, urban-dwelling class-defined character of both might conclude that the English, or some of them, north and south, have rather a lot in common). It is tempting to date these ludicrous caricatures from the industrial revolution that launched each half of the country on a different course but they stretch back to

These caricatures ... stretch back to Shakespeare and before

Shakespeare and before: the contrasting temperaments of the vol-
canic Hotspur and the roistering Prince Hal; the sturdy independence of the Northern lords; the tradition of revolt; the blunt
God-fearing character of the Mystery Cycles of Chester and York.

Today's electoral pattern of left-leaning cities and right-leaning
shires palely reprises the pattern. The Conservatives are largely unrepresented in the local government of Northern cities where
Labour's grip is very strong. They are well represented in the
county authorities however. The cities vote Labour at general elections while rural seats and market towns tend to fall to the Conservatives. The change in regional fortunes is reflected in the fact that
once-safe suburban Conservative parliamentary seats in parts of the
North have since the 1980s shifted to Labour, a counter-balance to
the displacement of Labour in parts of the South. In the 2016 referendum Leave votes were often returned by cities overshadowed by
larger neighbours: Bradford (by Yorkshire's commercial hub of
Leeds), Sunderland (by Newcastle, the North East's fulcrum). And
there is a further difference. The propensity to eat well (measured by consumption of fresh and processed
fruit and vegetables) broadly declines
across UK regions from
south to north, as do educational attainment and
work prospects. While
parts of the North are
and long have been dis-
tinctly prosperous, the North

The pub in the TV soap 'Coronation Street': first
broadcast in 1960, its portrayal of the North, part
realistic and part pastiche, confirmed traditional
peceptions

as a whole suffers from the perception that its 'best days' are
behind it and that it is in continued long-term decline – a
perception that the Northern powerhouse was intended to combat.
Balancing the need to sustain the UK economy as a whole with the
demands of Northern regeneration remains a challenge for any government.

5. Ireland and the Union

Ireland began the re-Christianisation of what are now Scotland and England in the 6th century. In the Viking era it attacked western Britain. It first suffered invasion by England in the 12th century, but mounted such resistance that new attempts at conquest were constantly undertaken. The reformed religion that captured 16th century England, Scotland and Wales never rallied a majority of the Irish. Their Catholic church, by its very success in resisting the Reformation, reinforced a sense of national feeling among the Irish and the 'old English' (early settlers) alike. This fixed the alien character of Ireland in English and Scots perceptions.

In the late 16th century adventurers from both countries, backed by the crown, seized land, especially in the northern province of Ulster. Their acquisitiveness was coloured by missionary zeal, founding colonial 'plantations' that continued into the new century and rooted Presbyterianism for the first time in Irish soil. Land seizures accomplished what conversion could not.

In the dynastic wars of the 17th century and the proto-revolutionary conflicts of the 18th, Ireland's national interest conflicted with the ambitions of an

The nineteenth century brought explosive conflicts over land ownership

ever more powerful and newly imperial British state. 1800 brought an Act of Union on the Scottish model, dissolving the Irish parliament in exchange for Westminster representation.

This assertion of UK parliamentary sovereignty suggested that any future Irish insurgency would directly confront central British power, and so it proved. The nineteenth century brought explosive conflicts over land ownership and sporadic but elemental eruptions

in protest at British rule. Attempts by Liberal governments to reform land ownership and devolve 'home rule' powers to Ireland
stumbled on the intransigence of English landowners, backed by
the Conservative Party, and the implacable opposition of Ulster
'loyalists' to any weakening of the Union. On the eve of World War
I the greatest crisis facing the British government was Ireland,
where tens of thousands of Ulstermen had formed the paramilitary
Ulster Volunteer Force to resist the plans of the Liberal government
to give home rule to the whole island – in which the mainly Protestant people of Ulster would become a minority. Led
by Sir Edward Carson, and with many open sympa-
thisers in the British military, their uncompromising
slogan was 'Ulster will fight and Ulster will be
right'; civil war seemed imminent. Only the onset
of the wider continental conflict defused the immediate crisis as the government suspended its
plans and many Irish from both North and
South volunteered to fight against Germany.
A chaotic insurrection in Dublin in 1916
(the Easter Rising) was quickly suppressed
by the British but after the pro-home rule
Irish Party was beaten by the republican
Sinn Fein ('Ourselves Alone') at the December 1918 general election, Sinn Fein re-

*Sir Edward Carson: 'Ulster
will fight and Ulster will be
right'. His statue still has pride
of place outside the Stormont
parliament building*

fused to take up its seats at Westminster, declaring the
independence of the whole island. Between 1919 and 1921 a brutal
if rather haphazard war, the Irish war of independence, was fought
between British troops and Irish police on the one hand and the
Irish Republican Army on the other. The military conflict was in-
conclusive but by the Anglo-Irish Peace Treaty of December 1921
most of Ireland was organised into an 'Irish Free State' (what would
later become the modern-day Republic of Ireland). Meanwhile the
UK retained six of the nine counties of historic Ulster; these six
counties brought into one polity (Northern Ireland, often referred
to simply as Ulster) most of the Protestant population, but also with
a substantial Catholic minority, a harbinger of future strife. Now
the two religious and political identities of Ireland had taken state

form there could be a new United Kingdom of Great Britain and Northern Ireland (1921).

This, the most recent territorial change in the UK's jurisdiction, reintroduced an armed border into the islands for the first time in three centuries.

the Republic of Ireland ... continued to formally assert sovereignty over the whole island of Ireland until 1999

This concession by a Britain weary of strife ended the Anglo-Irish war, but was the prelude to civil war in the Free State between the new post-revolutionary government and those unprepared to leave any part of Ireland in British hands. Despite these bitter internal differences, and the evident fact that Northern Ireland was a reality it could not change, both the Free State constitution and that of the Republic of Ireland (Eire, proclaimed 1949) nonetheless continued to formally assert sovereignty over the whole island of Ireland until this was abandoned in 1999 as part of the Northern Ireland peace process.

But the separation of the South from Britain was real and gradually the experiences of the two islands diverged yet further. Britain was transformed by World War II, the post-1945 inauguration of the welfare state, and increasing affluence, diversity and tolerance in the 1950s and 1960s; Eire chose neutrality, left the Commonwealth, suffered economic stagnation, dallied with Celtic obscurantism, and was culturally stifled by a socially conservative Catholic church, whose cultural paramountcy was for decades constitutionally guaranteed. Male emigration, primarily to Britain but also to the United States, boomed. Only in 1973, when both countries entered the then-EEC simultaneously, did common experience again start to shape them.

Northern Ireland within the UK

Meanwhile, within the territory of the new UK state a new front opened. Northern Ireland's Catholic minority was unreconciled to remaining under British rule. It now found itself at the mercy of an isolated Protestant majority determined to retain local power and a British identity, and quite unafraid to use sectarian methods. By the Government of Ireland Act 1920 Westminster delegated virtual autonomy to Northern Ireland. Mainland politicians like Winston Churchill, tired of the impact of the 'dreary steeples of Fermanagh and Tyrone' on British politics, sought to separate Northern Ireland from mainstream British affairs. Ulster was left to its own devices, subsidised but largely self-governing. The unionist majority were happy to have it that way. Though the term was then unknown, this was devolution, 1920s-style. Northern Ireland became locked into a relationship of permanent antagonism with the Republic, though in many respects the social and cultural norms of Ulster – the predominance of religion, the traditionalist view of personal morality – more closely mirrored those of its southern neighbour than those of a fast-changing Britain.

Until the late 1960s, by convention Northern Irish affairs were not even discussed at Westminster; the province trod its own dangerous path. Discrimination against Catholics in employment and housing was endemic. Constituency boundaries were gerrymandered to reduce nationalist representation at Stormont, the new local parliament. Naturally protests at this sectarianism occurred: they were brutally suppressed by a new and Stormont-controlled Royal Ulster Constabulary (RUC) from which

Ulster was left to its own devices ... the unionist majority were happy to have it that way

Catholics were absent. For some decades a sporadic low intensity border war continued, waged by republican volunteers (calling themselves the Irish Republican Army, IRA) and the RUC.

Gradually however the attractions of armed struggle waned. By the 1950s the IRA had begun to engage in conventional community politics and disposed of its guns. This was not, however, because sectarianism had declined for Protestant (in reality Presbyterian) ascendancy was constantly asserted. Its most vivid expression was the Orange Order, a masonic association whose frequent marches and bands noisily reminded everyone who was in charge. Very occasionally the conflict would even spread to the mainland, shaping politics and football loyalties in Liverpool until at least 1945 and Glasgow long after that. Meanwhile Ulster regularly sent 'Unionist' representatives to the UK parliament where they operated as part of the Conservative and Unionist Party. Like the republican South the unionist North seemed to be stuck in a timewarp while mainland Britain changed.

What triggered a new and wholly different war was the decline of deference. A new generation of university students, especially from Queen's Belfast, observing the civil rights movement in the United States, marched against discrimination closer to home. When Ulster received a new university as part of the UK's 1960s expansion of higher education, it was located not in Londonderry (Derry to Catholics), Ulster's Catholic-majority second city, but in the small mainly Protestant town of Coleraine. But the marchers were not concerned only with university access; they protested against the dire housing, employment and welfare prospects of the Catholic population. The RUC reacted with its customary violence, only to discover that the marchers were more articulate and sophisticated in handling the media: unwelcome and unfamiliar publicity attended Ulster, in Britain and beyond.

But this was a province riven by historic grievance: clashes between marchers and the police could easily be viewed through a sectarian lens and there were plenty of politicians willing to colour it. What had started as a professedly non-sectarian movement became engulfed by generalised majority/minority unrest. In the summer of 1969, the RUC was driven out a large Catholic area of Derry, and there were attacks by loyalists on West Belfast's Catholic population. Stormont had patently lost control and the British army was sent in to erect a *cordon sanitaire*. The troops received an overwhelming welcome from Catholics; it was the beginning of the end for unionist autonomy and the start of a quarter century of conflict which became known with grim understatement as 'the Troubles'.

> **Stormont had patently lost control and the British army was sent in to erect a cordon sanitaire**

This honeymoon with Catholic opinion was brief as the army quickly found itself embroiled in conflict with the Catholic population, who came to see it as an auxiliary of the Ulster rather than the British state. A new so-called 'provisional' IRA was created in December 1969, resuming the struggle of fifty years before. It steadily emerged as the main republican faction, edging aside what became known as the more cautious 'official' IRA. Ulster loyalists also armed themselves: among their paramilitaries was the Ulster Volunteer Force, which had adopted the name of those who had rallied against home rule before World War I. Atrocities mounted and the British government introduced internment without trial in August 1971 in a desperate attempt to get a grip on the situation, a tactic that acted only as a 'recruiting sergeant' for the IRA, most of those detained being from the Catholic community. (Seen as a failure, internment without trial was finally abandoned in 1975.) Areas of Belfast and Derry were effectively under paramilitary control and neighbourhoods were cleared of people not of the same sectarian community. The most damaging of all British army blunders occurred on 'Bloody Sunday' in January 1972 when troops fired on unarmed demonstrators in Derry, killing 13 and wounding many more. It took forty years to overcome cover-ups, achieve an honest account of the massacre and finally wring an apology from a British prime minister.

In 1971 Catholic 'free Derry' became a non-go zone for British troops; similar warnings and barriers appeared in loyalist areas

Sectarian violence intensified and 500 were killed by the IRA in 1972, the worst year of the Troubles. The pattern was set for two decades and more of bombings, shootings, maimings and intimidation at fluctuating levels of intensity: Ulster became an armed camp. In 1972 the UK suspended a discredited Stormont and imposed direct rule on the province. This action by a Conservative government alienated Ulster unionism: it sundered its organic connection to the Conservatives. Tension between the British government and hardline loyalists was underlined when in 1974 mass action by Protestant workers and businesses forced the abandonment of a British power-sharing initiative. On the nationalist side those who rejected the IRA's use of violence coalesced into the Social Democratic and Labour Party (SDLP). Both the SDLP and unionists sent representatives to Westminster. But the real struggle was in Northern Ireland where the paramilitaries and the political forces allied with them overruled all attempts to find peaceful solutions. One IRA prisoner, Bobby Sands, stood for and won a Westminster parliamentary seat at a by-election in April 1981 while on a prison hunger strike that ended with his death 26 days later. This electoral success paved the way for Sinn Fein, the political wing of the IRA, to begin to contest parliamentary seats both North and South, although it refused to take up its seats at Westminster.

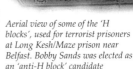

Aerial view of some of the 'H blocks', used for terrorist prisoners at Long Kesh/Maze prison near Belfast. Bobby Sands was elected as an 'anti-H block' candidate

Nor were these horrors entirely confined to Northern Ireland. Major British cities were bombed by the IRA, which also assassinated leading Conservative politicians and Lord Mountbatten, the queen's cousin, while he was in the Republic. In 1984 the British prime minister, Margaret Thatcher and members of her cabinet narrowly escaped when a bomb was detonated in a Brighton hotel at the time of the Conservative party conference. While bombings and killings by republican factions occurred periodically in Britain, for the most part the conflict remained confined to Northern Ireland, a place utterly unfamiliar to most British people.

The bombing of the Grand Hotel, Brighton, October 1984: five were killed, but the prime minister emerged unscathed

Until the wars of former Yugoslavia in the early 1990s, this was the worst internecine conflict in Europe since World War II. Total deaths between 1969 and 2001 reached 3,532. It is estimated (Malcolm Sutton's *Index of Deaths from the Conflict in Ireland*) that republican paramilitaries (principally the Provisional IRA) were responsible for 2,058 of these deaths, including 1,080 members or former members of the security forces. The asymmetrical nature of the conflict is demonstrated by the fact that the security forces killed only 145 members of republican paramilitaries – fewer, in fact, than the 187 republican paramilitaries killed by members of other republican factions. Loyalist paramilitaries were responsible for the deaths of only 14 members of the security forces but took the biggest toll of civilians, 878 compared with the 723 civilians killed by republicans and the 187 killed by the security forces.

The motivations behind individual killings were many and sometimes shrouded in obscurity: they included factional disputes between the terror groups on both sides, enforcement of protection rackets, personal vendettas settled under cover of a political cause and mistaken identities and blunders. But as a broad generalisation, the republican groups targeted mainly the security forces and loyalist civilians, the loyalists mainly Catholic civilians. There was, notably, minimal direct conflict between the two sets of paramilitaries: indeed more republican paramilitaries were killed by other republicans than by loyalists and more loyalist paramilitaries by other loyalists than by republicans. Little more than 10 per cent (363) of killings were at the hands of the security forces, whose exact mission and purpose often seemed unclear, reflecting political ambivalence at Westminster about whether this was a 'war' or a police action to contain civil strife and, if it was a war, whether it could ever be won and what victory would actually look like.

The peace process

While the overt posture of the British state was to refuse to 'negotiate with terrorists', it was privately doing precisely that. Such contacts dated back to the early days of the conflict, during the Edward Heath administration (1970-1974) but foundered on the conviction of the parties that they could 'win' and the sheer intensity of the ongoing violence. There were discreet contacts even in the time of Margaret Thatcher's tough 1980s government and in the next decade, under her Conservative successor John Major, the peace process became an open one as even the intransigents wearied of the never-ending impasse and sought a way out that would save face for both sides.

The IRA declared a 'complete ceasefire' in 1994 but as manoeuvring continued around the emergent peace process, in June 1996 it exploded a truck bomb – the biggest detonated in Britain since World War II – in the heart of Manchester; no one was killed (a warning having been given) but it caused immense damage and this and a another enormous explosion in London earlier that year focused attention on the mainland on the urgency of a solution. When in 1997 Tony Blair's Labour government succeeded John Major's Conservative government in London, it sought to comprehend peace-making within a wider devolutionary

While the overt posture of the British state was to refuse to 'negotiate with terrorists', it was privately doing precisely that

process. The form this took in Northern Ireland was a power-sharing executive containing representatives from all parties elected to a new Northern Ireland assembly. To ensure a close tally of seats to votes, members of the legislative assembly (MLAs) were chosen by the single transferable vote (STV) system, a form of proportional representation. This satisfied the demands of the Ulster Unionists for restored devolved government while placating nationalists and republicans with what could be sold as an Irish solution (though Sinn Fein's elected MPs still refused to take their Westminster seats). Only if all elected parties continued to participate would the executive (and therefore devolution) continue. All had a stake in its survival.

The 1998 Belfast agreement (more generally known as the Good Friday agreement) incorporated a new consensus and received popular endorsement in referenda held both north and south of the border. In referenda on the agreement held in May 1998, over 71 per cent voted 'Yes' in Northern Ireland on an 81 per cent turnout, while in the Republic, the 'Yes' vote neared 95 per cent on a 56 per cent turnout. It was followed by the awarding of the Nobel Peace Prize to two of the principal architects, the leader of the Ulster Unionist Party (UUP) David Trimble and SDLP leader John Hume, though in reality the key was the engagement or at least acquiescence of the various paramilitary groups, both loyalist and republican.

The Good Friday agreement also led to the release of hundreds of prisoners convicted of terrorist attacks, including the 1984 Brighton bombing. For political reasons, therefore, individuals from paramilitary groups convicted under UK law of crimes such as murder ended up serving much lesser sentences than ordinary citizens – thus effectively conceding the historic demand of the IRA that their campaign be seen as a war. In addition a curtain was de facto drawn down on

The Good Friday agreement ... led to the release of hundreds of prisoners convicted of terrorist attacks

the investigation of unsolved terrorist attacks preceding the Good Friday agreement.

The first assembly elections, in June 1998, reflected the long-standing Westminster division of seats between the unionist and nationalist communities, the Ulster Unionists with 28 seats in first place, and the SDLP in second with 24. However close behind with 20 seats were the Democratic Unionist Party (DUP) and Sinn Fein (18 seats). The DUP, formed in 1971 by a formidable Presbyterian minister, the Revd Ian Paisley, had been the most uncompromising opponents of any form of power-sharing and had wrecked all previous attempts. Now, its supple willingness to cooperate became key to sustaining the delicate and at times precarious peace process – as did the adherence of Sinn Fein. In the next assembly elections, in 2003, the DUP replaced the UUP as the leading party on the unionist side and Sinn Fein the SDLP on the nationalist/republican side. This dominance was subsequently reaffirmed and indeed strengthened at subsequent assembly elections: in the May 2016 elections the DUP won 38 seats and Sinn Fein 29, with the Ulster Unionists (16) and SDLP (14) very much the poor seconds in their own communities.

Sinn Fein/IRA's willingness to abandon the armed struggle did not, therefore, benefit the SDLP, which had always sought a peaceful resolution. On the contrary, in the eyes of many of the Catholic population, Sinn Fein/IRA had emerged a victor – not by uniting Ireland by force, an unachievable goal on any rational assessment, but by being undefeated by the British state and coming to be recognised by the British as a force they would ultimately have to strike a political bargain with. The SDLP was a clearly peripheral factor in that calculus. On the unionist side, the DUP, in perpetual conflict with the British government also emerged as the most powerful bargaining partner: the Ulster Unionists, paradoxically, had proved too 'loyalist' – to Britain rather than their own community. The assembly was suspended from October 2002 after a political breakdown – though with no resumption of general violence, reflecting the desire of their respective communities for an end to bloodshed; but when it resumed work in 2007 it did so with the remarkable spectacle of Paisley, famously the loudest and most unrepentant voice of intransigent unionism, taking office as first minister with Martin McGuinness of Sinn Fein – widely alleged to have been a former chief of staff of the IRA and self-confessedly a former IRA member – as deputy first minister. Thus it happened that peace was achieved not by 'moderate' voices coming together on an inter-communal basis but by ultimately unreconciled communities finding a sort of accommodation via their most hardline leaders. Whether in the long history of Ireland this marks a new beginning or is merely an interlude remains to be seen.

The Revd Ian Paisley: the leader of hardline unionism who sat down with Sinn Fein

Whereas devolved bodies in Scotland and Wales erected new and expensive buildings, the new Northern Ireland assembly is housed, ironically, at Stormont, the site of the former unionist-dominated parliament, where bronzes of past Orange champions still grace the building and park in which it sits. This symbol of the Protestant ascendancy, an imposing six storey 365 feet wide Grade-B listed building constructed in 1932 (and opened by the last king-emperor, George V) had accommodated the former government of Northern Ireland. It is now officially known as Parliament Buildings.

Devolution

The assembly is a genuinely devolved body though in Northern Ireland parlance this is termed 'transferred powers'. These allow it

The Stormont home of the Northern Ireland parliament, now the Northern Ireland assembly

to make laws in a wide range of areas, including housing, employment, education, health, agriculture and the environment. Its existence cannot be said to have established exclusively normal politics
(i.e. peaceful debate about distributional issues) in Northern Ireland. Political loyalties among voters still largely reflect national
and religious difference with few politicians non-aligned. However,
political violence has dramatically declined and bombings have
ceased; the RUC has been replaced by a new and overtly non-sectarian Northern Ireland Police Force while the British military presence has been minimised; massive public investment has been
made by successive UK governments.

Little noticed outside Ulster is the Irish dimension to its new system of government. A North South ministerial council (NSMC) brings
together ministers from the Northern Ireland executive and the Irish
government to develop consultation, cooperation and action within
the island of Ireland on matters of mutual interest. Common policies
and approaches on agriculture, education, environment, health,
tourism and transport are agreed in the NSMC but implemented separately either side of the border. Cooperation in this body was a major
initial concession by unionists who had always objected to the South's
territorial claims. However their path had been smoothed by the Republic's agreement to amend articles 2 and 3 of its constitution, effectively accepting as part of the Good Friday agreement process that the
territory of Northern Ireland could be transferred only by consent of
a majority of its people. Queen Elizabeth II in May 2011 made an en-
thusiastically-received four-day state visit to the Republic, the first

ever undertaken by a British monarch. Then, in 2012 Queen Elizabeth II met and shook hands with Sinn Fein deputy first minister Martin McGuinness. McGuinness also laid a wreath at the site of the Battle of the Somme in June 2016, a gesture to recognise both those soldiers from Ireland who fought in the British army and its importance to unionists (who had died there in large numbers).

27 June 2012: the queen and one-time IRA member Martin McGuinness shake hands. The IRA had assassinated her cousin, Lord Mountbatten, in 1979

The Good Friday agreement also led to the establishment of a British-Irish council comprising the British and Irish governments, the devolved institutions of Northern Ireland, Scotland and Wales together with representatives of the Isle of Man and the Channel Islands. To the council was added a British-Irish intergovernmental conference of senior representatives from each sovereign government to promote bilateral cooperation at all levels on matters of mutual interest. These bodies are not powerful though they might emerge in the context of broader constitutional change all round. Yet the shared interests of all in a peaceful Ireland and settled EU relationships are palpable. The 2016 Brexit vote occurred to expressions of great alarm from politicians in the Irish Republic.

Social changes

The scope of the cultural shift on both sides of the Ireland/Northern Ireland border is hard to overstate. The North still has a 'marching season' used by both sides to assert their competing identities. This retains sufficient electricity to require a Parades Commission, an independent, quasi-judicial body set up in 1997, to promote greater understanding by the general public of issues concerning public processions and be the means of resolving disputes about

them. The commission watches the details of marching and pre-
scribes a code of conduct, specifying every aspect of the conduct of
parades, including music, flags and
regalia. Religious observance – on **Catholics now**
both sides of the border – remains **outnumber Protestants ...**
high in comparison to the mainland. **within each age group**
In 2011 census compilers found 45 **under 40**
per cent of Northern Ireland's popu-
lation were either Catholic or brought up as Catholic, while 48 per
cent belonged to or were brought up in Protestant, other Christian
or Christian-related denominations. Since the 1960s however, the
number actually adhering to all religions combined has fallen from
almost 100 per cent to 82 per cent. It may be significant for the future of Ulster that among the oldest age groups, Protestants and
other Christians outnumber Catholics by around 2 to 1, whereas
Catholics now outnumber Protestants and other Christians within
each age group under 40.

The conflicted cultural and political character of the North is
nonetheless affirmed by the same statistics. Two-fifths of the population reported a 'British only' national identity, one-quarter 'Irish
only' and just over a fifth 'Northern Irish only'. Almost half included 'British' as a national identity, while 29 per cent included
Northern Irish and 28 per cent included Irish. Almost three-fifths
held a UK passport, with just over a fifth holding an Irish passport.
Among usual residents 3 or older, 11 per cent had some ability to
speak Irish while 8.1 per cent could speak some Ulster-Scots. There
remain political intransigents on both sides whose murderous ef-
Visitors ... may still forts the security services have so far
observe lurid murals been able to thwart. Visitors to East or
West Belfast and to Derry/Londonderry
commemorating one may still observe lurid murals commem-
or other side in the orating one or other side in the struggle
struggle and plentiful numbers of union flags or
tricolours (the Republic flag). And yet,
trends similar to the diversification evident elsewhere in the UK are
unmistakeable, albeit in diluted form. For example, the proportion
belonging to minority ethnic groups doubled in the decade to 2011,

though white ethnic background still accounted for 98 per cent of Northern Ireland residents and 94 per cent of those in Ireland.

In many ways the Republic has since the 1970s been more socially dynamic than the North; aspirations to greater human and civil rights were throttled in the North by the rise of sectarian politics while the Republic, joining the European Community at the same time as Britain, slowly became more open to liberal breezes from the rest of the world. Remarkably, the marriage rate across the whole island has now converged at 51 per cent, thanks principally to an increase amongst divorced persons of 150 per cent in the Republic compared with 47 per cent in Northern Ireland. Cohabiting couples are also more prevalent in Ireland. During half a century the average household size has fallen from 4.0 to 2.7 persons in Ireland and from 3.7 to 2.5 persons in Northern Ireland, the former clearly signalling the practice of birth control disapproved of by the church.

Indeed, it is hard to escape the conclusion that the most important social shift in the Republic has been the steep decline in the standing of institutional Catholicism. Once the cultural hegemon, the Catholic church has been dislodged from its constitutional preeminence, battered by revelations of appalling complicity in child abuse, unable to withstand liberal shifts in popular opinion. The record of constitutional amendments is instructive. In 1986 the Republic heavily rejected divorce in a nationwide referendum but less than ten years later the prestige of the Catholic church was insufficient to withstand it in a second vote. Homosexual acts were decriminalised in the Republic only in 1997, but in May 2015 it voted by over 62 per cent to legalise same-sex marriage, becoming the first country to endorse it by popular vote. Vehement clerical opposition met each of these proposals but with diminishing effect. The big exception to these changes is the absence of abortion rights. Strikingly, resistance to a woman's right to choose persists on both sides of the border. Northern Ireland was exempt from the 1967 Act which legalised abortion on the British mainland (see chapter 18). Though it is a transferred power, no attempt to harmonise with Britain has been made. The Republic voted no fewer than five times on one or other aspect of abortion rights. Legality under restricted conditions was allowed in 2013 but general lawful access is not

available. An unquantifiable number of Northern Irish women
travel to obtain abortion on the mainland.

Religion and culture

After the departure of the Romans from Britain it was Irish saints
who reintroduced Christianity to the mainland first on Iona, then
on Scotland's Western Isles, the Orkneys and the long Scottish and
English east coasts. The Northumbrian English church was to a
great extent an Irish church, at least until the Synod of Whitby (664).
Only in the 12th century was the direction of traffic switched. Now
Anglo-Norman culture and liturgy was exported by invasion. After
that Presbyterianism arrived in Ulster with the 16th and 17th century planters while a milder Protestantism was elsewhere incorporated into the Church of Ireland.

Seven of the eleven Catholic archbishops of Westminster ... have been of Irish extraction

In the history of modern times it can
be hard to draw an Anglo-Irish cultural
boundary as even a cursory survey of
religion, literature and music will illustrate. Irish Catholicism, so stubbornly
resistant to Anglo-Scots reforming zeal,
enjoyed a delayed revenge. It was 19th century Irish immigration
that restored both English and Scots Catholicism as mass move-
ments, boosting congregations but also, significantly, maintaining
the ranks of the priesthood. Until comparatively recently the English Catholic church seemed an Irish church. Seven of the eleven
Catholic archbishops of Westminster (primates, many of whom became cardinals) have been of Irish extraction.

The Irish ancestry of the English population at large is not com-
putable but its influence is great. The character and cultural history
of Liverpool, in particular, cannot be understood unless due weight
is given it. Liverpool might have had the world's second largest
Catholic cathedral if a building, designed by Edwin Lutyens and
started in the 1930s, had ever been completed; its scale may be imagined, if only dimly, from the vast 1933 crypt that underlies the more
modest but distinctively modernist 1960s edifice that was built instead

– Frederick Gibberd's Metropolitan Cathedral of Christ the King. As Liverpool in England, so Glasgow in Scotland. It was the huge influx of Irish after the potato famine (1845-on) and especially in the decade 1876-85 which altered the religious affiliation of the whole West Side. In the 20th century, however, Scots Catholicism owed little to Irish immigration, differing in this from the English variant, whose lifeblood it was (until replaced by late 20th century Polish immigration). Meanwhile the Presbyterian traffic of Northern Ireland and Scotland was a two-way affair.

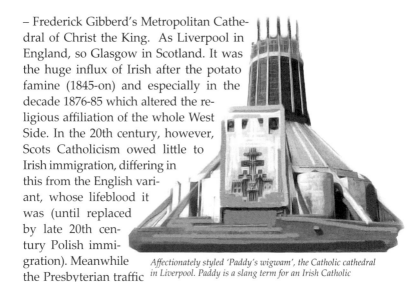

Affectionately styled 'Paddy's wigwam', the Catholic cathedral in Liverpool. Paddy is a slang term for an Irish Catholic

As with many Scots the national identity of Irish literary figures can be obscured by the existence of a 'United Kingdom'. It is quite difficult to imagine the English stage without Sheridan and Goldsmith in the 18th century, Wilde and Shaw in the 19th and 20th. Then there are poets: Swift in the 18th century; Heaney, MacNeice and Tom Paulin (all from the North) in the 20th. C.S. Lewis was from Ulster, Iris Murdoch from Dublin; even that celebrator of English arcadia Edmund Spenser was a colonist. Of composers Sullivan (born in England of an Irish father) and Stanford in the 19th century, are thought of as English. So too (sometimes) is the Hanoverian Handel, who spent most of 1742 in Ireland where his oratorio *Messiah* – that staple of English choirs – received its premiere during his visit.

The European dimension

In 1973 both the Republic and Northern Ireland (as part of the UK) joined the EEC, thenceforth sharing a new common space as the European Community by stages became the EU. Ireland's 2002 entry into the eurozone might have introduced greater separation for two currencies now circulated within the island of Ireland. In practice cross-border trade boomed and the wider European dimension offered new opportunities for contact between the Republic and Northern Ireland. But the latter was part of a UK determined to resist closer European integration and 2016 brought the referendum on revised terms of membership. In the campaign leading up to the vote, both first minister Arlene Foster (DUP) and secretary of state Theresa Villiers favoured the Leave option, but the Remain camp included Sinn Fein, the Ulster Unionists, the SDLP and the small non-aligned Alliance Party. Northern Ireland voted Remain by a majority of 56 to 44 per cent, one of only three UK regions to do so. Its 2016 vote closely resembled that in the 1975 referendum: nationalist and Catholic areas (the West and South) voted to stay while unionists and Presbyterians (the East) opted to leave on both occasions. It was noticeable that an increasingly prosperous Belfast returned a heavy vote to Remain. Foster welcomed the overall decision to Leave, but the Republic government expressed anxiety about reintroduction of a hard border on the island. Sinn Fein took the opportunity to call for a 'border poll' as provided for in the Good Friday agreement. This initiative was quickly rebuffed by Villiers who, in any case, was sacked by May soon after. Nevertheless, Northern Ireland will be taken out of the EU against the will of the majority.

6. Wales and the Union

Wales is the quiet minority territory of the UK. Conquered by England in the late 13th century it put up sporadic resistance until the early 15th. The 16th century brought administrative absorption by England and it posed no secessionist threat thereafter. Wales embraced the Reformation. In the centuries that followed it was culturally and linguistically separate from England, but 18th century industrialisation transformed a rural society as in much of Britain. The 19th century saw the establishment of large-scale extractive industry, notably coalmining, technical advances and an organised workforce. In the 20th century a nationalist movement emerged but its reach never extended beyond 20 per cent of the population and its commitment to achieving independence is qualified. In the 21st century, and in great contrast to Scotland, support for an independent Wales remains very much a minority cause. And in June 2016, Wales voted to leave the EU by 52.5 per cent to Remain's 47.5 per cent.

Contrasting fates

Wales was rapidly subdued by Rome, a brutal process culminating in a notorious massacre of druids on the remote north-western island of Mona (Anglesey). After the Roman legions left, local princedoms emerged, intermittently sharing kingship across western Britain: the Welsh language was spoken in Edinburgh in the 7th century.

The red dragon: the symbol of Wales since at least the ninth century AD.

Thereafter Welsh princes marauded into England suffering invasion in their turn. Even before that Germanic settlers had begun the remorseless population pressure that would push the Romano-British

Harlech castle, built to subdue the Welsh by King Edward I of England in the 1280s

ever westwards, though historians differ over how violent a process
this was. One version of the dubious legend of Arthur has him rallying the Christians of the West against these pagan invaders. Border wars continued for centuries, prompting one pagan Mercian
king to erect the island's second longest fortifications, Offa's Dyke,
against the fierce Welsh tribes. The Normans settled and fortified
only eastern Wales. Their work may be seen at Chepstow, whose
mighty castle still looms over the Wye. Nothing beyond this eastern
territory (later known as 'the Marches') was colonised.

The eventual conquest of Wales was the work of the aggressive
English king Edward I (1272-1307). Edward ringed the littoral with
coastal forts, military architecture that made Norman castles seem
puny: with such redoubts he could invade by land and sea. This
disaster eradicated the country's distinct political existence, leaving
no focus for national aspiration other than the empty title of 'Prince
of Wales' conferred by Edward on his eldest son. In the longer term
this may have fostered a national identity fastened upon a Welsh
language not spoken by the country's new rulers; a parallel perhaps
with the experience of the English under the Normans two centuries earlier. The language was so robust that the political changes
of later centuries could only be carried through in Wales by using
it as a vehicle. Thus the decision of King Henry VIII (of the Welsh
Tudor dynasty that seized the English throne in 1485) to break with

Rome and establish a national church was underpinned by the publication not only of an English but of a Welsh bible. How else was Henry to commit his monoglot Welsh subjects to the reformed faith? Politically however he simply absorbed Wales as an administrative region of England.

Cultural distinctiveness

Welsh remained the secure majority language of Wales until the 18th century. Its decline was a by-product of the rampant exploitation of natural resources that began in Blaenavon and spread across much of South Wales. The extraction of coal and iron ore fostered employment, demographic expansion, technological development and the growth of towns. The Welsh coalfields were a major source of Britain's only domestic fuel and steam coal for the powered ships replacing sail. Mining technologies and men were exported to North and South America. Coal, iron, steel and tinplate were traded from the new ports on the South Wales coast. Since much of this commerce was within the British empire it was unsurprising when English became, for the first time, the native language of choice.

Welsh speaking receded into agrarian and pastoral North, West and Mid-Wales. There it was celebrated culturally and offered a rallying point for those few who believed in independence. Literature, dance and song all flourished in these areas but their success could not disguise that national energy lay elsewhere – in the pits and ironworks of the South and the urban, chapel, sporting and labour culture that rested on them. In politics rural 19th century Wales backed the Liberal Party which in turn incorporated populist demands in its programme. Welsh liberalism advocated land reform, provided a Welsh-speaking prime minister (David Lloyd George, 1916-1922) and sought the disestablishment of the established Anglican church in Wales. By the time this was achieved (1920) Liberalism was in steep decline.

David Lloyd George, from North Wales, Britain's last Liberal prime minister; began the creation of the welfare state as chancellor of the exchequer (1908-1915); became prime minister in 1916, midway through World War I and led Britain to victory.

In South Wales the Liberal Party's heyday was brief, soon eclipsed by a burgeoning Labour Party that rapidly achieved majoritarian status. Labour was rooted in the trade unions which organised a huge industrial workforce. Since Labour was also a growing force across the UK this new Welsh political identity was a one-way bet; early nationalist figures appeared marginal dwellers in a Celtic twilight. Welsh Labour advanced as a wing of British Labour, most expressively in the person of Aneurin Bevan (1897-1960). Bevan, a son of the pits who left school at the age of 12, rose to be the cabinet minister who created the National Health Service. He was contemptuous of nationalism which he saw as a diversion from the class struggle and could not speak the Welsh language. Labour in 1964 introduced a Welsh Office but this was less a concession to national feeling than a move to streamline advocacy within the British government system. Unaffected by the party's fortunes in England, Labour has come first in Wales in every general election since 1922.

Labour has come first in Wales in every general election since 1922

Wales in modern times

However, the wider forces shaping the UK as a whole also left their imprint on Wales. Declining competitiveness in manufacturing narrowed traditional home markets for Wales's extractive industries. In the 1970s North Sea oil displaced coal as the principal fuel for domestic heating. Imperial decline, either directly or indirectly led to the loss of export markets. Since Wales's economic profile mirrored the classic heavy industry pattern of the industrial revolution its decline was especially severe. The country picked up some new light industries, often as a result of government intervention, but this did not compensate. By the 1970s calls for increased self-government and even home rule were being heard and, for the first time, they were not confined to the traditional nationalist areas beyond the populous South.

Starting in the 1970s, this changing mood produced several political effects. Plaid Cymru (PC, 'The Party of Wales', founded 1925) gained an audience for the first time in the 1960s, vying with the Conservatives and Liberals to offer an alternative to Labour outside South

Wales. Labour itself, though in government at Westminster for much of the 1960s and 1970s, had been unable to stem industrial decline. Meanwhile in a less confident Welsh Labour Party support for a measure of home rule gained traction. By 1979, a minority UK Labour government at Westminster, dependent in part on the three PC MPs, conceded a referendum on establishing a Welsh assembly and advocated a 'Yes' vote. In retrospect this move might seem to mark the birth of a new Welsh politics of identity. In the short term however it was a disaster for Labour, an expedient move interpreted as opportunism. Labour in Wales split, with many of its most influential figures opposing the line of their own UK government. Allied with traditional and implacable unionism (which rejected any constitutional shift) this opposition proved insuperable. Wales rejected the proposed assembly 4:1 in a vote nudging a 60 per cent turnout: nor was this a case of the populous South outvoting other areas – not one Welsh county voted in favour. This defeat (simultaneous with that of a proposed Scottish parliament) precipitated the fall of the UK Labour government.

A new political order

The new Conservative government of Mrs Thatcher was disinclined towards subsidy and increasingly willing to unleash market forces. This was a threat to the Welsh economy, dominated by heavy industry and public sector employment, in both of which the trade unions were strong. Wales participated fully in the major national strikes of the 1980s in steel and coal. While there was some inward investment, overall this and the following decade brought economic decline, with predictable political results. The Welsh voting pattern, like that of the Scots, showed an increasing attachment to a Labour Party which at the national (i.e. UK) level was marginalised, largely impotent and defeated in four straight UK elections. Within Wales, however, Labour's dominance increased at the level of local government, Westminster and (from 1979) European parliament representation.

Yet the Thatcherite legacy in Wales was complex. Her British government was willing to engage with and even encourage expressions of national identity outside politics. The Welsh language was encour-

aged and its cultural manifestations subsidised. The country gained
a Welsh language TV station, Welsh became a core subject of the national (*sic*) curriculum and eventually teacher employment in primary
schools was open only to the bilingual. Taxpayer support via the
British or proto-Welsh state has been crucial: S4C, the Welsh language
broadcaster, was by 2015 receiving public funding both via direct government grant (£6.8 million per year) and also via the licence fee (£74.5
million per year). Such measures, allied with the renewed attractiveness of Welsh-speaking to the young, ended its decline. By 2013 one
in five residents (572,000) could speak Welsh and nearly one in ten
used it as their language of choice.

When Labour swept back into power at Westminster in 1997,
Wales was part of a British political majority for the first time in two
decades: 34 of the country's 40 MPs were elected on the Labour
ticket. In the interim devolutionists had captured Welsh Labour and
so they all supported a new proposal to create a Welsh assembly
put to voters in Wales by referendum the same year. Now the divergent paths of the minority nations became apparent. Scotland's
strong vote for a much more powerful body – a parliament – threw
into sharp relief a knife-edge majority in Wales of less than 7,000,
and on a lower turnout (50.1 per cent) than in 1979. Clearly this
represented an important shift of opinion, most notably in some of
the strongest unionist areas, but it was still a very narrow basis for
constitutional change. Nonetheless the British Labour government
interpreted it as a mandate and the Government of Wales Act 1998
established a 60-strong assembly. This met for the first time the following year, elected on a mixed-member system.

From the assembly to Brexit

It took time for the new body to sink roots. Early administrations
were dominated by Labour either alone or in coalition with the Liberal
Democrats in a country where Labour had been the majority force for
so long; only the raised national authority of Plaid Cymru suggested
change. The first 'first minister' was perceived as handpicked by UK
prime minister Tony Blair, provoking a grassroots uprising and his
replacement by Rhodri Morgan. There were expensive administrative

shifts: an ambitious new assembly building (the Senedd, opened 2006) drastically overran its budget. Assembly debates appeared parochial; able and ambitious politicians preferred the UK stage. Perhaps reflecting doubts about the ability to carry popular assent it was not until a second act (the Government of Wales Act 2006, GOWA) that it gained the ability to make at least some laws from scratch rather than adapting legislation created in Westminster. GOWA also introduced a formal legal separation between the national assembly and the Welsh assembly government which took effect following the 2007 assembly elections.

The Senedd, the Welsh assembly
building, opened in 2006

These elections proved a watershed. Falling Labour representation was matched by PC's advance: the two parties negotiated a power-sharing agreement that reflected the junior partner's programme including new support for the language and demands for enhanced powers. As the assembly entered its second decade it became obvious that it had gained legitimacy. The Conservatives, who as in Scotland had benefited from the mixed-member system, had ceased to oppose; it had become a vehicle for implementing local priorities in health, education and social policy; unexpectedly it also emerged as an exemplar of equal gender representation, first in the elected body and then in government. The significance of this last point in a nation traditionally dominated by semi-skilled male manual labour and sporting endeavour cannot be overstated. All discussion about the assembly was now about strengthening it, even turning it into a parliament on the Scottish model.

A 2011 referendum showed how far opinion had shifted: the Welsh voted to give the assembly power to enact primary legislation with 21 out of 22 counties voting Yes, though the span of its responsibilities remained unchanged. While the fourth assembly elections returned Labour to a new spell of single-party government, the assembly as a whole displayed greater confidence. That

October the UK government established the Silk Commission to re-view the financial and constitutional arrangements in Wales. Its two reports (2012 and 2014) foresaw a new GOWA giving Wales all functions not reserved at Westminster plus enhanced influence over water, transport, energy and elections with new powers over polic-ing and youth justice.

Once enacted these measures would represent the fulfilment of a full devolution agenda, entirely compatible with unionism. It was noticeable that Carwyn Jones (successor to Morgan as first minister) was prepared to speak against independence on the (unionist) 'Bet-ter Together' platform during the 2014 Scottish referendum cam-paign. The new PC leader Leanne Wood, elected in 2012, personally advocated independence but her party still fell short of advocating it. The 2015 general election saw Welsh Conservatives pick up three Westminster seats to take their representation to 11 – their best re-sult since 1983. Labour's dominance continued with 24 seats while more than one in eight voters backed UKIP. In the May 2016 as-sembly elections the Conservatives lost the ground they had gained, but UKIP – favoured by a more proportional system – entered the Senedd for the first time with seven seats. Labour retained office but was rocked by losing the directly-elected seat of the Rhondda to Wood. It was forced to offer the education portfolio to the assem-bly's only elected Liberal; effectively she constituted the narrow ma-jority that allowed it to continue in government.

Two months later Wales voted again, this time in the referendum on EU membership. Turnout, at 71.7 per cent, was high. This time the official stance of the three British parties and that of PC was for Re-main but their advocacy succeeded only in five areas – Gwynedd, Cardiff, Ceredigion, the Vale of Glamorgan and Monmouthshire. 17 areas backed Brexit, including the vast bulk of Wales's Labour heart-lands dense with council housing. The significance of the steady ad-vance in the UKIP vote now became clear. Voters had rejected the advice of all the other party leaders including Plaid Cymru. In this respect Wales behaved in sharply different fashion from Scotland and Northern Ireland. Ostensibly the decision was to Wales's economic disadvantage: it had since 2000 consistently been one of the poorest parts of the EU despite the accession of new Eastern European member states. As such it attracted significant financial aid. The three structural funding rounds covering 2000 to 2020 brought it almost £5.2bn, the bulk designated for West Wales and the South Wales Valleys. The country may thus be said to have voted more like a deprived English region (where EU funding had also been generous) than like a minority nation, suggesting it found the nationalist stance less politically attractive.

Wales voted to leave the EU in the June 2016 referendum, but the country was divided (the dark areas voted to leave); the capital, Cardiff, voted Remain

Wales in the Union

In the wake of September 2014's Scottish referendum, all UK devolutionary arrangements seemed to be thrown into flux. The assembly felt confident enough to raise the stakes, and in its 2014 response to Silk, advocated a timetable for transfer of powers that would allow an enhanced body to be elected in 2021. An all-party assembly commission of January 2015 (formed to make recommendations about the institution itself) called for its size to be increased from 60 to 80-100 assembly members (AMs) and all electoral arrangements to be devolved as well. Remarkably both main parties, implacably unionist as recently as 1979, now advocated a very ambitious programme of self-government with Liberal Democrats and Plaid Cymru in support. In the fifth (2016) assembly however, they faced a small UKIP faction determinedly sceptical about enhancing assembly powers, proposing stronger local government as an alternative and newly-influential following the Brexit vote. The devolved budget for 2016-2017 is £15 billion and includes responsibility for the entire NHS in Wales. After nearly two decades of increasing devolution Welsh governments increasingly have to defend their track record as well as criticise Westminster. With independence still apparently a minority aspiration, the subject matter of politics may shift away from constitutional preoccupations in favour of social and economic outcomes.

More than 250,000 men worked in the Welsh coalmines in the

early 1920s. There is not a single underground mine left. The economic focus of Wales is now on tourism and public services, the main employers. Growth areas include environmental protection and regeneration and creative industries. These are growing faster than they are across the UK, and combined with cultural businesses now employ 17,500 people, contributing £400 million annually to the economy. Yet Wales remains significantly less prosperous than much of the UK, with lower employment, house prices and pre-tax personal incomes. Indeed, at £17,573 per head Wales's 2014 gross value added was the lowest of any UK region. There are large areas of economic deprivation, many concentrated in the Valleys where the economy collapsed following the closure of the pits and the population continues to decline.

Yet the national population exceeds three million, the highest it has ever been, three-quarters of them concentrated in the south-east around the cities of Swansea, Cardiff and Newport. These three places all grew as ports, outlets for coal from the Valleys to their North. Cardiff, with almost 350,000 residents is easily the largest city yet was designated capital of Wales only in 1955. It gained a clutch of impressive civic buildings early in the 20th century when it was the greatest coal exporter in the world. In the 21st it added a new waterfront on Cardiff Bay that houses the Senedd. Swansea, its only serious rival, has almost a quarter of a million inhabitants: it achieved city status only in 1969. Newport, with 150,000, is an even more recent city (2002). Wales's two other cities, Bangor and St David's, are small. Like Aberystwyth (home to the National Library of Wales) and Llangollen (which hosts the International Eisteddfod – the Welsh festival of literature and music) they owe their status to their role in Welsh cultural history. In North Wales, Wrexham, an industrial town of 60,000 and the Deeside industrial belt have significant populations.

The Welsh population is for the most part highly concentrated. Much of the country is given over to farming, to uncultivatable natural scenery, and to its two national parks. There are three World Heritage Sites: the Edward I in Gwynedd Castles and Town Walls, the Blaenavon Industrial Landscape (which exhibits early coal, iron and rail workings) and Thomas Telford's extraordinary Pontcysyllte

Aqueduct which carries the Llangollen Canal over the River Dee. Wales's coastline is extensive, nourished by substantial rivers flowing south (Wye, Usk, Taff, Avon, plus the mighty Severn); west (the Teifi) and north (Dee, Clwyd, Conwy). Rivers and mountains have combined to make travel between North and South difficult, an obstacle that neither Wales's road or rail system has yet surmounted. By contrast, transport links with England from both North and South are good. There are two crossings of the broad Severn estuary that marks its southern boundary with England; the M4 stretches from Swansea to London, and electrification of the Great Western main line is scheduled to match it by 2018.

Dylan Thomas (1914-1953), Welsh poet who found fame throughout Britain with his radio broadcasts for the BBC.

If Wales's political destination is uncertain, its cultural identity is conflicted for it cannot be equated to creative achievement in Welsh, a language which, though thriving, is inaccessible to 80 per cent of the population. Dylan Thomas, a poet unmistakeably Welsh in subject matter and rhythms of speech, wrote entirely in English.

Much the same might be said of the output of 'Cool Cymru' bands like the Manic Street Preachers or Catatonia. This little nation reaches out culturally, building on a song tradition by hosting the 'Cardiff Singer of the World' competition (a contest for classical singers) and regularly producing fine classical voices such as Geraint Evans, Gwynne Howell and Bryn Terfel; in the 1930s it provided refuge to Paul Robeson. A different succession of powerful singers – Shirley Bassey, Tom Jones – excelled in popular entertainment. Indeed song has been powerfully woven through Welsh history, sustained by the male voice choirs to be found in every pit village when coal was king. There may be no other part of

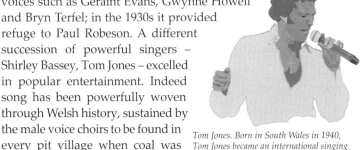

Tom Jones. Born in South Wales in 1940, Tom Jones became an international singing star fusing Welsh musicality with the earthiness of American soul

Song has been powerfully woven through Welsh history

the UK where song, sometimes in Welsh, sometimes in English but Welsh-accented, is so expressive of community life.

The establishment of the University of Wales by royal charter in 1893 was regarded, with the University of Wales Press, as one of the most important political and social developments in the nineteenth century. The further development of regional learning centres, through the establishment of colleges in Aberystwyth, Bangor, Cardiff and Swansea was a significant development and reinforced the regional presence of the University within Wales. The people of Wales regarded their University as a national institution to be nationally and globally celebrated. Its Centre for Advanced Welsh and Celtic Studies (CAWCS), *Geiriadur Prifysgol Cymru* (The Welsh Dictionary), and the University of Wales Press, helped to promote and celebrate language, heritage and culture. However, once the newly-established government of Wales had determined that universities should validate their own degrees the need for a federal structure began to evaporate. Today the country has ten universities and the University of Wales is building a new unitary identity.

Welsh sporting achievement is discussed in chapter 16. Undoubtedly rugby is the country's premier sport, if measured by participation, crowds and general interest. The Welsh team has at times been the best in the world. Like operatic singing, it was nourished by the fertile milieu of the densely populated South Wales Valleys, now in economic decline. In 2016 football gained a rare chance to compete for popular affection on equal terms when a swashbuckling Wales national side not only qualified for the finals of the UEFA European Championship but reached the semi-finals. Whether this will permanently raise the status of the game to the same level as rugby remains to be seen.

7. Scotland and the Union

On 18 September 2014, Scotland voted in a single question referendum by 55 to 45 per cent to stay within the United Kingdom.

At 82 per cent the turnout was not only comfortably higher than that in any other British plebiscite; it was 20 percentage points higher than the turnout in the British general election four years earlier. Moreover, this dazzling participation rate was achieved by an electorate which, for the first time, included 16- and 17-year olds, and after a thrilling and high-level national debate. The relatively narrow result followed an unprecedented all-party drive to avert an independence vote in which the three major British parties – the Conservatives, Labour and Liberal Democrats –combined on behalf of the Union against the Scottish National Party (SNP) and its small allies. In its wake serious consideration was given to constitutional change across the UK. This came after twenty – some would say forty – years of changes to the structure of a British state that until then (putting the question of Ireland to one side) had seemed to be among the most enduring in the Western world.

Eight months after the independence referendum Scotland went to the polls again, this time in a UK-wide general election. The result was a disaster for unionism: the same three victorious referendum parties retained but one Westminster seat apiece: every other MP for Scotland (56 of them altogether) was now a Scottish Nationalist. How did this extraordinary state of affairs come about and what are the implications for the United Kingdom?

The Union

Scotland today has a population of 5.3 million. It united with England to form the Union of Great Britain in 1707, but before that had enjoyed a millennium of independence. Indeed, the Scots were united in one kingdom a century before the English, whose unwelcome attentions they later fought off in the war of independence (1286-1328). From 1603 the two otherwise independent countries coexisted in a 'Union of Crowns' under a Scots dynasty reigning in London. This strange arrangement initially secured the English dynastic succession and the Church of England but steadily sucked Scotland into the gathering English Revolution: the two separate states actually fought several wars during the Union of Crowns. By the 1707 Union the Scots voluntarily dissolved their parliament in exchange for representation at Westminster.

Even though they had given up an independent state the Scots retained a separate legal and educational system and an entirely distinct church settlement. Some Scots ('Jacobites' *the nation entered on a century of cultural achievement rightly known as the Scottish Enlightenment*

for their adherence to King James of the ousted Stuart dynasty) made three violent challenges to the Union in the first half of the 18th century, but failed to rally the entire nation. All foundered, the last ('the '45') being put down with the utmost brutality. After this all opposition to rule from London took a peaceful and constitutional form and the intellectual and artistic leaders of the nation entered on a century of cultural achievement rightly known as the Scottish Enlightenment.

Adam Smith, author of The Wealth of Nations (1776), the foundation of free market economic theory: a towering figure of the Scottish Enlightenment

After this the only constitutional change before 1999 was the creation of the Scottish Office (1885), headed by a UK cabinet minister, as a government department assuming responsibility for the country's health, education, justice, agriculture, fisheries and farming.

England's careful conduct towards Scotland contrasts with its attitude towards Wales and Ireland. This explains two key facts about the 2014 referendum campaign. First, it referred to a voluntary union of the two countries: Scotland's right peacefully to withdraw from the Union was always implicit, as was the willingness of England to tolerate politically advocated change. England's murderous suppression of Highland culture after 1745 was made easier for being pitched against an identity (feudal, authoritarian, Catholic, Gaelic) that most Scots had already rejected. Second, the national identity acknowledged by a partial union was now reinforced by it. To some observers the peaceful conduct of the referendum campaign signified the maturity and confidence of the British state. In reality it had little choice and badly overplayed its hand.

The first surge of modern-day nationalism

In 1970 the national minorities of the United Kingdom were travelling on divergent tracks. Scotland's national consciousness was reinforced but also given respectability and acceptability by distinct institutions and some political exceptionalism. In Wales national consciousness was embodied in the survival of its language and attendant culture of writing, poetry and song. In both those countries overtly separatist nationalism dwelt at the margins. In Northern Ireland, in contrast, two competing identities were locked in intensifying conflict as Catholics looked to Dublin and Protestants to London – or their own parochial identity as Ulstermen. Against this background it was the UK economy – its growing debility and changing structure – that opened the door to a revival of Scottish nationalism.

By 1975 the UK economy as a whole was only too evidently falling behind the economies of the other G7 countries. Political paralysis at Westminster fed a pervasive sense of (British) national decline. But in Scotland, the discovery and extraction of North Sea oil and gas gave a fillip to the fortunes of the SNP (founded in 1934). It startled the Westminster establishment by gaining 11 (out of 70) parliamentary seats at the October 1974 general election. By the end of the decade a minority Labour government was surviving only with support from smaller parties including the SNP and the Welsh nationalist party Plaid Cymru. When each demanded a referendum on representative national bodies the government had no choice but to concede. In contrast to Wales, Scotland voted on 1 March 1979 for a more powerful parliament, only to fall foul of a blocking clause in the enabling legislation which required votes in favour to pass a minimum threshold. The delayed effect of these disastrous plebiscites was to be felt decades later and bring the UK to the brink of dissolution.

In the short run however Labour and the nationalists were all punished by the electorate; nationalism as a political cause seemed to have received its quietus. A renewed and more right-wing Conservative Party, now led by Margaret Thatcher, swept into power at Westminster just two months after the Scottish referendum, going on to win three successive general elections with commanding majorities. Her eventual successor John Major added a fourth victory, though less convincingly. Thatcher believed in the traditional unitary British state and the authority of central power backed by a parliamentary majority. There was no place for devolution in this vision: the decisions of a sovereign Westminster parliament would apply across the entire territory of the UK.

As the Conservative grip tightened on England so it faltered in Scotland

But now Scottish exceptionalism steadily asserted itself. As the Conservative grip tightened on England so it faltered in Scotland. The Conservatives had come first in Scotland in a general election with 31 MPs as recently as 1959, the year Mrs Thatcher entered parliament. They still took 22 seats in the election that made her prime minister. By the time of her third and last victory (1987) the Conservatives had shrunk to a mere 10 seats. Ten years later they disappeared entirely, doomed by their opposition to a Scottish parliament. This fateful development eliminated them as the party of the Union, once their principal identity and *raison d'être*. The unionist mantle now fell on Labour, chief beneficiary of anti-Thatcher feeling in Scotland. Labour's Westminster star waxed as that of the Conservatives waned. What made this possible was the formation in 1989 of the Scottish Constitutional Convention (SCC) by a broad range of representatives from civic Scotland and many political parties. It devised a detailed blueprint for devolution including proposals for a directly elected Scottish parliament with wide legislative powers. The SCC's report of 1995 formed the core of the parliament proposal made by Scottish Labour and the Liberal Democrats two years later.

The devolution era

Labour stormed back to office in 1997 as the biggest party in all three British countries. In Scotland its commitment to a devolved parliament was its central pledge and the bedrock of its appeal. While this was sincere, Labour also saw devolution as an insurance policy against a future nationalist surge: change in order to remain the same. It proposed a hybrid (mixed member) electoral system for the new parliament which was intended to prevent one party gaining a majority. The Conservative argument that devolution would not marginalise but feed nationalism was ignored. Labour legislated rapidly to authorise a new referendum in which the Scots voted heavily for a parliament (74.3 per cent) and to give it tax-varying powers (63.5 per cent).

This was duly enacted at Westminster and in 1999 Scotland's first parliament since 1706 met in Edinburgh. It installed a Labour-Liberal administration, termed the 'Scottish executive'. With the Conservatives marginalised, new political fault-lines emerged in Scotland. Opposition to the new devolved government was headed by the SNP which monitored and criticised its timidity in order to make the case for all-out independence. During the next eight years (two fixed terms of the new parliament) the SNP steadily gained ground in Scotland, ridiculing cautious Labour administrations, questioning their loyalty to Scottish priorities and positioning itself to the left of Tony Blair's increasingly right-wing UK Labour government.

This approach paid off. The 2007 elections were a major turning point in Scottish politics. The SNP narrowly emerged as the largest party but without an overall majority, apparently confirming the wisdom of the designers of the hybrid voting system. Since the SNP could not take practical steps towards independence, it focused on delivering competent government and a clear Scots identity, beginning with potent symbolism: the Scottish executive became the Scottish 'government'. SNP first minister Alex Salmond easily out-shone the lacklustre (and short-lived) leaders of the other Scottish parties and was undoubtedly helped when in 2010 the UK general election was lost by Labour's Scottish prime minister, Gordon Brown.

Salmond believed Westminster's new Con-servative-led administration was unlikely to appeal to Scots. Within a year he was proved right. The fourth Scottish election not only returned the SNP to office but equipped them with an overall majority. Scots voters were not ignorant of the SNP's commitment to independence. The crisis of unionism began.

The wily Scottish National Party leader Alex Salmond: he consistently out-manoeuvred London politicians

The referendum campaign

The degree of self-government yielded to Scotland within the Union was increasing even before the referendum campaign opened. By the Scotland Act 2012, the new Conservative prime minister, David Cameron's first government had devolved administration of the land and buildings transaction tax (LBTT), replacing UK stamp duty, and the landfill tax, effective from 2015. Many foreign ob-servers were surprised when Cameron conceded an independence referendum the same year, but he had little choice. John Major, an earlier Conservative prime minister, had conceded the point in a House of Commons exchange with Salmond himself two decades earlier. The SNP had a majority for a referendum at the very least but it chose to behave with perfect constitutional propriety, and not to emulate the behaviour of Sinn Fein which had in 1918 gained a ma-jority in Ireland and promptly seceded. Both sides needed a referen-dum: Edinburgh to achieve independence, Westminster to thwart it.

Now Cameron made an almost fatal error. Convinced Scots vot-ers would shun a leap in the dark, he resisted SNP and other pressure for a three-question referendum (status quo, full powers short of in-

dependence – often called 'devo max', and independence) and insisted on a straight yes or no to the proposition. Salmond conceded
but gained enfranchisement of 16- and 17-year olds. After this 'Edinburgh agreement' Scotland entered a lengthy campaign that would
culminate in the 18 September 2014
plebiscite. At that point support for inde- *Now Cameron made*
pendence was running at only about *an almost fatal error*
30%, for unionism approximately 60%. *... and insisted on a*
Why, then, did this comfortable lead *straight yes or no*
evaporate?

First was the demeanour and confidence of the nationalists. They
were not confined to the SNP; many prominent individuals outside
politics, as well as two smaller political parties – the Greens and the
Scottish Socialist Party (SSP) – spread a positive message in a 'Yes
Scotland' campaign. Pro-independence workers fanned out across
Scotland optimistically combining traditional public meetings with
the SNP's sophisticated voter database. Their sunny outlook gained
authority from the SNP government record. Its leaders ran Scotland
from the social-democratic position formerly occupied by the Scottish
Labour Party, to the latter's extreme discomfort.

In contrast to the populist and positive tone of the Yes campaign,
unionists offered a less attractive face. Though named the 'Better
Together' campaign their task was essentially a negative one – to
create anxiety about the consequences, especially economic, of independence, 'Project Fear' as it was privately described. A third
ballot question (remaining within the Union but with extra self-governing powers) might have allowed more positive advocacy, but
this had been ruled out. The unionist forces, though disparate, were
advocates of the status quo, and their leaders awoke to the frailty
of their position only at the eleventh hour. When they then tried to
craft a positive message they were left awkwardly arguing that a
No vote meant extra powers for Scotland.

A further inhibition shackled the Better Together campaign. The
three unionist parties – Labour, Conservative and Liberal Democrat
– were united on this issue only. Labour cleaved to a traditional
unionist position and kept tight political control of its Scottish party;
the Conservatives, rebuilding in a country that had entirely rejected

them, were free to develop policy; the Liberals were the most internally devolved and had always favoured a federal Britain. Moving to a devo max position would expose major fault lines, as post-referendum developments were to reveal. By campaigning in general terms Better Together had little appeal for the broad mass of Scottish opinion that, while not instinctively pro-independence, certainly thought Scotland fit for self-government.

A further advantage held by pro-independence campaigners lay in the political colour of Scottish identity. The UK's London-centric media and political establishment did not appreciate this until the eve of polling. Communitarian values were certainly stronger in Scotland which had a different school system and past religious settlement; hostility to the market forces favoured by UK governments for thirty years was greater too. The marginalised Conservatives could no longer rally Scots unionists. What mattered now was Labour's British (critics said English) and 'New Labour' character: it had shed much of its socialism leaving

Labour was now the principal unionist party: its bedrock vote was critical

space for the SNP, adopting elements of traditional socialist rhetoric, to fill. Labour was now the principal unionist party: its bedrock vote was critical.

In the final days of the campaign Yes Scotland's incrementally rising support became a surge, gaining ground precisely where Labour had dominated for more than four decades and exposing widespread disillusionment among its traditional supporters. Had this been an election this feeling might have been expressed by a fall in turnout. But the referendum excluded a 'don't know' response, and it was hard to argue that 'all politicians are the same' (another refuge of the apathetic): people faced a simple choice, yes or no.

Once it grasped, belatedly, that the existence of the Union was at stake, the British establishment was galvanised. A succession of business leaders, normally wary of overt political statements, issued dire warnings of lost jobs and investment; the London media turned with fury on the Yes campaign; Labour revitalised its creaking electoral machine and, on the eve of poll, the previously largely-absent Gordon Brown introduced some fervour. To the stick was added a carrot: the leaders of the three unionist parties issued a joint signed statement of undertakings promising new powers. It turned out to be enough to gain victory by 2 million votes to 1.6 million, but it was a victory dearly bought.

Scotland's future

Considerable unionist effort was put into projecting the 55:45 margin as a major political triumph but this was no emphatic victory for 'Project Fear'. Nine voting Scots in 20 had voted to reject the Union, and that on an 82 per cent turnout. Westminster's initial response was to reiterate the promise of devo max, but then Cameron, fearful of an English Conservative backlash, seemed to make it conditional on 'English votes for English laws' and the all-party front collapsed: splits between the unionist parties appeared to vindicate those who had argued that they would not deliver. This maladroit response, together with a growing appreciation of its achievement in raising support for independence from below a third to almost half, seemed to empower nationalism. The SNP's Salmond had resigned, but its membership had more than quadrupled in just two months. Even the SSP and Greens were boosted by a membership surge.

Cameron had appointed Lord Smith of Kelvin to flesh out the devolution commitments and he moved fast, publishing an agreement on further devolution in two months. The government's response of January 2015 was optimistically entitled 'Scotland in the United Kingdom: an enduring settlement'. But by then it was apparent that a referendum intended to scotch the snake had settled nothing. As minds turned to the approaching UK-wide general election the dismal prospects for unionism became all too clear. Scottish Labour had squandered its political capital on achieving a No vote and was now indelibly identified with the Conservatives and Liberal Democrats, neither of whom could withstand the SNP on their own. It compounded its errors by installing a leader of Blairite colour. By contrast the SNP, now confidently led by new first minister Nicola Sturgeon, broadened its appeal.

by then it was apparent that a referendum intended to scotch the snake had settled nothing

The Scottish general election campaign of 2015 was quite unlike that elsewhere in the UK. At the end of it the SNP had captured 56 of Scotland's 59 Westminster seats. 50 per cent of Scots had backed it. Labour had lost 40 seats; like the Conservatives and Liberal Democrats it kept just one seat. It was a rout.

Though rejected in Scotland, the Conservatives had polled sufficiently strongly in England and Wales to govern as a single party at Westminster. The Scotland Act 2016 incorporated Smith's recommendations, increasing the Scottish government's financial responsibility, yielding significant new financial powers, including over income tax and VAT (the UK's only sales tax), devolving substantial parts of the welfare system plus new constitutional powers and discretions in energy and transport policy. It would now be responsible for raising over 50 per cent of its own budget. These changes, all scheduled to take effect before 2020 will transform the Scottish parliament into one of the world's most powerful devolved bodies. Had such concessions been offered in September 2014, they might have captured the Scottish imagination.

Ahead of this radical transfer of powers, the Scottish government treasurer was cautious in his November 2015 budget. Attention was already turning to two further electoral tests. The SNP was a clear winner in the Scottish parliament elections of May 2016, taking 63 of the 129 seats in the Holyrood parliament and staying in government. But they had lost their overall majority and for the rest of their term (which stretches until 2021) will have to seek parliamentary assent from other parties. The real drama lay elsewhere with the displacement of Scottish Labour as principal antagonist of the SNP by a resurgent Conservative Party that had gained 16 seats. Even these results, which opened the prospect of 14 years of unbroken one-party rule by the SNP, were dwarfed in their impact by the next visit of Scots to the polls: the June 2016 referendum on Britain's terms of EU membership.

Nicola Sturgeon, leader of the Scottish National Party and Scotland's first minister since 2014

For once the major parties in Scotland were not split: all four advocated accepting Cameron's renegotiated terms. The SNP had for 20

years been a pro-European advocate, skilfully advocating a European identity for Scotland to offset the risks of independence. First Minister Sturgeon was seen by TV viewers not just in Scotland but across the UK as a principal and persuasive advocate of Remain. She did not fail to point out that Scots would resist being plucked out of the EU against their will. Just 21 months

The Scottish parliament building at Holyrood in Edinburgh; it was designed by the Catalan architect Enric Miralles

earlier, Better Together campaigners had insisted Scotland's continued EU membership turned on rejecting independence. On polling day turnout, no longer embracing 16- and 17-year olds, passed 67 per cent but did not scale the giddy heights of 2014. However, the result was much more emphatic with 62 per cent voting for Remain: every single counting area voted to remain in the European Union.

In this respect Scotland was the least divided country of the four constituent parts of the UK. To the SNP, arguing from the fundamental principle of nationality, any attempt to extract Scotland from the EU against its will would be illegitimate. To unionists however, and especially to the new Theresa May led government of July 2016, the UK had entered, and must now leave, as one unit. Nationalists were not slow to argue that such a fundamental change in Scotland's material circumstances should trigger a new independence referendum.

To the SNP... any attempt to extract Scotland from the EU against its will would be illegitimate

Scottish identity

An unshakeable national identity is the enduring feature of Scottish politics. In the 2011 census, 62 per cent of the total population reported their identity was 'Scottish only' – a proportion varying from 71 per cent for 10 to 14 year olds to 57 per cent for 30 to 34 year olds. The second most common response, 'Scottish and British identities only', was far behind at 18 per cent and most common among the 65 to 74 age group (25 per cent). 'British identity only' was chosen by a mere 8 per cent of the population and most evident among the 50 to 64 age group (10 per cent). A Scots identity may have been reinforced by the relatively low (4 per cent) proportion of the population belonging to ethnic minorities. In addition, the EU referendum result suggests a big majority do not feel there is a conflict between Scots and European identities.

If Scotland's national identity is clear, what are its roots? Certainly it was acknowledged, even guaranteed, by the Act of Union. The retention of a distinct church settlement, education and legal systems and the implications of a certain communitarian spirit have been noted. Scotland's national church, the Church of Scotland is Presbyterian: in that church no one person or group is preeminent and so it has no head of faith, taking its lead from the bible. Neither Holyrood nor Westminster is involved in its appointments. Its status as the national church dates from the re-establishment of Scottish Presbyterianism in 1690, guaranteed by the 1707 Union. Yet today, fewer than 30% attend its services and 37% of Scots profess no religion, compared with 25% in England and Wales.

Scotland's education system contrasts sharply with England's. It may owe its distinctive character to the Scottish Reformation, whose charismatic leader John Knox demanded an elementary school in every parish. Knox wanted to spread the study of the bible and literacy was a prerequisite but his views became part of the institutional memory. Right on the eve of the Union, a 1696 act of the Scots parliament – believed to be the world's first national education act – provided for a school in every parish, a fixed salary for the teacher and financial arrangements to cover the cost. This and later additions ensured that by the mid-19th century very large numbers were literate. Scotland appointed the first inspector of schools in 1840 and from 1872 all children between 5 and 13 had to receive education, a service funded by the local property tax.

Education now left church hands and the right to opt out of religious education was enshrined in law. All head teachers

In the 2011 census, 62 per cent of the total population reported their identity was 'Scottish only'

had to hold a certificate of competency and all teachers were trained. Since 1890 primary education has been free.

Consequentially, nearly all Scots share a common educational experience. Today, pupils overwhelmingly attend publicly funded schools, while less than 3 per cent of primary-aged and barely 5 percent of secondary-aged pupils attend private schools. Catholic schools came into the state education system in 1918 but were allowed to continue as denominational schools. A later key reform established a single external examination system (the 'highers'). The higher is Scotland's gold standard certifying a broad general education: it has been the main route to higher education since 1888.

Scottish higher education is highly distinguished. Among its 19 autonomous institutions are some of the oldest universities in Europe: St Andrew's (established in 1411), Scotland's first university and the third oldest in the English-speaking world; Glasgow (1451), with seven Nobel laureates and in 1840 the first British university to appoint a professor of engineering; and Aberdeen (a merger of universities founded in 1495 and 1593), highly distinguished in medical research and the UK's fifth oldest. The University of Edinburgh enrolled its first students in 1583 and was pivotal to the Scottish Enlightenment, intellectual home to David Hume, philosopher, economist and essayist; Joseph Black, the chemist behind the discovery of latent heat and carbon dioxide; and James Hutton, the 'father of modern geology'.

Scots law has a complicated history that goes back as far as Roman times. Roman law principles were used to develop Scots law which, at the moment of union was basically a system of rights and obligations. These basic principles are still applied in modern day courts though the long common history with England (where law rests on precedent and legislation) has had a significant impact over the three centuries of the Union – see chapter 19 for a broader discussion.

Other expressions of identity

Beyond those features endorsed by the Act of Union, stretch profound cultural identifiers. In contrast to Wales, which found consolation for political impotence in the robustness of its language,

Gaelic is marginalised, its speakers fewer than 60,000 (1.5 per cent of the population) in 2013. It receives sympathetic treatment from the Scottish government via official document bilingualism and a radio and television station. MSPs may use it to address the Holyrood parliament. Scots is quite another matter. The 2011 census for the first time asked respondents whether they could understand, speak, read or write Scots. 1.5 million people reported that they could speak it and 1.9 million reported that they could speak, read, write or understand it. Scots (sometimes dismissed as a mere dialect) came to Scotland in the 7th century as 'old English', then diverged from English during the wars of independence and eventually became a separate language. Generally, it was spoken in the Lowlands while Gaelic was the dominant language of the Highlands. After the Act of Union, English was encouraged and became the dominant language, used in writing and by the wealthy. However, versions of Scots remained in common use, sustaining a rich tradition in poetry, song and literature. This includes both the oral and written work of authors and poets, from the Renaissance (Barbour, Henryson and Dunbar) to the Enlightenment (Ramsay, Fergusson, Burns and Scott) to modern figures: R.L. Stevenson, George MacDonald, J. M. Barrie, Hugh MacDiarmid, Lewis Grassic Gibbon, John Buchan, Irvine Welsh and Liz Lochhead.

Scots identity has also been reinforced by many experiences which might have been expected to inculcate unionism: Scottish regiments named for regions (the Highlands) or counties (Sutherland) were prominent in both world wars. Edinburgh is home to the UK's second most significant financial centre, albeit on a far smaller scale than London, and three of Scotland's banks still produce legal tender (though under the control of the Bank of England, the UK's central bank). In one distinctive feature the country takes little pride. Scotland's unhealthy diet is widely cited as a factor in its poor health record. After smoking, Scottish eating habits are the second most

Robert Louis Stevenson (1850-1894): author of Treasure Island, Kidnapped *and* The Strange Case of Dr Jekyll and Mr Hyde

important cause of the nation's woeful health. While the 'deep-fried Mars Bar' may be an urban myth, children and the young follow a diet less healthy than that of other European children. Food Standards Scotland has recommended tougher targets for healthy eating after finding 'little or no progress' over the years 1999-2014.

The cities and beyond

Edinburgh's dramatic landscape is unmistakeably that of a capital city, celebrated architecturally by those who embraced the Union. The extinct volcano that forms its heart was a capital for Scots kings from the 7th century. But adjacent to this 'Old Town' is a wonder of the Scottish Enlightenment, the elegant, planned and proportional 'New Town'. By 2011, Edinburgh's population had reached 475,000. It benefits hugely from the emergence of Holyrood as Scotland's chief political focus. The proportion of Edinburgh residents holding a degree level qualification (41 per cent) is bettered in the UK only by Cambridge, inner London and Oxford. The relatively large number of Edinburgh residents born in such Western European countries as Germany, France and Spain reflects the city's status as a major business, learning and culture player. Few other UK cities have a higher proportion. Edinburgh hosts national galleries, two royal palaces, two cathedrals, the national rugby union ground (Murrayfield) and the Scottish parliament. The city became more ethnically diverse between 2001 and 2011, when non-white ethnic minorities doubled to pass eight per cent of the total population. This is well above the Scottish average (4.0%), but far lower than the England & Wales average (14.0%).

Glasgow (600,000, but with at least 1.2 million in a wider Clydeside) is Scotland's largest city, dating from at least the 12th century. It is architecturally graced by the work of Robert Adam, Alexander 'Greek' Thomson, and Charles Rennie Mackintosh. Unsurprisingly, it was European City of Culture in 1990, UK City of Architecture and Design in 1999 and is a World Heritage City. Admirers of its friendliness contrast it with what the novelist Muriel Spark once described as Edinburgh's 'cold, Calvinist heart'. Where Edinburgh

Glasgow ... was a formidable rival claimant to England's Birmingham to the title of 'second city of the empire'

occupies the south bank of the vast Forth estuary flowing east, Glasgow straddles the formidable Clyde estuary that flows west. It grew great on the industrial revolution, the Atlantic and imperial trade. Strong in manufactures, engineering and shipbuilding, it was a formidable rival claimant to England's Birmingham to the title of 'second city of the empire' and on the eve of World War II the population of the city proper stood at its peak of 1,128,000, many of them crammed into dense tenements later bulldozed.

Glasgow overtook Edinburgh in size because of immigration, above all due to the vast influx of Catholic Irish in the 19th century; there was a corresponding – though smaller – inflow of Presbyterian Northern Irish. Of all the mainland cities none exhibited the symptoms of sectarian conflict more than Glasgow where discrimination against Catholics was rampant in the 19th and early 20th centuries, most notably in employment and schooling. For a long time the city even had lay associations – Orange Orders, the Knights of St Columba – linked to the rival faiths in dismal echo of Ulster. They had mass support. Today the city has four cathedrals. Political and religious loyalties translated easily into support for the city's two great football clubs, the best supported in Scotland. (Glasgow) Celtic has moved beyond its confessional base but its great rival (Glasgow) Rangers still struggles: no Scots Catholic has ever played for its first team, though these days the make-up of the teams is more international than Scottish. In more attractive reflection of sporting feeling, Glasgow is also home to the national football stadium Hampden Park.

Memorial at Glasgow Rangers' ground at Ibrox: 66 fans were crushed to death at a match involving Glasgow rivals Rangers and Celtic in January 1971, the first of a succession of disasters in British football grounds in the 1970s and 1980s

Aberdeen (225,000) is an ancient Scottish burgh that initially developed as a place of learning and a port. In the 20th century, when the economic importance of fishing declined it found a new role as Europe's oil capital, base for exploration and extraction of fossil fuels from the North Sea. Dundee (150,000), dramatically stretched along the north coast of the broad Tay estuary built a distinct identity from empire imports and re-exports, notably in jute and jam manufacture. It was for a time an important media centre and is now the centre of a resurgent computer games industry. Stirling (90,000) and Inverness (60,000) are the only other cities of any size.

But Scotland's cities, like those of Wales, are an imperfect reflection of the country. Most Scots live in the central belt, which includes both Edinburgh and Glasgow. Proceeding north from this belt, the traveller soon reaches the Highlands and off the west coast, the Islands. Scotland's western coastline is sheltered by innumerable islands and houses countless sea lochs. There are many freshwater lochs too.

The Highlands are the classic terrain of deer celebrated by Landseer's famous 19th century painting of a stag, 'The Monarch of the Glen'; their moors are also favoured by grouse-shooters. The rugged impact of the glacier also shaped the contours of Britain's highest mountains, the tallest of which (Ben Nevis and the Cairngorms) exceed 4,000 feet: though modest in height by US or continental European standards, Scotland's northerly latitude and stormy weather can at times make these forbidding environments. The most celebrated industry of the Highlands (and some of the Islands) is the distilling of whisky, drawing on a great natural legacy of pure water and barley as well as ancient skills. It is an industry that also contributes to Highland Scotland's attractions as a tourist destination.

Distilling Scotch whisky, Scotland's iconic export: the Highlands in particular are thickly sprinkled with distilleries

The Highlands are not Scotland's only mountains: plenty (of gentler elevation) are to be found in the 'Lowlands' of the border country between Edinburgh and England. To the far north are two important mini archipelagos: the Orkneys (visible from the mainland) and the Shetlands, 200 miles distant and closer to Oslo than to London. Each bears traces of the Neolithic, Viking, and paleo-Christian past. The Western Isles of the Outer Hebrides arc around Scotland's north-western coast and shelter the Inner Hebrides. Further south, peninsulas and other islands (including Iona) point towards the nearby coast of Ulster. The east coast, less complex than the west, mostly lacks islands and is cut by broad handsome rivers that empty into the North Sea: Tweed, Tay and Dee. Scotland has five UNESCO World Heritage sites: neolithic Orkney, St Kilda (an abandoned island of the Outer Hebrides with a distinct culture), the Antonine wall (of the 1st century AD), New Lanark (an 18th and 19th century model town) and Edinburgh's Old and New Towns.

8. London

London, capital of England and the UK, is exceptionally dominant over both. Germany's Frankfurt is its financial centre, Hamburg its trading focus and Munich its commercial hub, all with architectural and art resources of world renown and their own media. Berlin, the actual capital, regained this status only in 1990 after a 45-year interval. Paris may dominate France more completely, but Bordeaux (trade and wine), Lyons (manufacturing) and Marseilles (sea freight) remain sturdily independent. French and German cities all have robust links in a transport network that does not depend on the capital. In Chicago, Los Angeles, New York, San Francisco & the Bay Area and Washington DC, the United States has five world cities – perhaps more – if we are to judge by economic weight, political influence and cultural assets. In the UK London combines capital city status with political, financial and cultural domination as well as vastly greater size: no other British city can match it in any single sector.

From this unrivalled position it commands the lion's share whenever new resources become available and so extends its lead. Its preeminence leads some to suggest London is best understood as a city state. With a population of 8.6 million it is home to nearly 1 in 7 of the UK population, generating 22 per cent of the UK GDP, and the inner dynamic propelling its chaotic growth is forecast to increase its population to ten million by 2031. It is also in many ways very different (as the 2016 EU referendum showed) in attitudes and interests to most of the rest of England.

Capital city

London was the major port and administrative centre (though not the capital) of the imperial province for the Romans, its founders over two millennia ago. It was almost certainly their largest settlement both before and after the Boudican sack of 61 AD. It was the largest English town, displacing Winchester (the Anglo-Saxon capital) when the invading Normans needed to dominate England. Their leader William ('the Conqueror') could not feel secure until he had concentrated power there against a sullen and dispossessed population. His 11th century court, executive and legislature all in one, was the principal centre of political influence. Medieval courts travelled on circuit in later centuries but London's capital status was never subsequently in doubt. Parliament's 13th century origins as advisor to the crown required proximity to the court. 16th and 17th century England may have been a second-division player among the European powers but London was rivalled only by Paris as the largest city.

The 1640s saw a London-located parliament wrest ultimate authority from the crown in the Civil War: when the king switched his capital to Oxford it was only because he had to, with the parliament side controlling London. Persons or organisations seeking to influence policy, gain wealth or personal advancement continued to gravitate there as the centuries passed. The emergence first of 19th century cabinet government and then the powerful 20th century core executive changed nothing: the city continued to host both law-making and decision-taking. Today 'SW1', the Westminster postal district, represents a colossal concentration of executive power and legislative influence. All central government buildings are located there. When in the 21st century the judiciary was extracted from the legislature it was promptly relocated next door. Britain's weak centrifugal forces cannot match the magnetic attraction of the centre: like medieval courtiers, organisations and individuals aspiring to influence must maintain a London presence.

London's dominance over UK policy-making was dented neither by devolution nor by almost half-a-century in the supra-national EU. Such relocation of government functions as has taken place has been minor (the Royal Mint) or fraught with problems such as key staff not being prepared to leave London (the National Statistics Agency). While political devolution to Scotland and Wales is increasingly real, administrative devolution within England is not.

Financial hub

Inside London is 'the City', a great concentration of financial power, the global hub, vastly more powerful than continental European centres like Zurich, Frankfurt or Paris. The historic City, with its own system of local government, spans a mere square mile yet houses the Stock Exchange, the Bank of England (the UK's mis-named central bank), several commodity and financial product exchanges, Lloyds (the dominant shipping insurers) and many private finance majors.

In the 1690s Lloyds, the Exchange and the Bank virtually invented modern finance-capital

In the 1690s Lloyds, the Exchange and the Bank virtually invented modern finance-capital. From here they spawned a dense network of global relationships expanding across – and beyond – the British empire. After World War II the empire disintegrated and the City entered a period of relative decline before recovering strongly in a new era of deregulation and innovation that began in the 1980s and gained pace thereafter – a transformation visually symbolised by the change from a skyline still dominated in the 1970s by the 17th century St Paul's cathedral to the mushrooming glass and steel skyscrapers of today.

London's financial preeminence has been restored but its scope is now global rather than imperial. It is as committed to making money from markets as ever and well-placed to benefit from future sources of income: it is easily the largest exchange and derivatives centre in the world, the only one that trades in renminbi-denominated financial products, the only Western centre of Islamic trade. World time is measured plus or minus

The Bank of England: founded in 1694 and the bedrock of British financial stability, as expressed in the old saying 'as safe as the Bank of England'

hours to Greenwich Mean Time (GMT) on a line of longitude running through the Royal London borough of that name. This is a great advantage for the City: London's capital markets open as Tokyo's close but hours before Wall Street starts to trade.

A few miles east of the historic City is 'Docklands', a new financial quarter fashioned out of London's derelict docks and neighbouring areas. Dominated by towering office blocks, it is home to many large venture banks and media conglomerates as well as affluent riverside urban-dwellers. In twenty years a central government initiative (at first not without local opposition) transformed a vast district of over eight square miles from decay to modernity. It has its own (driverless) light rail system and is the focus of new high-speed public transport connections with a major social impact on the deprived adjacent boroughs of London's East End. Now restored to local government, Docklands rivals the congested City for inward investment. Its dramatic architecture began the transformation of the riverscape and is increasingly echoed in clusters of new tall buildings on other stretches of the Thames.

Local government

London first gained elective government in 1888, when the boundaries of the London County Council (LCC) encompassed a far smaller city than today, establishing small boroughs to dispense local services on the rates, as local property taxes were called. The Greater London Council of 1965, the LCC's successor, swallowed the county of Middlesex and parts of Surrey and Essex, amalgamating the small LCC boroughs into 32 larger ones. It lasted just 21 years until its abolition in 1986 removed city-wide government entirely.

Elective London government returned in 2000 in the shape of the Greater London Authority (GLA) comprising an executive mayor and assembly each with a four-year term. The first two mayors, Ken Livingstone (Labour) and Boris Johnson (Conservative), were accomplished publicists but their high profile disguised their

The first two mayors ... were accomplished publicists but their high profile disguised their rather meagre powers

rather meagre powers. London is frequently compared with New York but is a political pygmy, its tax income raised not directly but as a precept on the council tax (the revised version of the rates) raised by the boroughs. Londoners pay many other taxes to central government, leading Boris Johnson (mayor in 2008-16) to claim that while New York retained 50 per cent of the taxes raised within it, London kept just five per cent. While the GLA has its own income, notably from public transport (see below), its spending power is actually pitiful: like other sub-national branches of UK government, it is fed from the centre.

Despite this limitation, the GLA is a strategic body. The mayor's £17bn annual budget supports investment in public transport, fire services and policing as well as the work of City Hall (its striking home and metaphor for transparency). This budget is funded by central government grants, transport fares and other charges, business rates and the council tax precept. Public transport takes pride of place because its agency Transport for London (TfL) runs the most extensive urban transport system in the world. TfL encompasses not only the famous underground railway (the 'tube') but whole sub-systems, buses, trams, the overground, the DLR. It also regulates those parts of the system in private hands – taxis (black cab and minicab) and boats, enforces a congestion charge zone on roads in the centre, and will introduce a low emission zone in 2020. TfL accounts for some two-thirds of GLA income.

The GLA is also London's police authority, though it has no role in the wider criminal justice system. Johnson established a Mayor's Office for Policing and Crime (MOPAC) to deliver the police

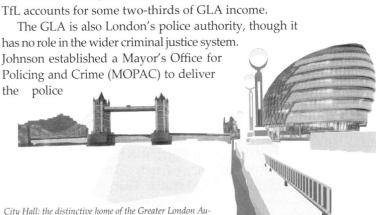

City Hall: the distinctive home of the Greater London Authority sits on the now bustling South Bank, previously an area of wharves and warehouses

and crime plan, and hold the Metropolitan Police Service and other law agencies to account for efficient, effective and fair policing and crime reduction. Fire and emergency planning and regulation of the River Thames complete the portfolio of strategic functions. Under the law that set up the GLA, the mayor must hold two public 'people's question time' events annually; mayor's question times, in front of the assembly, occur ten times a year.

Beneath the GLA sit London's 32 boroughs, varying in size in 2015 from the 158,000 of Kensington and Chelsea to the around 380,000 of Barnet in the north and Croydon in the south. They are obliged to deliver local services within a broad framework set by central government: housing, environmental, educational and other responsibilities. Like local government

Transport for London (TfL) runs the most extensive urban transport system in the world

elsewhere they increasingly act as licensing authorities rather than direct providers. Like the GLA, borough councillors are elected for four-year terms. The City, with barely more than 8,000 residents, enjoys its own form of government – the City of London Corporation – and claims to be the oldest continuous municipal democracy. Its unusual system of government comprises 25 wards, each electing an alderman and two or more common councilmen, depending on population. The small resident population shares the franchise with businesses, and has a figurehead – the lord mayor, quite distinct from the mayor of London, to promote the City's financial and business role. For 800 years he (and a few shes) have travelled in colourful medieval pageant to Westminster to swear loyalty to the crown.

Diversity and cohesion

London has always been diverse, a natural consequence of its role as an entrepôt. But the driving forces for that diversity have changed, in recent decades being the end of empire and the cashing in of citizenship rights by former colonial subjects or their descendants; the huge importance of London within the UK economy; its global significance as a financial centre; and its status as Europe's anglophone world city, open to all citizens of the European Union.

While English is the common language, London is home to a vast array of languages and dialects. It has the lowest proportion in the UK of residents whose main language is English (78 per cent), and the highest proportions of usual residents born outside the UK and non-UK nationals. Polish is the most common 'other' main language followed by Bengali (with Sylheti and Chatgaya) and Gujarati. London is also the most ethnically diverse region of the UK and has the highest proportion of people affiliated with a religion other than Christian. One in eight children is of mixed race. All this was given a concrete expression in the 2016 mayoral election which returned Sadiq Khan – a London-born Muslim – on the Labour ticket. His opponent sought to capitalise on Khan's Muslim identity. Most Londoners, far from being alarmed, just shrugged.

London has been described as a collection of villages and their outline may still be discerned, with the remnants of traditional ancient village high streets and greens cropping up in the most unlikely urban landscapes. London grew by filling in the gaps between these villages, by increasing density and by municipal spread. Faced with such diversity, there can seem to be many Londons, not one. It can be difficult to see factors in common between the City or Westminster and most outer London boroughs. The latter are increasingly becoming the only locations cheap enough to accommodate service workers, tenants and the low paid – three categories in which London's ethnic minorities are strongly represented. To some extent the inner/outer dichotomy is concretised by the tube which divides the city into five principal fare zones: zones 1 and 2 are a useful definition of inner London though they are widely regarded as arbitrary and are certainly geographically misleading. Yet inner vs. outer does not capture the huge social and financial gulf separating, for example, Enfield and Croydon (the northern and southern extremes) from, say, the green acres of Richmond along the upper Thames.

Sadiq Khan, elected the mayor of London in May 2016

To complicate matters further, the boroughs themselves are poor analytical units. All have areas of both poverty and wealth, as illustrated by the great variety (age, condition and architectural distinction) of housing stock. One reason why London is said to 'work' (i.e. not dissolve into periodic riot or be awash with criminality) is the proximity of rich and poor. 'Gentrification' – the occupation of formerly despised areas by the affluent – keeps street status fluid, and has transformed many once dilapidated areas of inner London. Elegant Georgian terraces may be around the corner from municipal es-

'Gentrification' ... has transformed many once dilapidated areas of inner London

tates where poverty prevails. Gated estates do exist, as do gated individual dwellings, but they are exceptional. The 'poor doors' lamented by New York's mayor are, as yet, few.

The experience of housing and housing tenure sharply divides London. For a city heading for a ten million population its house-building record is poor. An absolute scarcity of residences has driven up their price, whether for rent or purchase, with the effect that London property ownership is a one-way bet to accumulate wealth. This is to the satisfaction of longstanding residents across the city, but has also attracted the attention of those seeking to park 'hot' money in a central location. Transparency International claims the percentage of homes bought through offshore companies in Westminster is over nine per cent, in Kensington & Chelsea over seven per cent and in the City nearly five per cent. Since they are not acquired for use, such properties are often vacant. This is the opposite of the experience of many London residents, who often endure multi-occupation in private or social housing of doubtful quality.

The city is so large that local identities and appellations may be the only way to make sense of it. 'North London' is a geographically imprecise term intended to convey a population of affluent persons of liberal outlook inhabiting a belt embracing certain parts of Camden, Islington and Haringey: to this day, some such north Londoners would hesitate to live in the tube-starved terra incognita of 'south of the river' (though some south-of-the-river localities are in truth now distinctly more 'north London' than most of the northern boroughs). The East End is equally undefined, but its shifting boundaries are always associated with gritty inner-city poverty married to immigrant exoticism: Huguenots (17th century French protestants fleeing religious persecution), 19th century Jews, 20th century Bangladeshis all found a home there before moving on. The West End is not a residential but a shopping location – the giant department stores of Oxford Street and nearby. Inner south-west London contains Chelsea, haunt of young rich women said to determinedly roam its upmarket emporia, the 'Sloane Rangers' made famous in the 1980s (for Sloane Square, its principal shopping hub). Identities like these help to make sense of a large city.

And yet there are factors that unify. The most immediately visible is Transport for London (TfL). Stand on any thoroughfare and you will soon see the familiar red livery of a London bus. The tube conveys more than 90 million passengers annually through each of Waterloo, King's Cross/St Pancras, and Oxford Circus, its busiest stations: they might be office cleaners or the governor of the Bank of England. Tube services become patchier away from the centre and tend to be concentrated north of the river, but TfL runs an outer orbital system (the overground) that haphazardly traces the old LCC border. This overground is its vehicle for an ambitious municipalisation project to integrate outer London's surface railways. If it is completed it the social impact will be incalculable. In time the whole DLR network may do the same for the outer-east boroughs. In outer south London two boroughs – Croydon and Bromley – even have their own tram system. This ambitious transport network has drawbacks. It penalises longer journeys, hitting poorer peripheral residents hardest, but it is used by all.

London's river, the Thames – nearly all its tributaries have been built over and disappeared from sight – also symbolises unity. The Thames was the reason for the city's original settlement, though London long existed only on the north bank and managed with only one bridge (London Bridge, crossing to Southwark, then considered a different place) for many centuries. Today, as depicted in the TfL roundel, London is a blob equally divided by the blue band of the river. Bigger ships ended the Pool of London's commercial role but it is slowly recovering tourist trade courtesy of an ever-improving boat service. Bridges and high-end waterfront residences are proliferating. The public has regained access to virtually its entire length on both banks. Being by the Thames is a pleasure enjoyed by walking Londoners who can observe its remarkable tidal rise and fall of 23 feet. It is a river more looked upon than travelled, with today's docks located far away where its broad estuary empties into the North Sea.

London residents also have public services in common. Huge general hospitals allied to universities may be seen across central London perpetuating a presence that stretches back to the 18th century. While London is home to the densest concentration of private hospitals too, most Londoners are patients of the state-provided National Health Service (NHS). The education services of the LCC enjoyed a world-class reputation but reverted to the boroughs upon its abolition and for a time performance in many areas faltered. More recently London schools have performed strongly after a sustained programme of investment and intervention by government. Grades in London schools, from being lower than national averages in the 1990s, are now higher.

There are 11 London underground lines, with 270 stations: most of the network is north of the Thames, south London being poorly served

London's wealth of public spaces is another common resource. They can take many forms – the elegant Georgian square or the more familiar green guise of a park. The 5,000 acres distributed across eight royal parks in central London receive millions of residents and tourists each year for a simple walk, picnic, sport, entertainment, or to visit the historic buildings within. Hyde Park, Regent's Park and Kensington Gardens break up and divide central London. Despite their collective name they are managed by a central government agency. Meanwhile the City and Corporation owns and manages almost 4,500 hectares of historic and natural open space for public recreation and health. These are scattered across the wider city, among them famous spaces like Hampstead Heath and Epping Forest. Such green oases, though distributed more widely across London than the royal parks, cost local communities little. They are funded principally by the City, mostly function as charitable trusts and attract 23 million visits annually to their wildlife habitats, sites of scientific interest and national nature reserves. Most parks are locally run by their boroughs. They too exist in great number: the north London borough of Haringey, for instance, has over thirty, most quality-stamped with a 'green flag'. Others, especially in south London, are known as 'commons', important social signifiers in this property-conscious city. Largest of all the enclosed parks is Richmond Park, in the south-west, created as a royal park by King Charles I in the 17th century for hunting and where deer still roam.

Some green spaces, and many squares, fall under private ownership but still permit public access. In deprived east London the 560-acre Queen Elizabeth II Olympic Park has risen from derelict land reclaimed for London's 2012 Games. It is adjacent to Lee Valley Regional Park, 10,000 acres sprawling 26 miles along the course of one London river that has not disappeared (other than in its lower reaches where it approaches the Thames), created by act of parliament as a 'green lung' for the city.

Public space – space that does not require an entrance fee – is not necessarily open to the elements. In a millennial project the British Museum opened up – then covered – its great court (though it did not fail to provide opportunities to spend money). The atrium of the British Library is similar and anyone may likewise wander into the great flagship art and science museums without paying. London provides immense opportunities to sightsee without paying a penny.

The arts

London's concentration of arts institutions is unmatched in the UK, or even Europe. It has three of England's seven large-scale lyric opera or ballet companies and is the only British city with two dedicated opera houses. Theatres defy enumeration: the famous West End alone hosts more than fifty and this excludes the subsidised houses, 'off West End' (a category for large private theatres not centrally located), and the numberless venues above or behind pubs that stage live performance. Live music – rock or classical – is as widespread. There are huge venues (the O_2 arena or the Albert Hall), medium-

sized (the Barbican or Royal Festival Halls) and tiny ones (the Wigmore Hall or Kings Place). Many buildings have become concert venues: few conveniently-located churches fail to host classical concerts, sometimes entrance-free. A new classical concert hall is planned to address perceived poor acoustics in current spaces.

Named in memory of Queen Victoria's consort, Prince Albert, the Royal Albert Hall is famed for the annual summertime 'Proms' concerts, one of the world's greatest festivals of classical music

London is home to the Royal Academy, the National Gallery, the National Portrait Gallery, Tate Britain and Tate Modern, the Hayward Gallery and the Courtauld Gallery. It offers the British Museum, the Victoria & Albert Museum (the V&A), the Natural History Museum, the Science Museum and the Imperial War Museum. This astonishing concentration of immense museums and galleries in the capital reflects the distribution of power relative to the provinces. A 2013 report concluded that 'the centre' in England makes decisions on 75 per cent of the public's funds available for the arts – a far higher proportion than in comparable countries. Nor does this arise merely from public policy: in 2011-2012 some 82 per cent of private sector arts funding also went to London-based organisations. Indeed, a feature of the 2010s has been the expansion or establishment of very large private art galleries. They may feature more and more as the public sector languishes for lack of funds.

Nearly £600 million flowed from government to London galleries, museums and theatres in 2012-2013 while arts organisations elsewhere in England made do with barely one-third this amount. Arts Council England (ACE) (see chapter 15) distributes 45 per cent of National Lottery money to

The National Gallery on Trafalgar Square

The vast Tate Modern, dedicated to the display of modern art, is housed in a former power station on the South Bank

the arts in London, leaving 55 per cent for the rest of England. Indeed Arts Council spending since 1946 reveals a consistent London bias that has tended to grow despite contrary protestations. At the Department for Culture, Media & Sport (DCMS), which funds 16 major 'national' cultural organisations directly, 90 per cent of available funds directly benefited London. One critical assessment puts combined DCMS and Arts Council spending at £69 a head compared to under £5 a head for the rest of England. Rectifying the imbalance is not simple: London's cultural capital has accumulated over centuries to the prestige of the country as a whole and the galleries and theatres in London are far more accessible to visitors from overseas (or indeed most parts of the UK) than are those in provincial cities. Of the world's ten most visited museums in 2014, London was the only city with three (the British Museum, the National Gallery and the Tate Modern).

The public transport system

The main UK rail and road trunk routes fan out from London. The main rail termini are all located there, recipients of a giant refurbishment programme that has restored St Pancras International and King's Cross to more than their former glory. By rail it can often be quicker to travel from one provincial city to another via the capital. This illustrates London's success in attracting public infrastructural investment.

Around the capital a densely-woven quilt of suburban rail lines conveys large numbers of commuters daily. The Elizabeth line, Europe's largest construction project running from Berkshire and Buckinghamshire to Essex, will increase central London rail capacity by 10 per cent. Its east/west route stretches 100km with ten new stations, bringing an extra 1.5 million people within 45 minutes of central London: 200 million passengers will use it annually from 2018. A new north-east/south-west line is also planned: little wonder London's share of national transport spending is already one-third.

The city was the first in the world to open a metro system in 1863. Like many pioneers the transport authority has the curse of being first, yet it has responded by installing new technologies and the system has never stopped growing. Londoners grumble constantly about the tube, but it carries 1.3 billion passengers annually and for many journeys is the fastest possible route. Not even Paris's famous metro badges its capital as effectively as the tube expresses London, a PR success powered by the longstanding willingness of London Transport/TfL to sponsor contemporary art and design. The famous map (in reality a diagram), the posters pictorializing exciting city life or tranquil semi-rural suburbia, above all the famous logo are fruits of this enlightened policy. London's late 19th/early 20th century growth was above all due to the building of fast transit routes conveying commuters into the centre: over time their home areas became London too. The famous and distinguished London Underground posters of the 1920s and 1930s fostered an idea of attractive suburban life facilitated by public transport, simultaneously projecting distance from and participation in metropolitan life. City and transport system are inseparable.

Today's TfL no longer runs two bus systems – red for London and green for those running out into the country. Areas newly arrived in London enjoy the familiar red bus. The 2011 census revealed that in an area of London roughly corresponding to the old LCC, i.e. the more inner boroughs, more than 40 per cent of people lived in households with no car – far above the level in any other part of Britain. Almost 600 million bus journeys are made annually. As the city stretches ever further outwards, nibbling at the 'green belt' on its way (see final chapter), new transport needs become apparent and novel schemes are hatched.

The familiar London 'double-decker' bus. The double-deckers run on the main routes, with single-deckers on subsidiary routes, especially in the suburbs

Ideas and sport

It is not surprising then that the media are concentrated in London. The BBC (see chapter 17) and all other major broadcasters are based in London. National newspapers have shed any regional identities they might have had; if they are repositioning themselves it is either towards global markets or into digital. The UK's major publishers are nearly all in London.

At the dawn of the 20th century London had only one university. Today London University's 19 colleges are largely self-governing and for all practical purposes function as universities in their own right. Imperial College, King's, the LSE and UCL regularly appear at the top of global rankings. In addition, there are 29 other higher education institutions located in the city. In 2014 government funding was promised to 'Olympicopolis', a new education and cultural district centred on the Queen Elizabeth II Park. Partners include University College London, University of the Arts London (UAL), a new V&A museum, Sadler's Wells and a London College of Fashion campus. London has four cathedrals (if Westminster abbey – which functions as one in every respect except the ecclesiastical – is included); no other English city has more than two.

The 2012 Olympic Games focused many issues entwined in the city's identity. London was awarded the games seven years earlier for a bid resting on pledges to leave a legacy and transform the city. A proposed new East End Olympic park would be wrapped around the new national athletics stadium, aquatic centre and velodrome. This would be a compact, non-wasteful Games, with several temporary venues relocated beyond London and no white elephants. The bid victory was speedily followed by the July London bombings but revelations that the perpetrators were British-born seemed to focus efforts to integrate the ethnically-rich, money-poor East End. However, while Team GB's 2012 achievements glittered, the promised legacy of a fitter nation proved elusive. Four years on, other more tangible inheritances are real enough: the Olympic village is becoming new housing, the Premiership football side West Ham has moved into the Olympic Stadium and the Queen Elizabeth II Park is available for all.

The London Eye: constructed as a temporary feature for the millenium celebrations, it has since be-come a landmark tourist attraction

It will be no surprise that the UK's principal sporting venues are in London (for sport generally, see chapter 16). Indeed, London has a greater concentration of internationally-famous historic sporting venues than anywhere else on earth. England's national football stadium is at Wembley (north-west London), Wimbledon (in south-west London) hosts one of world tennis's four 'grand slam' competitions (and the most prestigious); rugby union's HQ is at Twickenham (also south-west London); Lord's (Marylebone) is the headquarters of world cricket. London is home to major football Premiership sides – Arsenal and Tottenham Hotspur (Spurs) in north London, Chelsea in west London – as well as many smaller clubs. But London does not have quite the same monopoly in sport that it has in many other areas: the historically most successful football sides (Liverpool and Manchester United) are in the north of the country, as is the most renowned cricketing county (Yorkshire), while the British Olympics medallists in 2016 trained in all parts of the United Kingdom.

9. Brexit!

On 23 June 2016 the UK voted by 51.9 to 48.1 per cent to leave the European Union, a clear margin of over 1.25 million votes. Forty-three years of reluctant compromise with the European project had ended with victory for those calling for what had become known as Brexit.

Theresa May, who took office as prime minister after the resignation of David Cameron in the immediate aftermath, responded to the huge turnout and substantial margin for Leave by confirming that 'Brexit means Brexit'. She went further and restructured her government to deliver the exit negotiations, installing Leave campaigners in the three principal posts responsible (see chapter 3). Within three months she committed to triggering Article 50 of the EU Lisbon Treaty – the exit clause – by end-March 2017. This may take the UK out by around March 2019. To some in the UK, and many outside it, the result was a huge shock or disappointment; to others it was unsurprising or a cause for great joy. Explanations proliferated but tended to have a common thread: the multiple divisions and differences woven through the fabric of the ancient British state, its nations and people. As discussed elsewhere in this book, there were immediate and dramatic political, social and economic consequences. This chapter surveys UK experience and perceptions of 'Europe' before, during and after this dramatic vote.

Forty-three years of reluctant compromise with the European project had ended

How the UK came to join

From an American perspective the very existence of a European Union can be puzzling – why would proud national states want to compromise their sovereignty in the first place? From a German or French perspective the continent without the Union is a fearful prospect, its creation having been an historical necessity.

The central axis of the Union is a bond between France and Germany, two countries which fought three massive wars in 1870-1871, 1914-1918 and 1939-1945. After this an exhausted generation of politicians sought reconciliation. When it was achieved, the objections of their neighbours subsided. Thus Holland, Belgium, Luxembourg and Italy – all of which had suffered occupation – joined the principal protagonists first in a European Coal and Steel Community (ECSC, 1951) and then in a European Economic Community (EEC, 1957).

The initial aims were a mixture of the prosaic and the heroic. Coal and steel were the raw materials of war and a joint authority to control them would put one obstacle in the way of further conflict between France and Germany. But ambitious idealism was not absent: two Frenchmen – the civil servant Jean Monnet and the politician Robert Schuman – foresaw growing international collaboration that would foster mutual confidence; Monnet explicitly anticipated a 'United States of Europe'; founding EEC documents aspired to 'an ever closer union'. This enthusiasm was reciprocated by the German chancellor (1949-1963), Konrad Adenauer. Until the end of the 1980s this fitted conceptually into the framework of a 'free' (and free market) West contrasting with a state-planned East in a European continent divided by the Cold War.

The war that shattered continental Europe's confidence in its institutions reinforced British self-belief

The UK had also suffered greatly in World War II, but it had not been invaded, occupied or succumbed to fascism. Indeed, its stubborn continuance as a parliamentary democracy proved a prerequisite for the eventual defeat of Nazism. The war that shattered continental Europe's confidence in its institutions reinforced British self-belief. National consciousness was fed on Churchill's wartime speeches, his alluring narrative of an 'island race' with global reach and a special bond with the United States. The UK stayed aloof from the early stirrings of European collaboration. Churchill, in opposition after 1945, himself envisaged a 'kind of United States of Europe', but this would be a continental project not involving the UK, whose ambitions remained global, imperial even.

But by the 1960s the country was less confident: the empire was rapidly being dismantled, economic self-doubt had grown, alternative international ventures had disappointed and influential voices increasingly advocated joining the 'Common Market', as the Community was generally referred to in Britain at that time. But successive bids to join foundered on French resistance. France's President de Gaulle doubted UK willingness to commit itself to the European 'project' and was wary of the threat to French domination of the Community. Only in 1973 did the Conservative government of Edward Heath finally enter the EEC (alongside Ireland and Denmark) as part of the first enlargement.

Winston Churchill: content with European unity, but with Britain standing aloof

Britain's entry was not without domestic opposition. Heath was a long-term Europhile but faced considerable opposition among sections of his own party, especially on the right, where some still clung to the imperial vision. The main opposition Labour Party was predominantly against or unenthusiastic about entry but contained a determined Europhile minority, especially on its more centrist, social democratic wing. In 1972 both parties split in a key Westminster vote on the Treaty of Accession: it needed a cross-party majority to get through. There was also vociferous opposition from much of the press, then extensively North American owned. Eurosceptics (as they would later come to be labelled) believed the UK unsuited by history and global role to a continental project; above all, entry compromised the national sovereignty only the British people had the right to relinquish. Europhiles sometimes advanced the idealistic case but more

Ted Heath took Britain into the European Community. He had served in World War II and shared much of the vision of the Community's 'founding fathers'

often played down the prospect of a closer union; they preferred the pragmatic language of trade and growth at a time when the major continental European economies were manifestly doing better than the British.

Labour returned to government in 1974: it now sought to overcome its own internal divisions by renegotiating minor changes to the UK's membership terms. Most of the Labour Party (and one-third of the Labour cabinet) remained irreconcilable and in the ensuing national referendum in June 1975 opposed their own government. (For the wider significance of referenda in UK politics, see chapter 3.) Despite this, and vehement campaigning by the Conservative right-wing, the government achieved a striking victory. The Yes side, to endorse the government's renegotiation and continued membership of the European Community, triumphed by 67.2 to 32.8 per cent on a respectable 65 per cent turnout. Over the next four decades this huge majority was gradually to evaporate.

The path to the referendum

The path to Brexit may be discerned through the development of British party politics, and especially those of the Conservative Party. In the 1980s Labour's hostility to the European project subsided. The party was electorally unsuccessful at home and needed other platforms; the 1979 introduction of direct elections to the European parliament also offered it a new opportunity. Meanwhile it was painfully refashioning itself in the European social democratic mould. But the Conservatives had begun a long period of government under the redoubtable Margaret Thatcher. Like Heath she had campaigned in 1975 for a Yes but now – seizing victory after victory at the British polls – she became alarmed at European ambitions.

Early in the 1980s Thatcher had scored some negotiating successes, for example achieving a rebate on Britain's EC contributions. In 1986 she signed the Single European Act, a milestone on the path to closer union; she was the driving force behind the creation of the single market. As late as 1989 she even acquiesced in sterling's participation in the Exchange Rate Mechanism (ERM, an attempt to co-ordinate European currencies). But her resistance to other integration proposals grew ever more vehement, compounded by frustration at her inability to stop them. When the fall of the Berlin Wall was rapidly followed by German reunification her unease grew. She trenchantly opposed what she perceived as an embryonic European state in a celebrated House of Commons outburst:

> 'The President of the Commission, Mr. Delors, said at a press conference the other day that he wanted the European Parliament to be the democratic body of the Community, he wanted the Commission to be the Executive and he wanted the Council of Ministers to be the Senate. No. No. No.' (30 October 1990).

This was almost her last statement before her party's still-powerful Europhiles overthrew her the following month. Yet there was a growing mood of Euroscepticism. Her emollient successor John Major appeased with 'opt-outs' (derogations) from the Maastricht Treaty (1992, converting the European Community into the European Union); without them UK welfare and employment policies would have been harmonised with those of other member states. However, he spent much of his premiership in a rearguard battle to avoid submitting the treaty itself to a new referendum, a potential threat to UK membership. It was trench warfare: at one point Major resigned the party leadership, defying Eurosceptics to fight him for it.

In 1997, the divided Conservatives were routed electorally by an initially Europhile Tony Blair. Euroscepticism seemed marginal in his 'New Labour' party. Major's

Margaret Thatcher: took Britain deeper into Europe, but became alarmed at the prospect of a European state

opt-outs were reversed and the UK put few obstacles in the path of migrants from new accession states in Eastern Europe. When in 2002 14 member states relinquished their national currencies for the euro, it seemed the UK might even join them. But caution, orbiting around Blair's formidable chancellor of the exchequer, Gordon Brown, gradually reasserted itself. 'Tests' were laid down for measuring the UK national interest in Eurozone membership. After 2007 the recession snuffed out any lingering prospect. Brown (now prime minister) became distracted by emergency economic measures and the favourable moment passed.

2010 brought the Conservatives, now led by David Cameron, back to office. During 13 years of opposition the party that took Britain into the EEC had become predominantly Eurosceptic. It was no longer a matter of opposing further European convergence: a noisy minority now clamoured for withdrawal. This led Cameron to take a fateful step. In his 2013 'Bloomberg speech' he committed himself to renegotiating the terms of entry. After laying down a series of treaty change demands that would effectively exempt the country from the goal of ever-closer union, he pledged to obtain them and submit the results to a new referendum. This pledge, uttered while governing in coalition with the Europhile Liberal Democrats, was reiterated in his party's 2015 election manifesto. When the Conservatives unexpectedly returned to office with a single-party majority it had to be honoured. A prime minister who had once promised to stop his party 'banging on about Europe' faced absorption of all his energies by this very issue. The electorate would soon have to confront the question: 'Should the United Kingdom remain a member of the European Union or leave the European Union?' Inevitably, talks now opened with the UK's European partners in search of revised membership terms he could plausibly recommend.

UK negotiations and domestic public opinion

Three factors loomed in the background to Cameron's EU talks as they really got under way: the transformation of the ruling Conservatives into a mainly Eurosceptic party; the rise, partly at the Conservatives' expense, of the Europhobic UKIP (both these factors are discussed in chapter 3 above); the long-term failure of government to control immigration, and especially EU immigration (see also chapter 12). Though fearful of a UK exit, his fellow EU heads of government were not free agents: they had to sustain the principles of the EU while distracted by a protracted Eurozone crisis and the arrival in Europe of an avalanche of refugees from war-torn Syria.

The negotiations ran from autumn 2015 to the following February. Cameron set his own goals: a formal opt-out from the drive for ever closer union, which was conceded; drastic reductions in the right of EU citizens to claim UK benefits, which was yielded only in part; absolute separation of the UK from the finances of the Eurozone, which was achieved, though exemption of the City from EU financial rules was not; and a promise, easily conceded, to cut bureaucratic 'red tape'. He had been careful not to ask for the impossible. But had he asked – indeed, had he achieved – enough?

Cameron reported the results to a distinctly underwhelmed House of Commons. Many of his backbenchers had felt all along that his negotiating agenda failed to capture the breadth of concerns of the British people. 'Is that it?' one of them derisively enquired. Here exposed, before the campaign had even begun – but only four months before the fateful vote – was a fundamental weakness of the Remain case. The scattered discontents evident across the country could not be encompassed within realistic goals and even these were only partially obtained. Cameron sought revised EU membership terms he could recommend in a nation-wide campaign but many of the discontented had objectives that were simply incompatible with membership.

'Is that it?' one of them derisively enquired

The campaign

The four months of campaigning from February to June 2016 drew together in concentrated form the country's conflicted feelings. The cabinet split with six members permitted to break collective responsibility and campaign against government policy. In this Cameron followed the precedent set by Labour prime minister Harold Wilson in the 1975 referendum, but with very different results. The government itself made no pretence of neutrality, doggedly defending the prime minister's negotiated terms and reinforcing the argument with an array of official advice from authoritative national and international bodies. The British public was bombarded with advice from each government department, the Bank of England, the IMF, the World Bank, major British corporations and foreign multinationals located in the UK. It was of course no secret that the EU itself as well as its national heads of government wished the UK to vote Remain; the pleas from the Irish prime minister were especially urgent. On his valedictory visit to the UK, US president Barack Obama added his voice to theirs. Generally, this advice came with warnings, sometimes apocalyptic, of the consequences of not taking it.

Divisions opened up around the UK. The Scottish government campaigned strongly for Remain and was supported by the other three major parties in the country. This pattern was repeated in Wales. In Northern Ireland the Ulster Unionists, SDLP and Sinn Fein backed Remain while the province's largest political force, the Democratic Unionists, led by the first minister, Arlene Foster, advocated Leave. Since Theresa Villiers, UK secretary of state for Northern Ireland, was also a rebel cabinet minister, two of Ulster's most prominent politicians were Leavers. In England the largely Eurosceptic Conservative grassroots mainly supported Leave and were enthused by former London mayor Boris Johnson, a particular favourite among them; Labour and the Liberal Democrats worked for Remain, though not a few on the Labour side, including the party's own leader, Jeremy Corbyn, were lukewarm.

During the final weeks campaigning was organised along the lines of a British general election, with the umbrella organisations for the opposing sides recognised by the Electoral Commission (Vote Leave and Britain Stronger in Europe) allowed to spend up to £7m, get a free mailshot, TV broadcasts and £600,000 of public funds. Less familiar was the spectacle of the right-wing press opposing a Conservative leader, the only national campaign when Cameron suffered this handicap. Vote Leave's main slogan was 'Take Back Control'. It promised that 'we will be able to save £350m a week'; 'we'll be in charge of our own borders'; 'we can control immigration'; 'we'll be free to trade with the whole world'; and 'we can make our own laws'. Britain Stronger in Europe promised more jobs, lower prices, protection of workers' rights and a better future.

This heavily economic focus on the Remain side, sometimes backed by alarmist threats of the consequences of a Leave vote, imparted a dual character to the debate. The Remain side seemed to think it sufficient to marshal the weight of official opinion; the Leave side gradually gained the confidence to ridicule experts and speak to anxieties that were deeply felt across large parts of the country. It fed a gathering 'us and them' mood. Two parallel narratives unfolded; their tangents were few. In the final days, opinion seemed to harden and the tone of exchanges became bitter; members of parliament complained of being 'trolled'. A week before the vote the country was stunned by the assassination of Jo Cox, Labour MP for Batley & Spen (in Yorkshire), at her constituency office, an event attributed by many to the harsh feelings engendered by an ill-tempered campaign. Activity was suspended for several days amid a sense that the atrocity might slow the gathering momentum of Leave. It was a subdued UK that went to the polls on 23 June.

> *The Leave side gradually gained the confidence to ridicule experts and speak to anxieties that were deeply felt across large parts of the country*

The decision

72.2 per cent of the electorate voted, more than in any recent general election and far higher than in the 1975 referendum. Opinion polls, while generally wrong in predicting the overall result, had nonetheless accurately enough identified broad trends revealing a sharply divided country. In Scotland not a single counting area had voted for Leave, Scotland as a whole going 62/38 for Remain. Northern Ireland had also voted Remain by almost 56/44 though here the east/west distribution of votes seemed to echo the sectarian divide (see chapter 5).

But England had voted 53.2/46.8 to Leave, as had, less decisively, Wales: these two countries also had the highest turnout. In Wales the only counting areas to vote Remain were two rural counties on its west-facing coast, the border county of Monmouthshire and the capital Cardiff and its suburbs. But it was England, much the largest

Region	Remain	Leave
Scotland	62.0	38.0
London	59.9	40.1
N. Ireland	55.7	44.3
Wales	48.3	51.7
South East	48.2	51.8
South West	47.4	52.6
North West	46.3	53.7
East	43.5	56.5
Yorkshire & Humber	42.3	57.7
North East	42.0	58.0
East Midlands	41.2	58.8
West Midlands	40.7	59.3

0%   50%

The Brexit referendum: how the regions voted

home country and therefore decisive in voting weight that revealed the sharpest division between capital and provinces. London voted almost 60/40 for Remain with only five of its boroughs voting Leave. This was true of most major English cities: Liverpool, Manchester, Leeds, Bristol and Newcastle had all voted Remain. However, Leave votes returned by Birmingham and Sheffield confounded any easy urbanist interpretation, while smaller cities had mostly voted Leave. Rural areas in the main voted Leave, with the exception of a thick wedge of countryside from the south coast to the Severn estuary. London excepted, every single English region had voted Leave and the vote was particularly decisive in the Midlands, home of many key marginal parliamentary constituencies – a fact that could hardly escape the attention of Labour and Conservative strategists planning their parties' response to the vote.

In the wake of the result much confident generalisation was made but at the time of writing there is little hard evidence beyond the results. During the campaign, polls had strongly suggested that the likelihood of voting Leave increased with a person's age. Since the propensity of older voters to actually cast their vote had been established over many years this was a great advantage. Graduates were thought more likely to vote Remain, and this sits well with the concentration of Remain votes where their numbers are high. This factor is however difficult to disentangle from age, as the graduate population is also significantly younger.

Many commentators reached beyond social factors to attitudes. The referendum offered an opportunity to voters to give a verdict on their own prospects, the state of the country and where they thought it was heading. Large parts of the UK – smaller towns with poor transport connections, declining coastal resorts, the outer-edges of cities – seem to have relished the chance. Some of the highest Leave votes were recorded in areas with a low proportion of people holding formal qualifications or marketable skills. Where low wages coincided with strong feelings towards immigrants, especially EU migrants, the Leave vote was particularly emphatic: in Boston (Lincolnshire) it exceeded 75 per cent.

London excepted, every single English region had voted Leave

The heavy Remain vote in cosmopolitan London was no suprise, even though its 800,000 residents born elsewhere in the EU were not entitled to vote. Some of its boroughs, emblematic of metropolitan diversity, with large numbers of highly educated professionals and ethnic minorities, returned over 75 per cent for Remain. Here, indeed across the UK, areas with high numbers of graduates, high median average income, large numbers of middle-class people, or with high numbers born outside the UK all backed Remain.

London is not England, yet the characteristics concentrated in the capital were not absent elsewhere. The wider population had become incomparably more diverse, addicted to (cheap) international air travel and habituated to most varieties of European cuisine, especially the 'continental' diet. (Its stubborn refusal to speak other languages and expectation that other nations' citizens will speak English remained unchanged.) British companies had and have a global reach and London remains the world financial centre. The EU had long been the single biggest market for British exports. Foreign students (including many EU citizens seeking to acquire

English) were flocking to the country's prestigious universities. The UK seemed to have an increasingly outward-facing population and 1.3 million of its citizens actually lived elsewhere in the EU. Why, then, did it return a majority for Leave?

Early answers are inevitably tentative. It is clear that the growing diversity of the country was not welcomed by all. Frequently the presence of immigrants was the cause of anxiety, even active resentment. In some areas the presence of EU migrants from Eastern European states in particular attracted powerful dislike, especially so if coupled with the prevalence of low wages or meagre job opportunities. David Cameron's two governments had made quantified promises to curb immigration, one of them to reduce it below a net figure of 100,000 annually. Within the EU and its free labour market, such targets were completely infeasible, as Leave campaigners were not slow to point out. In calendar 2015, net long-term international migration was no less than 333,000, maintaining a rate in evidence for some time. Net migration of EU citizens was 184,000, roughly the same as non-EU net migration. While the number of

The UK seemed to have an increasingly outward-facing population and 1.3 million of its citizens actually lived elsewhere in the EU

British nationals in employment had greatly increased and that of non-EU nationals marginally so, over half the growth in employment was accounted for by foreign nationals. These explosive numbers appeared four weeks before polling day, though disgruntled British job-seekers dwelling in poor areas hardly needed their views confirmed.

Nevertheless, over 17 million votes for Leave cannot be reduced to an anti-immigrant spasm. An increasingly introverted political context also played its part. The UK had never comfortably settled into the EU. European idealism was largely absent from its political debate. Even before the referendum campaign began, Cameron himself drew a contrast between the passion for the Union that had animated him in the Scottish independence debate and his cold-blooded calculation that EU membership served the national interest. Instead, relations with the EU were viewed through a transactional prism. He

Cameron ... was merely the latest politician to present successive negotiations in adversarial terms, Britain against the Rest

was merely the latest politician to present successive negotiations in adversarial terms, Britain against the Rest. For decades the print media had gleefully written up this pre-sentational ploy. At successive EU heads of government meetings – negotiations that always seemed to plough on into the night – a British prime minister always emerged to claim 'victory', the content of which was usually a block on EU 'interference'. It is not hard to discern echoes of the post-war narrative.

But the Brexit vote did not express complacency about the state of the country. It must surely also be read as a revolt of the disap-pointed or dispossessed. The long boom of 1992-2007 that en-compassed 60 consecutive quar-ters of growth may have been a rising tide, but it had not raised all boats. Tracts of Britain were

The long boom of 1992-2007 ... may have been a rising tide, but it had not raised all boats

still dogged by persistently high unemployment and reducing op-portunity, visible in abandoned industrial sites, poor housing and public transport, dismal high streets populated by charity shops and 'pound shops'. As boom turned to recession, the austerity measures afflicting the poorest made things worse for such areas, disproportionately dependent as they were on public spending. Overall, incomes rose from 2013, but there was a persistent sense of relative deprivation. The contrast with London, seat of power, influence and wealth could hardly have been greater. This was rich soil for the 'them and us' narrative of the Brexit campaigners who con-nected the capital's remoteness with that of the even more remote EU – 'Brussels' as it was scornfully labelled. They could point out that many areas were not getting their share as prosperity slowly returned. They at-tracted large crowds in peripheral areas: the

Nigel Farage: as leader of the United Kingdom Independence Party he relentlessly beat the 'anti-establishment' drum

West Country, smaller towns and lesser cities, the coast. All would poll heavily for Leave.

And yet, there is more to it than that. Relatively prosperous English shires voted for Leave, just as poorer cities, like Glasgow, in Scotland, or Derry, in Northern Ireland, voted Remain. Perhaps a different interpretation offers itself? That the different parts of the UK voted to affirm their seperate identities. Scotland in 2014 had voted to stay in the UK only after dire warnings that it would have to apply for EU membership as a new entrant if it did not. In that campaign both sides had claimed to be the best protector of Scotland's European identity. The majority population of Northern Ireland had for decades maintained an implacable determination to stay in the UK, but a quarter century of peace had brought cross-community appreciation of the economic and other advantages of an open border with the Republic, a continuing EU member. Hardline unionists favoured Brexit, but some pragmatists voted with the Catholic minority.

Perhaps a different interpretation offers itself? That the different parts of the UK voted to affirm their separate identities

London's success within the EU has already been noted: many of its people instinctively felt part of a wider world. The other English regions, however, might be said to have affirmed that they were not London, to have asserted that England's national identity was not one with that of the capital. In Wales, the national question has never been posed as sharply as in Scotland, but it shares the English regions' sense of distance from Westminster and rejected the advice of all its party leaders.

10.   Facing the world

Britain has always had global connections. Neither its first (18th century) nor its second (19th century) empire was a continental entity, unlike those of Russia, Germany or Austria. Of European imperial nations France alone had similar pretensions to global reach, until Napoleon fatally attempted to subdue all of Europe to his will: this resemblance partly explains why the two countries were constantly at war with each other during the 'long 18th century' (1689-1815), though never in the two centuries thereafter. It also illuminates how both survived World War II despite occupation (France) and isolation (Britain) in a Nazi Europe.

England's early colonial conquests owed more to buccaneering opportunists ... than to state policy

The British empire has been described as acquired 'in a fit of absence of mind'. Certainly England's early colonial conquests owed more to buccaneering opportunists (Drake, Frobisher, Hawkins, Raleigh) than to state policy. A consciously imperial course was charted only after 1700 as Britain developed global economic interests and pioneered financial services. Far-flung colonies were bound to it by intense trading links: it needed a powerful fleet to defend them. France's single successful 18th century fleet action against the Royal Navy led directly to Yorktown and the one involuntary colonial loss before the 20th century – that of the United States.

Much of the empire was acquired on an ad hoc basis at the initiative of private individuals and business interests: for decades India was essentially the fiefdom of a private company, the British East India Company, while Cecil Rhodes later acquired vast tracts of Africa for the crown in pursuit of his commercial interests – a

Victorian buccaneer. Only in the late 19th century did the UK truly assume an imperial style when Queen Victoria in 1877 adopted the title 'empress'. Even then, the empire in question was not the whole collection of overseas possessions but India, the 'jewel in the crown'.

The protection of possessions across the world needed sea power. Until as late as 1923 naval doctrine dictated that the Royal Navy maintain a 'fleet in being' capable of destroying a combination of the second and third largest. This axiom rested on the supposed invincibility of the (highly expensive) capital ship. But the submarine and the aircraft carrier rendered battleships obsolescent, and in any case once economic supremacy had been lost, naval supremacy inevitably eventually followed. During World War II the Royal Navy was very much the junior partner to the US navy.

In the aftermath of World War II empires were out of fashion and a debilitated UK could not hope to retain one in the face of the global growth of national consciousness. The fleet was also unaffordable and seemed to have lost its *raison d'être*. Foreign policy tilted towards accepting the inevitable: there was a new policy of shepherding 'developing countries' to independence. The UK abandoned India in 1947 and progressively thereafter its other possessions, though the process was at times messy and on occasion involved dealing with guerrilla insurgencies, not least in Aden, Malaya and Kenya. Each choreographed exit from direct rule mollified domestic opinion by bequeathing political institutions inspired by the 'mother country'. Since newly grown-up ex-colonies were seeded with British civic culture, trade links looked set to continue; a legacy had been left. The empire now became the Commonwealth, reflecting more equal international relationships. This 'managed decline' soothed domestic opinion, disguising necessity as choice. And certainly the British decolonisation experience was less disastrous than the French, though great brutality was used in Kenya and elsewhere.

This 'managed decline' soothed domestic opinion, disguising necessity as choice

Decolonisation

This dignified retreat before the inevitable was also epic in scale: by the 1970s 'the empire on which the sun never set' had shrunk to a small collection of willing dependencies ('British Overseas Territories'), mostly dots on the world map: Anguilla, Montserrat, Bermuda, Hong Kong, Pitcairn Island, British Antarctic Territory, St Helena and its dependencies – Ascension Island, Tristan da Cunha – the British Virgin islands, the Cayman Islands, South Georgia and the South Islands, the Falkland Islands, the Turks and Caicos Islands and Gibraltar.

Raising the flag in the recapture of the Falklands in 1982; but British losses were heavy

Sovereignty issues subsequently appeared in the different guise of territorial claims by rival states. Argentina's seizure of the Falklands in 1982 was reversed in a brief but bloody conflict which cost over 900 British and Argentinian lives – the equivalent of half the population of the islands. Hong Kong was peaceably returned to China when the UK lease expired in 1997. Gibraltar remains resolutely British but, mindful of Spain's claims, recorded the highest Remain vote in the 2016 EU referendum in which, by a quirk of history, it alone of overseas dependencies had a say. Otherwise when these places hit the headlines it is most commonly because of their role as offshore tax havens (the British Virgin Islands and Cayman Islands in particular).

Yet the cultural impact of two and a half imperial centuries survives in attitudes to defence, foreign policy and world trade. It is obligatory to refer to the armed forces as 'the finest in the world'. Britain is an habitual participant in global foreign policy initiatives even when its national interest is obscure. The 2016 EU referendum debate was shaped in part by perceptions of lost commercial opportunities beyond the continent. Bewildered foreign observers of the Last Night of the Proms are regaled with a sequence of nautical ditties culminating in an anthem asserting that 'Britannia rules the waves'. Nostalgia and delusion abound but Britons of all political persuasions retain a relish for global influence. The reverse migratory flows that have brought multiethnicity to the mother country itself offer a permanent reminder of the imperial past. At the policy-making level the UK's ambitious political class sees the country in global and not regional terms.

Nostalgia and delusion abound but Britons of all political persuasions retain a relish for global influence

Foreign policy

In the mid-Victorian era of Lord Palmerston (d.1865) and his ilk the British foreign secretary was arbiter of nations. The Foreign Office, built in the 1860s, reflects the confidence and ambition of the era, with its magnificent, richly decorated Durbar Court, India Office council chamber, Locarno suite and grand staircase. Today's Foreign & Commonwealth Office (FCO), no longer with an empire to oversee, nonetheless retains a worldwide network of 270 embassies and consulates across 168 countries.

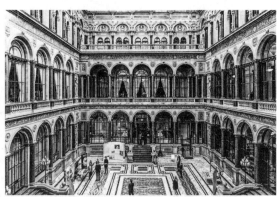

Palmerston's foreign policy rested on overwhelming naval might and apparently limitless wealth.

The splendid Durbar Court at the Foreign Office

He intervened freely in the affairs of weaker countries. But within a generation Britain's economy was overtaken by those of Germany and the United States. After a century of successfully avoiding 'continental entanglements' in Europe while it pursued its ambitions on other continents, Britain was dragged into a great European war in 1914, which turned it into a debtor nation. Two decades later World War II virtually bankrupted it. In the ensuing Cold War (1945-1989) that matched two nuclear superpowers, Britain's role shrank to that of spear-carrier for the USA. In 1973 – at the third attempt – it entered the European Economic Community (EEC), seemingly signalling an acceptance of a European identity as the one-sidedness of the 'special relationship' with the USA became ever more apparent and the last bits of empire were shuffled off. But as the Com-

In the ensuing Cold War ... Britain's role shrank to that of spear-carrier for the USA

munity evolved into the European Union (EU) Britain began to drag its feet and Euroscepticism became a potent factor in domestic politics – as seen in chapter 9.

At the end of the 20th century a tripartite foreign policy was briefly projected, pivoting between the United States, the EU and the Commonwealth. But the strategic imperatives of transatlanticism (see below) soon reasserted themselves. Britain aligned with the United States in Afghanistan, then – fiercely opposed by France and Germany, the other two principal EU nations – in the Iraq War. A century and a half on from Lord Palmerston, following the Brexit vote to leave the European Union, Britain seems about to enter a new era where it tries to avoid 'continental entanglements'.

The Commonwealth

In 1914 imperial Britain declared war without consulting the wider empire, though the empire did not fail to rally to its support. After World War II it decolonised and in 1949 its former colonial and dominion relationships were repackaged as the 'Commonwealth'. This term was already bracketed with empire in the pre-war period; indeed it badged the first Commonwealth Games in 1930. In the new organisation Britain had no coercive power yet retained the loudest voice and the British monarch became head of the Commonwealth. More fundamentally, traditional trading pat-

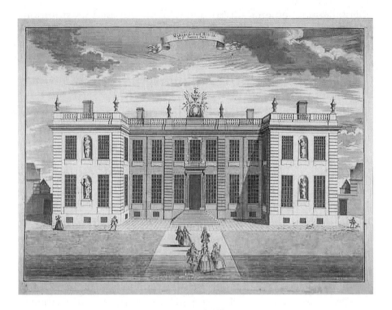

Marlborough House in London, built for Sarah Churchill, the Duchess of Marlborough, at the start of the 18th century; it is now the headquarters of the Commonwealth

terns did not realign for another generation, so the Commonwealth cohered around economic reality. UK and Irish entry into the EEC signalled an important shift towards Europe and away from the larger dominions and colonies of the Antipodes. Yet they themselves were already slowly disengaging. Canada moved more closely into the US orbit; South Africa and Britain were estranged over apartheid; India and Pakistan were preoccupied with their own rivalry. Traditionally strong bonds with Australia and New Zealand, both of which had contributed greatly to the British cause in World War II, were inevitably weakened as these countries of necessity sought new economic relationships in their own Asia-Pacific backyard.

By 2016 the Commonwealth had 53 member countries, of which 31 were small states, and was home to 2.2 billion people. While each state has one vote this scarcely signifies in a consensual organisation. It has an active secretariat with a network of over 80 intergovernmental, civil society, cultural and professional organisations, but most attention is focused on its Heads of Government Meeting (CHOGM). The Commonwealth styles itself as a voice for small states, a champion for youth empowerment, promoting democracy, the rule of law, human rights, good governance and social and economic development. Yet it lacks an armed wing and so cannot impose its principles. When suasion fails, only one sanction remains – that of parting company.

The decolonisation endgame illustrated this perfectly. When apartheid became South African state policy (1948) and white settlers seized power in Rhodesia (Unilateral Declaration of Independence, UDI 1965), member states – overwhelmingly non-white – naturally sought to rally opposition. In 1961 South Africa turned its back on Britain, withdrew from the Commonwealth and became a republic. Rhodesia was ejected. Could the Commonwealth move beyond moral exhortation to an economic role? In fact, attempts to impose Commonwealth sanctions on South Africa yielded only patchy results, primarily due to lukewarm support in Britain, whose government viewed the rebel African National Congress (ANC) as a terrorist front. Britain was also blamed for the protracted failure to end UDI though it was finally resolved (and a new state, Zimbabwe, formed) by a process begun at the 1979 CHOGM. White rule still had more than a decade to run in South Africa, but after it ended the new majority-rule country triumphantly rejoined the Commonwealth (1995).

Faced only with moral condemnation recalcitrant states have had relatively little to lose. Pakistan pulled out from 1972 to 1989, sensitive to condemnation of its actions in the 1971 war over the secession of Bangladesh; the latter joined the Commonwealth. Pakistan was excluded twice more, once after imposing martial law (1999). Fiji has been excluded three times on similar grounds. In 1995 Nigeria was suspended for two years, as was Zimbabwe in 2002 following irregularities in that year's presidential election. The following year it simply withdrew. The two most recent entrants – Rwanda and Mozambique – were not former British colonies, but several of their regional neighbours were, indicating the enduring significance of the Commonwealth in that part of Africa. Meanwhile multicultural Britain has found new uses for the Commonwealth. Trade and state visits regularly occur from and to the UK; in a 2015 state visit Indian prime minister Narendra Modi addressed a rally of 60,000 of Britain's 1.2 million ethnically Indian residents. India accounts for half the Commonwealth's population and has a fast growing economy with vast potential. Meanwhile the Commonwealth reflects, but also provides space for, British 'soft power' (see below).

The United States and 'transatlanticism'

The USA and UK fought two wars between 1776 and 1814 and came close to a third during the US Civil War of 1861-1865. Indeed, the Royal Navy was war-gaming a possible American conflict as recently as 1920. But the two were close allies in both world wars and since 1945 the 'Atlantic alliance' has been a cardinal principle of British policy. This has channelled UK military strategy, as in the Korean War (1950-1953). The country has undertaken no initiatives disapproved of by Washington since the Anglo-French Suez fiasco (1956) though it resisted pressure to assist the USA in Vietnam in the 1960s. A sceptical USA, wary of damaging relations with Latin America, merely acquiesced in the unilateral British recapture of the Falkland Islands (1982). Especially since the end of the Cold War, the default position of British governments has been an alignment with US policy: the first Gulf War (1990), Afghanistan (2001-2009), Iraq (2003-2012), Syria (2015-).

In these ventures the British military contribution was small in absolute terms, though it stretched UK capacity (see below). But UK participation in US-led ventures had a political value for both countries. For America, British participation provided political cover for what might otherwise have seemed unilateral initiatives. United States politicians are also susceptible to the romantic version of the Anglo-American partnership projected in speeches, books and even his own person by Sir Winston Churchill (UK prime minister 1940-1945, 1951-1955). British governments wish to be regarded as first among the USA's many allies: they refer habitually to a 'special relationship' resting on cultural empathy and many wartime partnerships. Personal affinity periodically refreshes it. Churchill and F.D. Roosevelt (president 1933-1945) shared an elevated social position, a background in naval strategy and finally the experience of supreme leadership in World War II; Ronald Reagan (president 1981-1989) and Margaret Thatcher (prime minister 1979-1990) radiated mutual admiration in the later Cold War despite Reagan's reservations about the Falkland Islands war; Tony Blair (prime minister 1997-2007) worked closely with successive US presidents, Bill Clinton and George W. Bush. Underlying these personal affinities is a tension between the wish of policy-makers to align with the United States and domestic popular resistance to military ventures where the national interest is opaque. On the eve of the 2003 Iraq War up to two million Britons marched in opposition, thought to be the largest demonstration in the country's history.

The European Union

The basis of the EU is a large common market in goods, services and labour, but periodically it has sought to add political coherence to its economic power – a foreign minister, an armed wing. It was quite unable to prevent the bitter fighting on its borders following the breakup of Yugoslavia. Efforts to make the EU a military power have generally been resisted by the UK, which regards the North Atlantic Treaty Organisation (NATO) as a more useful military vehicle and is opposed in principle to the creation of a European army. Among EU members there are only two nuclear powers, France and the UK, both of which remain permanent members of the UN Security Council. Great prestige attaches to both attributes and neither country would contemplate giving them up. France and the UK are also the preeminent conventional military powers of the EU so in practice any Union initiatives requiring the exertion of force will draw on them. EU Common Security and Defence Policy does enable it to participate in, even lead peace-keeping and conflict prevention and international security operations. Such missions are rather ad hoc but UK troops and warships have taken part in them, most recently in operations to disrupt cross-Mediterranean people smuggling.

During the 2016 EU referendum campaign, both the prime minister and the Ministry of Defence expressed fears that defence spending would have to be cut in the event of the UK leaving. But if security worries fed the Remain vote, concerns about the UK's sovereign ability to deploy forces in its own defence may have bolstered Leave; voters primarily concerned about immigration were certainly sceptical about the UK's ability as an EU member to protect its borders. If the UK withdraws in 2019, this triangulation seems likely to end.

Conventional defence

The Ministry of Defence (MoD) is the government department responsible for the country's armed forces. Its self-defined military tasks are: defending the UK and its overseas territories; providing strategic intelligence; providing nuclear deterrence; supporting civil emergency organisations in times of crisis; defending UK interests by projecting power strategically and through expeditionary interventions; providing a defence contribution to UK influence; and providing security for stabilisation. From a linear perspective defence is a declining priority for Britain: in the two world wars, with three million men under arms, it accounted for almost 50 per cent of GNP. Ernest Bevin (UK foreign secretary 1945-1950) was the acknowledged father of NATO. No national government since has questioned continuing membership, even when the end of the Cold War removed the ostensible reason for the alliance. Britain is (with Estonia and the USA) one of only three NATO member countries sustaining defence expenditure at 2 per cent or more of GNP.

Yet the UK has slowly reassigned its priorities. The late 1960s saw it consciously relinquish a global military role: strategic imperatives were defined more nearly to home, 'West of Suez' and the administration of air, land and sea forces gathered into one government department. That same decade defence spending was outstripped by education expenditure and numbers in the now-integrated forces dipped below one-third of a million. Since the 1990s the defence budget has been only the fifth largest element of government spending, well behind welfare, health, education and general public services. The prowess of Britain's armed forces is still proclaimed, but all is not well with them. The early 21st century brought two lengthy wars in Afghanistan and Iraq. The army suffered significant defeats in both theatres and its capacity was considerably run down. Britain's involvement in these wars can be explained only by determination to sustain the special relationship. While its logistical contribution was small the human cost was great. The Iraq War (179 dead during 2003-2009) shook public confidence in government decision-making. Thirteen years of the Afghan War (453 dead and 616 serious injuries) wearied it and the inadequacies of British military equipment, especially compared with that of its American allies, were at times cruelly exposed.

The prowess of Britain's armed forces is still proclaimed, but all is not well with them

By 2014, the number of full-time trained personnel in the UK armed forces was below 150,000 – 30,000 fewer even than in 2010. Within the country respect for the military remains fairly high. Remembrance Day (marking the World War I armistice) powerfully commemorates a huge loss of uniformed lives then and since. In preceding weeks, volunteers from the British Legion (the veterans' association) collect for military charities, giving in exchange a fabric poppy to be worn. (After the Western Front fighting, red poppies had grown spontaneously in the Flanders soil containing so many British dead.) However, the armed forces are now an entirely professional body of volunteers and there is no form of compulsory military service such as exists in most European countries or national guard on the American model. For the first time in a century, few Britons remember military service: a decreasing number even know soldiers. But governments continue to commit their depleted armed forces in conflict zones: Libya (2011), Iraq (2013) and Syria (2015). Public reluctance was evident in August 2013 when Prime Minister David Cameron unsuccessfully sought parliamentary backing for a very limited military intervention against President Assad's Syrian regime; nonetheless Britain still became a bit-player in the Syrian conflict, though in the event targeting Islamist opponents of Assad. British troops have been engaged somewhere, on some scale, almost continuously for generations.

Defence equipment is getting scarcer as its costs rise. In 2014 there were 11 submarines and 65 surface vessels in the Royal Navy, with 13 auxiliary craft, five fewer than in 2010. Britain's two aircraft carriers were out of commission. The army had ten armoured regiments in the regular army and four in reserves, unchanged since April 2000. RAF squadrons numbered 44, their combat aircraft numbers, declining since 2006, reduced to 149. Those under Joint Helicopter Command decreased to 174. Poorly-scheduled purchases by the Defence Ministry left the country without an aircraft carrier in the latter 2010s. But two are being built in UK shipyards: the 65,000 tonnes HMS *Queen Elizabeth* and HMS *Prince of Wales* will eventually be the country's largest-ever warships.

Nuclear weapons

In 1941 Winston Churchill authorised development of an atomic bomb but progress was slow. In 1943 it was subsumed into the US Manhattan Project and the UK lost control. When the USA unilaterally ended wartime nuclear collaboration in 1946 the Attlee government resumed an independent atomic programme, the UK testing its first bomb in 1952. That year however the USA raised the stakes by testing a thermonuclear weapon (the 'H-bomb'), and the USSR soon followed suit. The UK again felt it had to catch up, testing its own weapon in 1958. Only after this was bilateral UK-USA collaboration resumed under a Mutual Defence Agreement (MDA), still the cornerstone of UK-USA nuclear defence cooperation.

Britain's early nuclear weapons were air-launched but its attempts to switch to a missile programme were fatally hampered by dependence on US technology. From 1962 the US submarine-based Polaris missile system became available to the UK under the MDA with the submarines and warheads designed and built in the UK. In 1980, Britain decided to procure the Trident missile system to replace Polaris, and from 1994 onwards built four UK-designed Vanguard-class submarines to carry them. Britain thus retains the capacity to launch a seaborne nuclear attack, though with only one submarine sure to be at sea at any one time the capability is on a scale designed to deter rather than defeat an aggressor.

All major political parties attach great importance to maintaining what they perceive as an independent capacity. Prime ministers proclaim that firing Trident does not require US permission, satellites or codes. The MoD adds that 'decision making and use of the system remains entirely sovereign to the UK; only the prime m inister can authorise the launch of nuclear weapons, which ensures that political control is maintained at all times'. However, possession of nuclear weapons has been actively opposed by some since the launch of the Campaign for Nuclear Disarmament (CND) in 1958. CND and other critics argue Trident is technically dependent on the USA, serviced at a Georgia (USA) port and uses US warhead components. The decision in principle to upgrade to a more modern system was taken in 2016; it may commit HM government to a £41bn outlay. US Defence Secretary Ash Carter commented that Trident aided the special relationship, supporting the UK's 'outsized role on the global stage … because of its moral standing and its historical standing'.

A Vanguard class submarine, carrier of British nuclear weapons

Security and intelligence

The National Security Council (NSC), established in 2010 along with the new post of national security advisor, is the main forum for collective discussion of the government's objectives for national security. The NSC meets weekly with the prime minister in the chair. Its principal focus is on acts of terrorism affecting the UK or its interests; cyber-attacks; major accidents or natural hazards (for example an influenza pandemic); an international military crisis between states, drawing in the UK and allies. Although sharing a name with the much older National Security Council in the USA, the British NSC is little known to the public and the national security advisor is not a powerful role.

MI5 is the UK's domestic national security intelligence agency, answerable to the home secretary. Its role is comparable to, though far less extensive than, that of the Federal Bureau of Investigation (FBI) in the USA. The role of MI5, as defined in the Security Service Act 1989, is 'the protection of national security and in particular its protection against threats such as terrorism, espionage and sabotage, the activities of agents of foreign powers, and from actions intended to overthrow or undermine parliamentary democracy by political, industrial or violent means'. As the Cold War came to an end, terrorist threats from Northern Ireland and states such as Colonel Gadhafi's Libya became priorities for MI5. The rise of Islamist terrorism at the end of the 1990s, culminating in the 9/11 attacks in 2001, led to major operational changes and the service gained its first female director general. MI5's work has been depicted in a number of films and TV series, notably the BBC's *Spooks* (*MI-5* in the United States).

MI6 headquarters in London: it has featured as a backdrop in recent James Bond films

The Secret Intelligence Service (SIS), often called MI6, gathers intelligence outside the UK in support of the government's security, defence, foreign and economic policies, answering to the foreign secretary. It is roughly equivalent to the Central Intelligence Agency (CIA) in the USA, though without the latter's scale and resources. It gives the UK government a global covert capability. While secretive it claims to operate within a strict legal framework and be politically accountable. It originated in the Secret Service Bureau created in 1909 in response to the threat from Imperial Germany (with which Britain went to war in 1914). In the Cold War era its effectiveness was compromised by Soviet subversion, not least by Harold (Kim) Philby, at one time Britain's leading intelligence officer in the USA. The fact that Philby was allowed to 'retire' despite suspicions of his role, before eventually fleeing to Moscow, was indicative of the gentlemen's club atmosphere that had characterised the service and caused mistrust on the American side. Now much changed, MI6 openly operates from an imposing headquarters on the South Bank of the Thames at Vauxhall Cross. MI6 is a favourite subject of fiction, most notably in the shape of James Bond, the louche agent 007 who, in the novels of Ian Fleming and half a century of blockbuster film-making, famously operates with a 'licence to kill'.

GCHQ (Government Communications Headquarters) is responsible for electronic monitoring activities, equivalent to the role played by the National Security Agency in the USA, with which GCHQ has close and longstanding ties, effectively dividing up the globe for some aspects of intelligence gathering. It was set up (originally as the Government Code and Cypher School) to acquire 'signals intelligence' and in World War II, based at

Sean Connery, the original screen James Bond, starting with 'Dr No' in 1962

Bletchley Park in Buckinghamshire it scored major successes. Bletchley Park heralded the information age by pioneering industrialised codebreaking processes: the Turing/Welchman Bombe and Colossus, the world's first electronic computer; it cracked the German Enigma code. Subsequently based in the quiet provincial town of Cheltenham – in sharp contrast to MI5 and MI6, in the heart of London – its very existence was kept secret from the public until the later 1970s. GCHQ and the NSA in America never attracted the limelight in the way of MI6 and the CIA yet both were more important in the Cold War than the more glamorous espionage agencies. Today GCHQ's work covers areas such as international crime and commercial cyber security as well as other traditional for-

GCHQ headquarters in Cheltenham, popularly known as 'the doughnut'

eign policy and national security concerns. While much of its work remains secret it has cultivated an open public persona in recent years, even collaborating in publication of *The GCHQ Puzzle Book*.

The United Nations, aid and global economic standing

In 1945 the UK was a founder member of the United Nations and it remains one of the five permanent members of the UN Security Council, all nuclear powers. On the Council or in the Assembly, it is generally in alignment with the United States. It differs from the USA however in its greater sensitivity to UN positions. Discomfort about UN condemnation was an important aspect of the Suez debacle; half a century on, unwillingness to seek a second authorising UN resolution weakened the domestic position of the British government in the Iraq War. Concern about adherence to international law remains a potent factor in domestic politics.

The UK adheres to the UN's 2000 target of contributing 0.7 per cent of national income (£11.7bn) to overseas development aid and this commitment is now enshrined in law. Most of the aid is channelled through the designated Department for Overseas Aid (DfiD). The UK is the second largest donor of aid after the United States, which gives considerably more in absolute terms despite falling short of the 0.7 per cent target. Only four other countries give a greater share of their national income as aid. Increasingly aid flows via international organisations, principally the EU. Nearly 60 per cent of Official Development Assistance (ODA) was bilateral, the rest multilateral.

Only four other countries give a greater share of their national income as aid

The size of the UK economy gives it access to the principal global economic forums. At the G8 it joins the biggest Western economies (Canada, France, Germany, Italy, Japan and the USA) plus Russia. The G8 discusses economic and trade matters annually: the UK held the presidency in 2013 and will again in 2021. There and at the G20, it is a consistent advocate of free trade. It is also prominent in the much larger International Monetary Fund (IMF), set up in the 1940s to regulate the post-war world monetary system. Relationships suffer when IMF assessments of the British economy fall short of the government's own view. At the World Bank, UK prestige is high due to its generosity as an aid donor.

Soft power

If defence ('hard power') is at a low ebb, what of 'soft power'? This term, an invention of American economist Joseph Nye, connotes the collection of cultural assets that can raise a country's reputation and make it attractive to others.

The British Council is a prime example of 'soft power'; it was established in 1934 in an effort to bolster British influence at a time when the ability to wield hard power was under threat, a conflict vividly portrayed in Olivia Manning's fiction. The Council is the UK's international cultural relations and educational opportunities organisation, with a presence in over 100 countries. In its view, 'the UK's language, arts, education system and civil society are the reasons for its international attractiveness ... strengthening its reputation as an open, vibrant country, with a thriving cultural scene and a world-class education sector'. Early in 2016, the then foreign secretary thought 'there is probably no country, other than the US, with a more influential global brand ... our influence can lie increasingly in the attractive power of our institutions, our language, our capital city, our legal system, our education, our creativity, our diversity'. In the second decade of the 21st century government ministers had to wrestle with the consequences of the UK's attractiveness when they attributed explosive inward migration to an unduly generous welfare system. Within the migrant numbers were counted the many students flocking to Britain's prestigious universities.

It is certainly an advantage to be a – indeed the original – English-speaking country, deploying the world's most widely-spoken second language as its language of choice. This is an invaluable legacy of the age, or two ages, of empire. The English language is a great economic asset and may be an even greater cultural advantage. The UK arts sector is a particular strength, containing the world's most visited (and largest) modern art gallery (Tate Modern), one of the three premier museums of civilisation (the British Museum), countless theatres and a matchless acting tradition. Recently these established excellences have been augmented, with new achievement in architecture, film, design and fashion. Eleven UK universities regularly appear among rankings of the world's top one hundred and Oxford and Cambridge are routinely at or very close to the pinnacle. The arts and higher education have a collateral (and frequently ignored) impact on economic performance but they burnish global influence as well. The British Council's list of soft power attributes is rounded off by UK civil society. The UK is law-abiding and ranks relatively low on any global index of corruption; British citizens have visa-free access to more countries than the citizens of any other country.

British citizens have visa-free access to more countries than the citizens of any other country

The British Broadcasting Corporation (BBC) – discussed in detail in chapter 17 – is the world's largest public service broadcaster and much else besides. Five of its six strategic objectives directly underpin soft power: sustaining citizenship and civil society, representing the UK, its nations, regions and communities, promoting education and learning, bringing the UK to the world and the world to the UK, and stimulating creativity and cultural excellence. In 2014 the FCO offloaded to it the funding of the 'World Service', a respected global radio station with a £250m annual budget. The World Service broadcasts globally in English but also maintains 27 foreign-language services regionally broadcast. It differs from Voice of America in not being a government outlet and so its prestige (and reputation for access) is higher. Former USSR President Mikhail Gorbachev has revealed that he first learned of the abortive 1991 coup by tuning into the World Service during a Russian radio blackout. Nor is the BBC alone in its international media prestige. The UK still hosts the most respected financial daily (The Financial Times – recently acquired by Nikkei) and weekly (The Economist) as well as several other public service broadcasters.

The Foreign and Commonwealth Office

The FCO itself is an exponent of soft power, a silkily-skilled 'Rolls-Royce machine', allowing the UK to enjoy disproportionate leverage in multilateral organisations. It employs the world's most sought-after diplomatic drafters and exploited this reputation in 2015 by opening a Diplomatic Academy – and not just for its own staff. The UK is represented overseas not by former politicians but by career diplomats up to ambassador level. They are admired for their suave and skilful management of international relations, and led the successful Iran nuclear negotiations. Before 2007 the FCO focused only on English discourse, but this was reversed in 2013 with the establishment of a new and enhanced FCO language school. The UK ranks fourth among nations by the number of diplomatic posts it maintains.

Yet there is a diminishing number of British diplomats in EU service and a major concern following the 2016 Brexit vote was a dearth of native trade negotiating skills, outsourced to the EU for more than four decades. Successive budgetary cuts have pared back FCO capacity. In the referendum campaign it strongly advised a Remain vote, declining to plan for the contingency of a Vote Leave triumph (the Commons foreign affairs committee later condemned this 'gross negligence'). Its recommendation spurned, it faced radical change. When Theresa May became prime minister she chose as the new foreign secretary Boris Johnson, the florid Brexit campaigner. Yet his writ did not seem to extend to all external affairs because two new government departments were created on its turf: one for international trade and one specifically for negotiating EU withdrawal. Tough Brexiters ran both.

Hard on the heels of these startling developments came publication of *The Report of the Iraq Inquiry*. Its chair Sir John Chilcot took seven years to explore UK involvement in the Iraq War and the lessons to be learned. His report probed policy from the background to the war decision, military preparations, conduct of the conflict and planning for the aftermath, when intense sectarian violence had erupted. The censure of Tony Blair and his government was forensically severe, concluding that Iraq was invaded before peaceful options had been exhausted; that judgements about the scale of the threat from Iraq's weapons of mass destruction (WMD) had been presented with unjustified severity; that the consequences of the invasion had been underestimated; that planning for Iraq after Saddam Hussein had been wholly inadequate; that stated objectives had not been achieved. Much press attention focused on Blair's July 2002 assurance to George W. Bush, 'I will be with you, whatever.' As the department directing UK external relations, the FCO was in the firing line: the failure of contingency planning lay at its door.

11. An open economy

In the 18th century Britain was the first country to industrialise and the first to develop a new demography based on industrial towns. By 1800 it was close to enjoying a global monopoly in some areas of manufacturing, losing its pole position only sometime in the 1870s. After this, though still industrially and militarily powerful, it entered a century of relative economic decline, at one point dropping to eighth in world rankings. Today the British formal economy has rebounded to fifth or sixth-largest, roughly similar in size to that of France and behind the USA, China, Japan and Germany. While some of its original features persist, much has changed. A manufacturing base survives (though often not its national ownership) but the country has largely bowed out of the extractive industries: today's Britons are much more likely to be employed in services than production. Yet, while the UK share of world trade has drastically shrunk since the days of empire, it has retained its strength in financial services. The UK remains a financial superpower, largely thanks to the dense concentration of companies and institutions in the City of London. Financial and related professional services (very broadly defined) are reported to be the country's largest provider of taxes, to employ 2.2 million and to account for 12 per cent of economic output.

Britain's economic decline had multiple causes. Geopolitics explains much: the penalty of being the first industrial nation, loss of empire, the human and economic cost of two total wars, the emergence of so many productive rivals. A country of 65 million people has a relatively small home market. It must export to sustain high output with economies of scale and hence has always has been committed to free trade. In 2014, 47 per cent of British goods exports went to the EU, 17 per cent to the USA and 25 per cent to the rest of the world. But export of goods (below 3 per cent of global share, and led by cars and pharmaceutical products) is not sufficient to keep the country solvent so it relies on income from a vast overseas investment portfolio. Overall it is the sixth largest trader in the world, and (if measured against the size of its economy) the largest exporter of services. The Brexit vote of June 2016 posed a series of searching questions for economic policy-makers: will the UK retain access to the single market of the EU; will the UK remain in the EU customs union; and if it does neither will it find adequate compensatory opportunities in faster-growing markets elsewhere?

Characteristics of the British economy

The British economy is markedly open. It is often contrasted to the French model of *dirigisme*, the defence of home country ownership of national champions. UK governments, sensitive to the country's need for access to foreign markets, have allowed key brand firms to be acquired by multinationals, mostly from the United States. Recent takeover victims include Burberry, Cadbury, Clark's Shoes, Land Rover and Rolls Royce. A further concern centres on technology when innovative UK firms are snapped up by multinationals: in July 2016 ARM, a large information technology firm was taken over by Japan's SoftBank. A quarter of foreign-owned businesses in Britain were owned from within the USA in 2012; 48 per cent of UK foreign direct investment overall originated from the EU. This overseas ownership varies greatly across sectors, covering only 4 per cent of construction firms but 61 per cent of services companies. There are no restrictions of the kind which force US media tycoons to be American citizens. The UK ranks eighth in a World Bank table of business-friendly countries. The Financial Times calculated the UK was by far the most 'open for business' economy among the G7, its employment protection laws the fifth weakest. As discussed in chapters 9 and 12, UK net migration in the 21st century has been large, sustained, and greatly powered by EU nationals.

Such openness goes hand in hand with deregulation as successive governments seek to increase the country's attractiveness to overseas investors. At 20 per cent UK corporation tax is relatively low. Her Majesty's Revenue and Customs (HMRC) is often alleged to adopt a light-touch approach to multinationals – a charge it disputes. Moreover, the scope for inward investment has been greatly broadened by the privatisations of formerly publicly-owned enterprises that have created new markets over nearly four decades. Sovereign wealth funds from the Middle East, China and elsewhere now have significant holdings in key infrastructural projects. But just as Britain welcomes inward investment, so UK companies in their turn hold extensive overseas interests, with consequent benefits in foreign exchange earnings. This has been a very successful rentier economy since mid-Victorian times, though doubts have mounted over the continued ability of UK overseas earnings to offset the country's chronic current account deficit.

doubts have mounted over the continued ability of UK overseas earnings to offset the country's chronic current account deficit

Finance

Finance is the great exception to the country's relative decline. The City of London became the world financial centre as early as the 1690s, prospering for a long time virtually without a rival. In the age of empire, it became banker to the whole world. Today it retains preeminence but now the key is an open economy. The capital value of companies trading on the London Stock Exchange (LSE) before 1914 was the world's largest; after that it fell behind Wall Street and (eventually) Tokyo. It remains the third largest however and still lists 529 foreign companies, 20% of global foreign equity listings. (To track the capital value of the top one hundred firms trading on the Exchange, follow the 'FTSE 100'.) Early in 2016, banks, insurers and asset managers yielded first place in this index to consumer goods companies, a demotion that reflected their punishing fortunes since the recession.

But the City has acquired other financial strengths. It hosts 251 foreign banks, is the global insurance centre and home to the third largest domestic insurance sector in the world. London houses 18% of global hedge fund assets and 85% of Europe's. It is the leading Western centre for Islamic finance, the largest centre for cross-border banking and cross-border borrowing and accounts for 41% of global foreign exchange trading (FOREX). More than four decades of EU membership did not even dent this preeminence: in 2015 London successfully defended at the European Court of Justice the right of clearing houses outside the Eurozone to handle euro liquidity. But in the wake of the 2016 Brexit vote the City faced possible new attempts by continuing EU member states to poach markets and staff. It was also anxious over the possible loss of 'passporting' rights (the ability to offer financial services across the EU, likely to be denied to non-citizens). It aspired to compensate by innovation and deeper penetration of high-growth markets.

The pace of internationalisation accelerated in recent decades. The growth of the LSE – the only significant UK exchange – illustrates this well. In 1981 barely 4 per cent of UK stock was owned by overseas investors; in 1986 it was liberalised and automated in a 'Big Bang'; by 2014 the overseas investor share had grown to 54 per cent (Japan 32 per cent, USA 16 per cent). Space for this inward financial investment has been left by UK individuals who have largely abandoned the stock market. There, their interests are held by great institutional investors such as pension funds and insurance companies. These bodies are themselves in retreat from equity, growing increasingly risk-averse and shifting holdings into gilts and property. However, the dependence of the UK on financial services has grown exponentially.

UK trade depends more on financial services than does that of any other G7 nation

Business services and finance, a mere 5% of GDP in 1948 accounted for 32% in 2013. UK trade depends more on financial services than does that of any other G7 nation, greatly helped by a time zone that allows connections to the Americas and Asia in the same working day.

Also in the 'square mile' of the City is the Bank of England, which despite its name is the central bank to the whole UK. This venerable institution (founded in 1694 and sometimes known as the 'Old Lady of Threadneedle Street', after its location) historically managed the national debt and maintained financial stability. It controls the issuing of the UK's distinctively elaborate sterling banknotes and determines denominations. (Three Scottish banks and four Northern Ireland banks also issue notes under their name but strictly under Bank of England control.) To these responsibilities it later added a duty to advise the chancellor of the exchequer (a politician) on interest rates and to supervise the private banks. In 1946 it was na-

tionalised and became wholly-owned by HM government. In 1997 its obligation to ensure financial stability was enshrined in law, and it became an independent monetary authority, henceforth setting interest rates itself and obliged to account for deviant shifts in inflation. By such means it was hoped to insulate monetary policy from political interference.

The Bank's financial policy committee (FPC) closely monitors micro-trends in the economy and, since the recession, has acquired important powers to supervise Britain's errant banking sector. Per-

Mark Carney, the Canadian who is governor of the Bank of England; he has become a more prominent public figure than any of his predecessors

haps the key event of the dramatic day after the UK's Brexit vote – arguably more important than the resignation of the prime minister – was a sombre press conference at which the Bank's governor Mark Carney calmed markets with a measured statement assuring them that all contingencies had been anticipated and that the country's entire reserves stood ready to be deployed, if necessary, to calm markets. It worked. The Bank of England remains one of the world's most powerful central banks, along with the Bank of Japan, the European Central Bank and the Federal Reserve in the USA.

Assisting the Bank in supervision of the financial sector are two key financial regulators. The Prudential Regulation Authority (PRA), part of the Bank itself, is responsible for the prudential regulation and supervision of around 1,700 banks, building societies, credit unions, insurers and major investment firms. The Financial Conduct Authority – independent of the Bank – is the conduct regulator for 56,000 financial services firms and financial markets in the UK and the prudential regulator for over 24,000 of those firms.

The City's preeminence in insurance, like the Bank, dates from the 17th century when traders needed to insure their ships and their cargoes. This business was conducted in coffee shops, notably that of Edward Lloyd. Lloyd's wrote almost £27 billion of premium business in 2015. It is the world's specialist market for insurance and reinsurance, licensed to underwrite business in over 70 territories and able to accept risks proposed from over 200 countries and territories in accordance with local laws and regulation. Lloyds is only one of 350 companies providing commercial insurance from the City and accounting for one-fifth of its output.

Lloyds of London: founded at his coffee house by Edward Lloyd around 1688, it is the marketplace at the heart of world insurance

Manufacturing, services, construction and agriculture

The UK has largely lost the defining industries of the industrial revolution – coal, iron & steel, engineering, textiles and shipbuilding. Where they have survived it is under foreign ownership; otherwise the country buys in its needs. The mass consumer industries of the 20th century – cars, white goods, audio-visuals – survive but usually as subsidiaries of global firms. According to the World Bank, during 2007-2014 the UK fell from seventh to ninth among manufacturer nations, overtaken by India and South Korea. Increasingly, UK growth areas tend to be those most closely aligned with design and the arts or linked to university research (life sciences). High value-added areas seem to be the most resilient. Britain's statistics agency the ONS found that 'UK manufacturing industry has declined at the fastest pace of the G7 economies … from having one of the largest

UK manufacturing industry has declined at the fastest pace of the G7 economies

Digging the foundations for yet another cotton mill in 19th century Preston in Lancashire: a once great British industry has now largely relocated overseas

shares in 1948, to the lowest in 2012. The pace of the decline in the relative size of manufacturing industries has been fastest in the most recent years – since 1995 its share of GDP has almost halved.'

Things are very different in the services sector which in 2012 contributed 79 per cent of the value of GNP; in 1948 it had been 46 per cent. Britain's service sector is broad – extending far beyond financial services – and it has excelled at global marketing. After business services and finance, the next largest service sectors are government services, distribution, hotels and restaurants, transport, storage and communication. As John Kay has pointed out, the UK has a trade surplus in almost every service sector except tourism. After World War II services accounted for 44 per cent of employment; today the figure has risen to 85 per cent.

the UK has a trade surplus in almost every service sector except tourism

Building is a bellwether of economic health, a large labour-intensive industry, hampered in the UK by a lack of skills, a shortage it mitigates with imported labour. It accounts for about 6 per cent of UK production. Many major building projects are in evidence in British city centres and especially London, though over the long term the UK has suffered the lowest level of investment in infrastructure relative to

GDP of the major world economies. UK property is generally expensive, primarily due to the high cost of land, a scarce commodity in the more crowded parts of a small island where there are strict restrictions on the use of agricultural land for development. Even when economic activity was at a low ebb during the 2007-2013 recession property prices continued to rise, especially in London and the South East. Beyond doubt there is a powerful appetite for home ownership. This, together with ever more ingenious government schemes to feed it helps to drive the market on.

The UK's highly intensive farming sector accounts for only 0.5 per cent of GDP (for farming's social role, see the final chapter). With the exception of the two world wars when food was scarce and home production boomed, the long-term trend has been one of relative decline. Taking agriculture and fishing together the ageing workforce has slumped to a record low of one per cent of the total UK workforce; in 1841, at the dawn of the free trade era, it was 22 per cent. The farm sector is in general highly productive. However, Britain is a significant importer of food due to year-round demand for seasonal products, relentlessly marketed by Britain's powerful grocery chains. Livestock rearing dominates the hillier North and West (including Wales, Scotland and Northern Ireland) where rainfall is higher. Crops are more likely to be grown in the drier and sunnier South and East. At almost 75 per cent, the East of England has the highest percentage of arable land and the largest area under wheat; Scotland has the largest area under barley. The North West has the most dairy farms while damp Wales has the least arable land but most sheep and lambs. The trend towards local sourcing has boosted UK farming, and the EU list of protected food names underpins it (see the appendix to this chapter).

Employment

The UK has a very high employment participation rate. Nearly three-quarters of those aged 16-64 (almost 80 per cent of men, almost 70 per cent of women) are in paid work, doing the UK's largest ever number of paid jobs (37.1 million). The median earnings of a full-time working Briton were £27,600 in 2015. The national living wage, starting at £7.20 and scheduled to rise to £9 an hour by 2020, replaced the minimum wage in April 2016. Once fully implemented it is expected to cover 18 per cent of workers. However, private sector earnings have remained consistently at around 85 per cent of public sector earnings since 2009. This matters because, by 2016, 83 per cent of the workforce were in the private sector, with public sector employment having dropped steadily as a proportion of the total. Full-time workers did over 37 hours per week in their main job; part-timers 16 hours per week in their main job.

Yet many are shut out from the workforce. The number of young people aged 16-24 who are 'NEETS' (Not in Employment, Training or Students) is ominously large for such a work-based society, even though unemployment among young people is lower than in most other European countries. Work and other prospects for NEETS are poor: while there are opportunities in the over-heating capital and broad South East, these are scarcer, require less skill and pay less in traditional industrial areas. Training and apprenticeships are discussed in chapter 14. In the EU referendum many blamed poor training opportunities on the large number of foreign workers. In the 19 years to March 2016, the number of non-UK nationals working in the UK more than trebled to 3.3 million, taking them nearly one in ten of the workforce. This partly reflects the admission of several new member states to the EU, as explained in chapter 9. Non-UK nationals from the EU working in the UK make up about two-thirds of the non-UK nationals working.

In the 38 years to 2016, the proportion of jobs accounted for by the manufacturing and mining and quarrying sectors fell from over 26 per cent to 8.0 per cent while the proportion of jobs accounted for by the services sector increased from over 63 per cent to 83 per cent. The old core workforce – semi-skilled, male – has shrunk. For many such individuals the loss of a coal-mining or steel smelting job meant the end of paid work or at best its replacement by a low-status, poorly-paid private sector service job.

About 25 per cent of the employed workforce are in trade unions, a fairly steep decline from the 32% of twenty years earlier. The reason is not hard to find since over half of employees in the public sector are in trade unions, whereas fewer than one in seven are union members in the much larger private sector which is the area of job growth. Though Britain's unions operate in a highly restricted environment this is less inimical to their position than private ownership, whether in former state enterprises or not. The rapid growth in self-employment is also a factor. Some self-employment is voluntary and *women have moved from one-third to one half of all paid workers in the space of just one generation* genuine, but controversy has arisen over the status of workers on zero hours contracts and in the 'gig' economy such as minicab drivers and couriers, who are nominally self-employed (and therefore denied employee benefits such as sick pay or redundancy) while de facto working for only one employer.

The gender pay gap of 9.4 per cent is the lowest ever. Female participation in paid work is high: women have moved from one-third to one half of all paid workers in the space of just one generation. To some extent this reflects the low level of wages, forcing all adults to earn. But other factors are at work: initiatives to raise the number of single-parent workers by enhancing childcare, the rising number of graduate women, shifting financial incentives, the 'de-genderisation' of working roles; the introduction of a national minimum wage. The sector with the highest proportion of women workers is public administration, education and health (70 per cent – areas of mainly public sector employment), while the lowest is construction (12 per cent).

After the referendum

The UK government currently intends to complete the process of leaving the EU by the end of March 2019. By that date it will have to resolve many key issues. One among them is membership (or not) of the EU customs union (which will govern UK trading relationships with the rest of the world). New trade negotiations must be undertaken with all countries across the globe, including the EU itself but they cannot properly begin until the process of withdrawal is complete. However, one assessment puts UK trade flows with the rest of the world outside the EU at 70 per cent: it is much less dependent than the remaining 27 members on intra-EU trade flows.

Leaving the EU internal market will have consequences for the UK's nonetheless substantial EU trade. Remaining within that market will likely require continuing observance of the free movement of labour, the very thing many in the Leave majority found objectionable. Remaining also implies continued subordination to the European Court of Justice (ECJ, see chapter 19) which enforces a level playing field in trade, but many Leavers also object to the ECJ on sovereignty grounds as it trumps the domestic courts.

The Nissan plant at Sunderland is the biggest car factory in the UK; 55 per cent of production is exported to the EU but the area voted strongly for Brexit

Key sectors of the UK economy (food processing, hospitality, catering) are greatly dependent on EU citizens who may not be skilled; in other sectors (the NHS, universities, scientific research) there is great dependence on those with scarce skills. Opportunities for UK citizens wishing to work in the EU (including passporting issues) will need to be resolved. In investment, the UK has greatly benefited from commitments by the European Investment Bank (EIB), lead financier of the Channel Tunnel, the second Severn Crossing and the Jubilee Line extension. The UK has a long list of infrastructure projects for which capital will have to be raised. If it cannot negotiate continued access to EIB funds then alternatives will have to be found.

Appendix: food products protected under the EU scheme

The EU protected food name scheme highlights regional and traditional foods whose authenticity and origin can be guaranteed, giving
legal protection against imitation throughout
the EU. There are 73 protected food names in
the UK.

Anglesey Sea Salt; Arbroath Smokies; Armagh Bramley Apples; Beacon Fell Traditional Lancashire; Bonchester Blue; Buxton
Blue; Cornish Pasty; Cornish Clotted Cream;
Cornish Sardines; Dorset Blue; Dovedale; East
Kent Golding; Exmoor Blue; Fal Oysters; Fen-
land Celery; Gloucestershire Cider and Perry;

*Rolling the cheese, the Stilton
village sign. Stilton is known
as the 'king of English cheeses'*

Herefordshire Cider and Perry; Isle of Man Loaghtan Lamb; Isle of Man
Queenies; Jersey Royal Potatoes; Kentish ale and Kentish Strong Ale; Lake-
land Herdwick; Lough Neagh Eels; Melton Mowbray Pork Pie; Native
Shetland Wool; Newmarket Sausage; New Season Comber Early Potatoes;
Orkney Beef and Lamb; Orkney Scottish Island Cheddar; Pembrokeshire
Early Potatoes/Pembrokeshire Earlies; Rutland Bitter; Scotch Beef; Scotch
Lamb; Scottish Farmed Salmon; Scottish Wild Salmon; Shetland Lamb; Sin-
gle Gloucester; Staffordshire Cheese; Stilton Blue and White; Stornoway
Black Pudding; Swaledale and Swalesdale Ewes' Cheese; Teviotdale; Tra-
ditional Cumberland Sausage; Traditional Farmfresh Turkey; Traditional
Grimsby Smoked Fish; Traditionally Farmed Gloucester Old Spots Pork;
Welsh Beef; Welsh Lamb; West Country Beef and Lamb; West Country
Farmhouse Cheddar; Whitstable Oysters; Worcestershire Cider and Perry;
Yorkshire Forced Rhubarb; Yorkshire Wensleydale; Traditional Ayrshire
Dunlop.

12. Social identities

Is Britain hamstrung by class? Visitors are bewildered by the subtle social gradations and behaviour patterns apparently determining life-chances. A Western world fed on period drama half-expects to find a whole complex social structure still intact, from kindly (or brutal) patricians to a servant class, a Downton Abbey world.

Class delineation certainly survives but no two people will agree on its exact contours. There is of course an hereditary aristocracy with a decorative monarchy at its apex. Law, politics, certain rarefied areas of culture and finance, and the upper ranks of the civil service in Whitehall are to

Downton Abbey: the outside world's view of Britain is heavily influenced by film and TV portrayals

this day dominated by the (largely male) alumni of a small number of top public schools and Oxbridge – the upper class or upper middle class, according to taste. A solid middle class is defined by university education, professional status, financial security and comfortable home ownership. There is a traditional working class of manual workers, shrunken numerically but still millions strong. Somewhere between the incontrovertibly working class and the indisputably middle class are other millions, many in private sector service jobs, who inhabit a grey area; the old 'white collar' qualification for lower middle class status has lost its meaning in a country where ever fewer work in 'blue collar' jobs. In America these people call themselves the 'middle class' but in Britain many such think of themselves as working class – or don't think in those terms at all. Increasing numbers are self-employed, some by choice, many of necessity; their circumstances are often precarious and to them the finer points of class distinction are meaningless. And it is common now to also identify an 'underclass' lacking the skills or drive to work, reliant on various forms of state assistance, increasingly impoverished, mercilessly lampooned as the 'chavs'.

Being born into any of these classes makes it more likely than not that you will stay there. Yet a class-based description would capture only half the picture. Society is divided in other powerful ways and the impact of traditional class divisions is blunted.

Classes

Britain's aristocracy is tiny, powerless and cautious of ostentation: its titles often unused, the famous 'cut-glass' accents coarsened. Even the queen, last word in 'posh', has learned to flatten her vowels a little. Largely excluded from the House of Lords, ineligible for the House of Commons, sometimes unable even to vote, the hereditary nobility has no power. Some do retain great wealth, usually in the form of landed estates and great houses. Much of this was levered by 20th century tax duties into the hands of the state, but sometimes the 'nobs' hold on, selling an occasional Canaletto to stay solvent. Primogeniture, that French import passing on at death the whole inheritance and title to the eldest son, curbed their numbers and may even have saved them from a British version of the guillotine.

But lack of visible power is not the same as lack of influence or access to power. And those aristocrats retaining their 'stately homes' even acquired a new legitimacy as their properties came to be seen as embodying the national past (see final chapter). In the words of Debrett's (the quasi-official guide to noble rank) 'while the (reform of the) House of Lords Act in 1999 has greatly reduced the political power of the peerage, their social influence remains undimmed, and their lives remain a source of interest and speculation'.

The House of Lords: tradition and splendour, but most members are now working life peers, nominated by the political parties

The privately educated business and professional elite continues to prosper in politics and beyond. Half the cabinet of David Cameron (Eton, Oxford, prime minister 2010-2016) was privately educated. Half also attended Oxford or Cambridge ('Oxbridge'), the two British universities most likely to draw students from such schools. Oxford's dominance in politics has been remarkable. Only three of the twelve prime ministers since Winston Churchill's second term in 1955 have not been Oxford graduates. Yet the private schools/Oxbridge focus is weakening: Tony Blair's 1997-2007 government was the least privately- and Oxbridge-educated ever. Even in Cameron's cabinet, 43 per cent had attended state schools and Oxbridge dominance was below its peak. While the House of Lords lingers on – against all the odds – as a useful outlet for patronage, the reach of the 'establishment' (a pejorative term coined in the 1950s for the network of wire-pullers linked by educational privilege) is shortening. In the 2016 EU referendum, vox pops rarely omitted denunciations of the 'Westminster establishment' and 'elite', sentiments the Brexit campaigners cheerfully fed, notwithstanding the fact that the Brexiters' two leading lights were both products of famous public schools (Boris Johnson, Eton; Nigel Farage, Dulwich).

Below the establishment lies Britain's wider middle class. The breadth of this class, the fact that

Only three prime ministers since 1955 have not been Oxford graduates

a significant proportion of the population had a stake in society, and that many others saw such status as within their reach with application and good fortune, has traditionally been seen as at least one factor in Britain's historical avoidance of social revolution (there are of course many other factors). While Europe was convulsed in the 1930s by the struggle between communism and fascism, Britain elected as its prime minister the reassuringly placid, Conservative, pipe smoking Stanley Baldwin. In the second half of the 20th century the rise of the middle class was driven further forward by economic growth, redistribution of wealth from the richest, and the demands of an ever more sophisticated economy for ever more educated workers. The escalator of social mobility seemed only to run in one direction, and that was up.

Over 40 per cent of today's young go on to higher education; 50 years ago it was 10 per cent. Sheer numbers give this new educated middle class great social weight. Its out-

this new educated middle class ... has benefited most ... from the post-1945 expansion of the British state

look, first formed by baby-boomers at universities in the liberal 1960s, may be said to underpin the tolerant values of official Britain. It is the class that on a long view has benefited most, in consumption and employment terms, from the post-1945 expansion of the British state. The numerical shrinkage of the traditional working class is its mirror image, stemming from the secular decline of Britain's extractive and manufacturing industries. The great expansion in the number of low-paid public sector service jobs compensated, but only in part.

The underclass, if such it is, consists of those whose educational attainments are limited and whose employment and earnings prospects are poor. It is a financial headache for successive governments ambitious to cut the welfare budget, railing against a 'benefit culture', eyeing slashed welfare benefits as the solution. The value and range of these benefits has diminished, causing real hardship; yet the welfare budget continues to grow. Multiple deprivation is concentrated in low-quality rentals and sink housing estates. The Social Mobility and Child Poverty Commission offered a startling profile of the poor in 2015: 1.5 million children in poverty because their working parents earned insufficient to secure a basic standard of living; 22 per cent of employees on low hourly pay (in the best-performing EU countries it is below 10 per cent); 24 per cent of poor white British boys gaining five good GCSEs against a national average of 57 per cent.

Yet for most Britons class stratification has weakened under the pressure of social mobility. There has been a huge growth in the number of 'first-generation' undergraduates (i.e. from non-graduate households), and an increasing number from working-class homes; but there has also been a great expansion in the numbers unable to work and in danger of sinking into the underclass. Perhaps for the first time, also, significant numbers of young people from middle class families face prospects, in terms of housing, job security and real incomes, that are worse than those of their parents – from whom, even if the parents are affluent, they may well inherit nothing until well into middle age as longevity surpasses anything known before. While in the 20th century social mobility was an escalator up, in the 21st century some are finding themselves on an escalator down.

Immigration

Britain like much of Western Europe experienced the late 20th century shift from an almost totally white to a multiethnic society. The scale and speed of this transition were remarkable. Small numbers distantly descended from slaves lived in the Atlantic-facing maritime cities – Bristol, Cardiff, Liverpool – before 1945, but it was only after that date that the real

The arrival of the liner Windrush in 1948 with nearly 500 West Indians on board; the start of large-scale immigration from the Caribbean

change occurred. From 1948 successive waves of immigrants from the Caribbean, East Africa and South Asia travelled to the UK, primarily to England, sometimes encouraged on their way by the governments of their countries of origin, sometimes fleeing them. It then took barely half a century to establish multiethnicity as a fact of life in all the major English conurbations except Tyneside; it is also an increasing factor in smaller towns, especially those radiating out from the big cities. Only in the deeper countryside are non-white faces still rare.

Immigration retains its political toxicity: no-one doubts its impact on the 2016 EU referendum vote. However, the issue has changed. In the 1960s and 1970s it was the colour of people's skins that caused friction: white immigrants from the old Commonwealth were welcome but 'coloured immigration' met a far more mixed response in an era when the open expression of the crudest racial prejudice was not uncommon. Nowadays, however, the issues are more to do with scale, the impact on jobs and housing – and many of the immigrants are white Europeans.

Annual immigration was 329,000 in 1991 but 630,000 in 2015, an increase of 91 per cent. In 2014, 13 per cent of people migrating to the UK were British nationals, 42 per cent were nationals of other EU countries, and 45 per cent were nationals of non-EU countries. House of Commons researchers have pointed out that this meant fewer than half were subject to immigration control. This is one reason why immigration has defied the restraining efforts of successive governments. While the gross numbers, which are inflated by including short-stay students and do not take account of emigration, can seem misleadingly high, the Office of National Statistics is on record that the recorded numbers of immigrants are an underestimate. It believes the 'largest single cause is most likely to be underestimation of long-term immigration from central and Eastern Europe in the middle part of the decade'. During that time the UK freely accepted migrants from the generally much poorer Eastern European countries that joined the EU in 2004 and 2007: even the of-

Sign for the 'Balti Triangle' of curry restaurants in Birmingham. The 'balti', an Indian-derived concoction perfected in the city is now a national dish alongside fish and chips

Brick Lane in East London; successive waves of immigrants have made it their 'high street'

ficial numbers show EU migrants accounted for 268,000 in 2014.

Immediate political pressures notwithstanding, it is the consequences of past immigration that have had the greatest social impact over the last half-century. Unlike most EU arrivals, West Indians, Indians and Pakistanis do not have white descendants and they may follow unfamiliar cultural, especially religious, practices. An American presidential hopeful was rightly ridiculed for suggesting that many English cities contained vast no-go areas for whites. Nevertheless, it is true that the visitor to Southall High Street (Ealing, Greater London), Belgrave Road (Leicester) or Manningham Road (Bradford) might momentarily feel in another country. Such an observation would certainly find an echo among some locals. Intriguingly the 2016 Brexit vote projects mixed signals: Ealing and Leicester voted Remain, Bradford voted Leave. But exotic unfamiliarity is not the same as insecurity: there are no 'no-go' areas.

Given the pace of post-war immigration Britain's success in assimilating it is remarkable. Relations are largely peaceful, not least because the state has promoted racial and religious tolerance for half a century. The familiarity of daily life has dampened down the instinctive prejudice once felt against the unfamiliar. Crucially most people in those places with most immigrants have seemingly come to embrace change, even welcomed its consequences. The social impact of immigration is familiar. In mid-20th century Britain shops were firmly shut on Sundays and for half a day midweek and few were open in the evening other than off licences selling alcoholic drinks. Now, especially in cities, it is possible to find small neighbourhood shops open every day of the week deep into the night.

This and the presence of varieties of curry in the cuisine of every Briton is attributable to past immigration by African Asians (ethnic Indians formerly resident in East Africa) and Bangladeshis. More broadly large parts of the public sector workforce – not only at the unskilled level – are of minority ethnic origin. A brain-drain from the poorest parts of the world helps Britain's public services to keep going. Personal names that still seem unpronounceable to older generations trip effortlessly off the tongues of the young. And anyone walking the streets of London or other cities will notice that the number of children who are born of one white and one black parent is ever-rising: the merging of races in this melting pot is a phenomenon that is making simplistic definitions of race and identity ever harder. Symptomatically, TV advertisers favour mixed-race children above all others as most likely to sell their products.

Yet while the shape of the issue has changed immigration remains politically combustible. The 2016 referendum suggests that beyond the metropolitan areas feelings of alienation abound: 'our country' is being taken from 'us' is a sentiment powerfully felt in declining seaside or old Northern industrial towns, indeed all towns where unemployment is high. For decades this could be loftily dismissed as racial prejudice but over time it has reached beyond colour. Large numbers of (white) East European males undertake seasonal crop-gathering for Eastern England's agri-businesses; the UK's largest minority group in 2015 was its 850,000-strong Polish population. That year's general election saw four million votes cast for the anti-EU party UKIP, which campaigned primarily on control of EU migration: more than four times that number voted Leave a year later. To many, especially in the underclass, immigration explains their personal economic plight.

Immigrants, past and present, tend to be younger than the indigenous population. They have a higher birth rate than UK-born women: in 2015, 27.5 per cent of live births were to mothers born outside the UK compared with only 11.6 per cent in 1990. The number of pupils in primary schools exposed at home to a language other than English is 15 per cent and growing at quite a fast rate. The 2011 census found that two per cent of

in 2015, 27.5 per cent of live births were to mothers born outside the UK

the population at large did not speak English well or at all. This was an average: for London and Leicester the figure was eight per cent.

Integration and ethnicity

For half a century, the state has officially encouraged integration of communities while adopting a policy of multiculturalism, allowing (and indeed requiring of the indigenous population) a broad toleration of cultural differences. For a time, British policymakers complacently observed France's troubled attempts to integrate even larger numbers from the Maghreb and elsewhere. It was easy to exaggerate the contrast between the French and British approaches: the former uncompromisingly secular, insisting that immigrants embrace a secular native culture; the latter celebrating multiculturalism. *Schadenfreude* faltered as doubts surfaced about the success of the 'British model'. British cities *did* burn – Toxteth (Liverpool) and Brixton (London) in 1981, Broadwater Farm (London) in 1985, Oldham (near Manchester) in 2001, Tottenham (London) in 2011. Such risings were variously read. Were they a reaction to racism or police brutality; were they expressions of economic discontent? When the Tottenham riots led to looting in several areas of London, with imitators in Birmingham, Manchester and elsewhere, sympathy was in short supply. But in each case the response of the state, once it had restored order, was to invest in urban renewal.

Schadenfreude faltered as doubts surfaced about the success of the 'British model'

Open racism persists in the UK even if it invariably meets official condemnation. It can be overt; more often it is unconscious or implicit. There have been numerous racially-motivated murders across the decades, though the criminal justice system was reluctant to acknowledge them. The police in particular were long indifferent to racial crime and racism was endemic among them. One case above all focused the problem. In April 1993, Stephen Lawrence, a young south London black man, was murdered in an unprovoked racist attack. The Metropolitan Police investigation was slow and inefficient. For years no one was convicted, though after a new trial the murderers finally received life sentences in 2012. Following years of campaigning by Lawrence's parents, a judicial inquiry was set up. Its 1999 report found the police performance 'marred by a combination of professional incompetence, *institutional racism* (my italics) and a failure of leadership by senior officers.'

These words electrified the situation: legislation established a new offence of hate crime. By 2009, reporting of such crimes had reached 60,000 alleged incidents a year (compared with 9,000 in the entire USA – clearly there are differences in definition or willingness to report). Police performance improved, doubling the hate crime detection rate to about 44 per cent. Yet in other respects progress was slow and sometimes went into reverse. Whereas in 1999 a black person – usually a young male – was six times more likely to be stopped and searched than a white person, in 2006-2007 it was seven times. As late as 2014 – 21 years after the murder – it was revealed that undercover police had spied on the Lawrence family during their campaigns for justice. A new inquiry was set up, this time into covert policing.

Across British society the employment prospects of ethnic minorities have improved, but their progress towards senior positions has been slow. The 2011 census showed that of those in employment, men from the Pakistani (57%), Black African (54%) and Bangladeshi (53%) ethnic groups were most likely to work in low skilled jobs. A 2014 report found that 'poverty and ethnicity are strongly related, with poverty higher among all ethnic minority groups than among white British people in the UK....' In most professions the proportion of minority ethnic members is far below the ten per cent it represents in the population at large. There is evidence that advancement and earnings prospects actually decrease during a career. In January 2016, Prime Minister David Cameron noted that Oxford's 2014 intake of over 2,500 included only 27 black students, that there were no black generals, and that 'just 4% of chief executives in the FTSE 100 are from ethnic minorities'.

Islamism

These concerns persist. They have however been overshadowed by new developments. From within the British-born Muslim population (ethnically Asian or African) have come murderers and terrorists in the name of Islam. Suicide attacks paralysed London for a day, killing 52 people and injuring more than 770 in July 2005; in 2013 a reserve soldier was randomly beheaded in Woolwich. The security services say they have thwarted many more plots. These incidents were especially disturbing because they could not be understood as inchoate economic protests. Some perpetrators were not low achievers, and all justified their crimes with explicit attacks on Britain, its way of life and its foreign policy orientation. The July bombers portrayed themselves in pre-attack videos as soldiers in a wider clash of Christianity with Islam. Turmoil in the Middle East, seen by many Britons (not just Islamists) as exacerbated by Western military interventions, has proved a further radicalising factor. From 2014 onwards, growing numbers of young Muslims, some with apparently good life prospects in the UK– men, women, even children – have left the country to enlist with ISIS/DAESH in the Syrian civil war; their return is viewed with apprehension.

The state has struggled to combine an effective policing response ... with defence of a liberal society

The state has struggled to combine an effective policing response to this loathing with defence of a liberal society. Politicians have sought to articulate a coherent set of 'British' values around which the whole population might positively unite. A new British decision of November 2015 to extend RAF bombing of ISIS from Iraq to Syria, the 2015 Paris terror attacks, the 2016 attacks in Nice, Rouen and across Germany, the huge numbers of refugees seeking to relocate in Europe, all heightened the tension. A BBC poll found that 95 per cent of Muslims felt a loyalty to the UK despite the fact that almost half believed their lives were made more difficult because of attitudes towards Islam – though other polls have suggested a less optimistic interpretation. Ironically, 2016's Brexit vote raised the possibility only of controlling migration from the EU.

Age

Forecasts suggest Britain's population of 64.5 million (2015) will reach 70 million by 2030. This steady increase owes as much to longevity as to fertility. In 2012 average male life expectancy in England and Wales at 65 was forecast to

Britain's pensioners ... are, on average, the most prosperous older generation ever

advance by one year every three years until 2030. Almost 18 per cent of the population is now aged 65 or over, up by one-fifth in ten years. The median age is now 40. The UK's 'old age dependency ratio' is 27, broadly average among EU members, meaning it has roughly one older person to every four people of working age. Such information as exists points to age as a strong indicator of a Brexit vote in the 2016 referendum. Among 16-24-year-olds there was a strong preference for Remain but the young were thought to have been less likely to vote.

But while many of Britain's pensioners face a long retirement on limited means they are, on average, the most prosperous older generation ever. Their state pensions, while modest, are inflation-proofed and they enjoy free local public transport and health prescriptions. Most of all, the home owners among them – three-quarters of them – have accumulated a degree of wealth from appreciating house prices. The Resolution Foundation says that the share of wealth enjoyed by the recently retired has overtaken that held by under-45s. Growing numbers of fit older people wish to continue in work; others, preferring freedom from work, boost leisure markets by spending their pensions. Yet with age comes a growing likelihood of debility. Already over four million households consist of a single elderly person. There are thought to be 6.5 million unpaid carers, some of them elderly themselves. Britain's atomised society lacks the extended families of Southern Europe where familial networks muffled the impact of austerity after 2007. Yet while people are living longer many are also living healthier. This, combined with their continuing purchasing power, is reshaping domestic markets, a development major high street retailers struggle to comprehend.

Housing

Ageing but still fit state pensioners are of a generation for whom home purchase was either the norm or the general aspiration: most have now purchased their homes outright. Freedom from mortgage repayments increases their purchasing power but their continued occupancy of owned homes restricts the housing supply. This comes at a time when the building of dwellings is at an historically low ebb and has been there for many years. Council housebuilding, once a major creator of new housing stock, has virtually ceased. Housing associations – the only possible alternative social housing builders – labour under growing financial restrictions. Private sector building is less restricted but this sector alone cannot meet demand for home purchase or rent. In 2015 Britain built 175,000 homes; fifty years earlier it built 475,000. Homes are scarce and, in more prosperous parts of the country, unaffordable to many.

Broader economic trends have also made home purchase increasingly difficult. Interest rates – kept at record lows since the recession began in 2008 – have made borrowing cheap, but curbs on lending have restricted banks' ability to offer mortgages. In large parts of Southern England, and especially in *especially in London ... the young have become 'generation rent'* London, house prices have scaled dizzying heights thanks to a cocktail of population pressure, lack of new housing, hot money associated with the City of London and the financial sector and property speculation. Excluded from home purchase the young have become 'generation rent'. Nor is this a cheap option: rents, like homes for sale, are subject to supply and demand. Those young people ineligible for mortgages and unable to afford rent may seek to remain in the parental home. This option too is fraught as reductions in housing support from the benefit system bite. Even when it is feasible to live at home, there are family pressures: the younger generation sees its aspiration to live independently receding; parents face crowding in limited space. Others live into their thirties in multi-occupancy with friends or strangers; some 'couch surf' with no fixed abode.

Two semi-detached houses: typically English, a style little known elsewhere in Europe

Thus independent living and home ownership, available on a rising trend to the baby boomer generation born in the 1950s and early 1960s, has become an increasingly remote option for many of today's young. By 2012-2013, according to the official English Housing Survey, the proportion of homes lived in by owner-occupiers had dropped to 65.2 per cent, down from 71 per cent in 2003 and the lowest level since 1987. However, this was essentially a phenomenon affecting the young. In 1991, 67 per cent of the 25 to 34 age group were homeowners. By 2011-2012, in a remarkable downturn, that figure had declined to 43%. In contrast, home ownership had continued to increase among older groups: among the 65-74 bracket to almost 80 per cent, compared with just 50 per cent two decades earlier.

Similar trends may be observed in a number of Western countries. However, the peculiar cachet attached by the British to property ownership has long been a dimension of middle class identity and skilled working class aspiration. This is not true of continental countries like Germany where rental (albeit of a very secure kind) is the principal form of housing tenure and favoured by all classes.

Spiralling house prices forestall even a heavily-leveraged entry into the property market for many. For established home-owners, across much of Britain, property has brought an increase in wealth. Over a lifetime this has been the most dependable form of capital accumulation, with average annual national prices falling only twice in 70 years. At or near retirement mortgagees pay off their debt, becoming owners of an uncompromised asset that is likely to be worth many times its purchase price. On their death the property passes to their heirs, releasing it as available housing stock but also enriching the heirs. UK inheritance tax is felt keenly by those who have to pay it, but the inter-generational transfer of property still represents a windfall on a scale that people whose parents do not

Property ownership may in the end become the biggest social divider of all

own property will rarely enjoy. Perhaps generational wealth transfer will reinforce class separation, with home-owners begetting home-owners just as graduates beget graduates. Property ownership may in the end become the biggest social divider of all.

Wealth and income

Wealth, an abundance of valuable possessions or money, is a static concept. It can create income, but income – a dynamic concept – is for most people received in the form of earnings. Housing for most provides basic shelter but in post-1945 Britain it has been a reliable form of capital accumulation, as we have seen. Property comprises 90 per cent of the wealth of most Britons; only the richest hold their wealth in other forms: luxury goods, art, yachts. The poor are poor very largely because they do not own property. Though UK poles of wealth are extreme, between the property-less and the mega-rich are tens of millions who have accumulated modest wealth from the relentless bull market in housing. Usually the family home has made them nominally wealthy, though a growing minority has bought ad-

total rents paid are now greater than total mortgage payments

ditional property either for investment or as a second home. These people, who reproduce themselves in the next generation, feel wealthy even if their wealth is not easily realisable.

Side by side with their wealth are the booming fortunes of landlords: in 2015 their total housing wealth (of nearly £1.1 trillion) overtook that of mortgage-paying owner occupiers for the first time. The Financial Times reports that total rents paid are now greater than total mortgage payments.

Either side of single-property owner occupiers are the poor and the very rich. London is home to the globally wealthy drawn by rising property prices in its most prestigious localities, sometimes in gated developments. Their investments are safe in a stable law-abiding society and they have access to the global financial capital. A London base may be very attractive to (say) a Russian oligarch who owns a Premiership club, an Arab oil sheikh uncertain of the stability of his home regime, an American or Chinese tycoon needing to watch over a global business. They belong to a mobile class of super-rich whose interaction with the host population is minimal, but whose consumption patterns have an impact on the city, its politics, architecture and traffic.

By contrast the poor may be found not only in London but across Britain. Not only do they not have assets, they also have low incomes. Principally because of advances in the real value of the state pension, the automatic nexus of poverty and age has been broken – a great success of the last 30 years of policy. But in its place has come extensive child poverty, stubbornly resistant to state efforts. A great number of children in poor households

> *the automatic nexus of poverty and age has been broken ... But in its place has come extensive child poverty*

have parents unable to enter the labour market. Nine years of austerity have increased the numbers of the working poor and followed 30 years in which the bottom 90 per cent of the population received barely 40 per cent of national income. In maintained nursery, state-funded primary, state-funded secondary, special schools and pupil referral units, nearly one in five pupils claim free school meals.

One of over 700 fund-raising shops operated by the children's charity Barnardo's; it says that 'poverty is the single greatest threat to the well-being of children and families'

The impact of a low income is reinforced by a poorer quality of life. The OECD found almost 90 per cent of adults in the top fifth of disposable income rated their health as 'good' or 'very good'; for the bottom fifth it was 64 per cent. Despite promises made at the time of the London Olympics, Sport England found the poor less likely to participate in sport than at any time since 2005. Some 55 per cent of poor males (47 per cent of such women) meet the Department of Health's aerobic activity guidelines as against 76 per cent (63 per cent for women) of the better off. The official Marmot Review (2010) concluded residents of poorest areas lived on average 17 years fewer of 'disability-free life'. Faced with persistent evidence of this kind, the UK state intervenes heavily in the distribution of income. In 2014-2015 the average income of the richest fifth of UK households before taxes and benefits was 14 times greater than that of the poorest fifth, but after taking into account taxes and benefits the ratio is reduced to 4 to 1.

Gender

Women are a narrow majority of the UK population. The World Bank reports that Britain's female to male ratio in paid work of above 81 per cent is high, even among rich countries. But their earnings diverge from men's after childbirth and fewer women reach senior posts. State initiatives to promote equality at work stretch back 40 years and are partly responsible for bringing women's earnings to 85 per cent of men's.

While outright and formal discrimination has long been outlawed, pay inequality stubbornly persists. One cause is the low number of women occupying senior positions in high earning professions: the law, politics and the civil service. There is only one woman law lord (out of 12), seven Court of Appeal judges (out of 38) and 21 women High Court judges (out of 108). Three-quarters of law firm partners are men. Among solicitors (whose status is lower than barristers) the sexes are almost equally divided. In Theresa May, the UK has its second woman prime minister, but the cabinet is only one-third female although the shadow cabinet for the first time has a majority of women. There are 150 women MPs (out of 650). In the wider public sector, more immediately subject to policy, the number of women appointed to senior positions has grown but HMRC suggests that the overall proportion of female high earners has not budged for four years.

Many government and government-backed targets exist to boost the number of senior women, especially in the private sector, but progress is slow. Women make up 47 per cent of the workforce but only 34 per cent of managers, directors and senior officials. Of the 280 executive directors at FTSE Top 100 companies, only 24 were women, though the proportion on boards (including non-executive positions) is above one-quarter. Large companies will have to disclose earnings differences under a system of audit to be introduced in 2018, and the FTSE top 350 companies have been set a target of one-third women on the board by 2020.

A major factor holding back women's career progression is the taking of career breaks to have children, and often then returning to work on a part-time basis. As a balancing factor, many women are having children later. In England and Wales, women aged 30 to 34 have had the highest fertility of any age group since 2004, whereas prior to this women aged 25 to 29 had the highest fertility. And in 2015 the fertility rate for women aged 40 and over rose above the rate for women aged under 20 for the first time since 1947, back in the era of large families before widespread contraception. Reflecting these trends, women are also having fewer children – by 2015 down to an average of 1.82 per woman – notwithstanding the upward boost to fertility given by the arrival of migrants.

13.   A nation of unbelievers

The growth of the modern English state is virtually the same thing as the growth of the English Christian church. Christianity certainly arrived in England in the 4th century under the auspices of Rome. At first overwhelmed by pagan invaders, it gradually re-established itself from the 6th century on. A millennium later King Henry VIII repudiated the papacy, the only global authority of the 16th century, asserting a national sovereignty centred on his own kingship in politics and religion alike: he was head of church and state. Historians have delineated how, in succeeding centuries, an English – then a British – Protestant national identity was fashioned.

Henry VIII (king from 1509-1547); he wrested control of the English church from the pope in Rome

This sentiment survived the curbing of the monarchy in the 17th century and the unions with Scotland (securely Protestant, but not Episcopalian) and Ireland (irreconcilably Catholic) in the 18th. The state simply ignored the political and other contradictions thrown up by union with Scotland and Ireland. After this the Anglican state had to tolerate rival Christian (though avowedly Protestant) churches even in England. In the 19th century Christianity's grip was finally loosened, not by a rival faith but by science: Charles Darwin's *On the Origin of Species* (1869), the work of a deeply serious and committed Christian troubled by his own findings, added rocket-boosters to doubt. In the 20th and 21st centuries Anglicanism came to face not only non-Christian rivals but a still

Anglicanism came to face ... a still more corrosive foe: indifference

more corrosive foe: indifference. In a 2012 speech of which Henry would not have approved, Queen Elizabeth defined the Church of England's role not as one of defending its own beliefs but as protecting the free practice of all faiths and none.

Church and state

Superficially the UK can look today like a theocracy: its head of state is also supreme head of the Church of England; the church's hierarchy (26 senior bishops each governing a diocese) sit by right in parliament's upper house, the House of Lords; its priests, politically represented by the hierarchy, are disenfranchised; the House of Commons begins each day with 'Prayers'; many political leaders formally profess Anglicanism. The new prime minister, Theresa May, is a clergyman's daughter and undemonstrative Anglican. State funerals and weddings – of royal personages for example – are overtly conducted in conformity with the church's rite, and its leaders feature prominently, even preside, at solemn or national public occasions such as Remembrance Day.

Where there is an established church the political becomes religious and vice versa. For centuries this led dissenters to operate their own highly successful schools outside those of the Church of England. But the 1902 legislation that for the first time gave control of universal elementary education to elected local authorities (the Balfour Act) also incorporated pre-existing Church of England ('C of E') schools. Dissenters and Catholics were exempt from imposed acts of worship, but all rate-payers were required to fund the schools, sparking outrage and mass disobedience. At exactly the same time the secularisation of education was being carried through in the French Republic. There, clergy became state employees, religious orders were disbanded and religious teaching ended in schools. At the dawn of the 20th century, neither country foresaw a multi-faith society but the divergence between French *laïcité* and English accommodation of religion might be said to date from this moment. In England it led to the 'voluntary aided' or 'faith' school of today.

In the modern era it is easier to separate national identity from professions of belief: the queen's remarks as noted above show how the UK, which once identified Britishness with Protestantism, now identifies it with multiculturalism. This has many consequences, not least that formal links with the Christian churches are waning. The number of UK residents identifying as Christian fell from 72 per cent in 2001 to 59 per cent in 2011; those reporting no religious affiliation rose from 15 to 25 per cent. A recent church study disclosed that 40 per cent of the English did not believe that Jesus even existed, let alone was God in human form. Formal Church of England adherence, as measured by regular attendance at its services is practised by relatively few: a 2013 report found that only one million people participated in its services each week. Thus a formally confessional state governs a nation of unbelievers. In the 21st century, with an urgent need to discover a common value system uniting good citizens, there has been little progress beyond a formal promulgation of religious tolerance.

> *a formally confessional state governs a nation of unbelievers*

The Church of England

The various Christian churches have not been inert in the face of an increasingly complex society. An early 20th century jibe depicted the Church of England as 'the Tory Party at prayer'. No-one would say that today: when, in 2015, Anglican bishops signed a letter condemning the impact of Conservative tax policy on the poor it was only the latest manifestation; 30 years earlier the entire hierarchy had publicly inveighed against Thatcherism, prompting ministerial mutterings against 'marxist bishops'.

The Anglican church has – not without internal opposition – had woman priests for many years. In 2015 it appointed its first female bishops, one of whom has entered the House of Lords as bishop of Gloucester. Since bishops ordain priests this is a potential flashpoint. The Catholic church is unlikely to follow. Nor will it emulate the Church of England's socially liberal outlook in respect of gay priests and gay marriage. These two issues – the ordination of women and acceptance of gay priests – have generated significant internal conflict

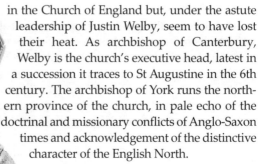

in the Church of England but, under the astute leadership of Justin Welby, seem to have lost their heat. As archbishop of Canterbury, Welby is the church's executive head, latest in a succession it traces to St Augustine in the 6th century. The archbishop of York runs the northern province of the church, in pale echo of the doctrinal and missionary conflicts of Anglo-Saxon times and acknowledgement of the distinctive character of the English North.

The Church of England is famously a 'broad church', comprehending a wide span of liturgy, if not actual belief. Some church interiors display florid decorations and follow practices once only associated with Catholi-

As archbishop of Canterbury, Justin Welby is head of the Church of England

cism; others in their plainness and evangelicalism evoke the spirit of 16th century Calvinism. While the church traces its roots back to the early Christian fathers, its specifically Anglican identity arose from the post-Reformation settlement. Out of the Reformation turmoil it emerged with two priceless liturgical assets: an English bible rendered from the Greek (and earlier English translations) into the most limpid and vivid prose (the 'Authorised Version' of 1610); and the Book of Common Prayer (1552). These seminal works rival Shakespeare's oeuvre as foundations of colloquial English. In shaping the language they shaped national identity too.

The built evidence of the church is one of the most enduring images of England. Of the 42 Anglican cathedrals, 38 are Grade I listed (and immensely expensive to maintain). Most are astonishing statements of medieval Christian certainty: York, the largest gothic structure north of the Alps; Wells, whose decorated west front rivals any in Europe; Salisbury with its 404 ft spire; Durham, notable for the unity of its Romanesque; the 1,000-year old Westminster (strictly speaking, an abbey); Canterbury which stretches back even further to St Augustine himself. The last three are all World Heritage sites.

King Henry's church began with all the property of the former Catholic church. Some of it – monasteries, abbeys, convents – was sur-

INCOLNIENSIS
FACIES OCCIDENTALIS.

Vt præclara hujus Ecclesiæ fama
amplius innotesat hoc posuit.
MICHAEL HONYWOOD
S. Th. D. ibidem Decanus.

Lincoln cathedral: for more than two centuries, before its central spire collpased in 1549, it was the tallest building in the world

plus to requirements, liquidated for its land value and survives (if at all) in the form of ruins, thanks largely to the state. But the cathedrals and 16,000 parish churches are the functioning fabric of the Church of England. Every English settlement of any longevity is constructed around its parish church, parts of which may be up to 1,500 years old. Enter a medieval church and you are by definition in an Anglican place of worship. Catholicism lost these places in the 1530s and never got them back. Three centuries on it had to build anew. Calls have been made for the two great Christian churches to share their places of worship, but little has happened. An ambivalence persists, perhaps best expressed in the polyphony and melismas that can be heard from choirs in the churches and cathedrals of either faith.

Every English settlement of any longevity is constructed around its parish church

Wales, once famous for the ubiquity of household bibles and its zealous chapel-goers, now reports the highest levels of unbelief in the UK and this affects all streams of Christianity. The Anglican 'Church in Wales', as it is called, has six bishops, one of whom serves as archbishop of the country. However, it suffered disaffection from the 18th century and by the 19th had lost the allegiance of most Welsh Christians, who referred plain chapel services. Disestablishment (1919) was a triumph for the chapel cause. A century on, the collapse in attendance even at chapels, whether Congregational, Presbyterian or Methodist, has been dramatic. With a chapel closing every week, attempts have been made to draw them all together on an ecumenical basis. Welsh Catholicism naturally stands apart from any prospect of structural merger however much it shares the social goals of the other churches. In 1916 Wales was created a Catholic province with an archdiocese in Cardiff and bishops serving West and North Wales.

The Church of England has spawned an international organisation rather like the Commonwealth. The Anglican communion has more than 70 million adherents in 38 provinces spreading across 161 countries. They are unified through their history, theology, worship and their relationship to the ancient See of Canterbury. These are all episcopal churches and include the Church in Wales and the Church of Ireland. However, they are also autonomous and in recent years the communion has been stressed by vehement disagreement, in particular over the issue of gay priests. A number of African episcopal churches are greatly estranged, especially from the American episcopal church, over this issue.

Outside Anglicanism

If unbelief is a formidable challenge, the Church of England also has Christian rivals: the Catholic church, Methodists and others whose adherents – together with Anglicans – make up the UK's ten per cent of active Christians. Catholic attendance at Sunday mass – mandated more strongly than Anglican attendance at Sunday communion – may even exceed Church of England congregations. Considered from an historical perspective, the recovery in the numbers of Catholic faithful is remarkable. Only a few are from 'old' Catholic families, especially in Lancashire, Sussex and the Scottish Highlands that defied the Reformation: it was 18th and 19th century mass immigration from Ireland that revived British Catholicism. The emigrating poor of 19th century Ireland, coming from lands where Protestantism never took root, brought their faith with them as they huddled in western British cities, above all in Liverpool (see chapter 4). A century on, English and Scottish Catholicism has again been boosted by immigration, this time from Poland.

The 1850 restoration of the English Catholic hierarchy provoked riots and hostile legislation, but within 50 years the sense of affront to national identity had faded. Today's hierarchy rules dioceses from towns and cities without a Church of England bishop (Liverpool being the single exception). The Catholic church's 22 bishops do not sit by right in the House of Lords though, like other religious leaders, they may be appointed in their personal capacity. Catholics in Scotland have always had an entirely separate church. With a hierarchy of six bishops and two archbishops (restored in 1878) it claims the adherence of some 670,000 out of five million Scots. Its implacable opposition to gay clergy was undermined in 2013 by the resignation of Keith O'Brien, only its third cardinal since 1560, following allegations of assault by four former priests.

Of the other longstanding Christian denominations, Presbyterians, above all those in the 400,000-strong Church of Scotland (or Kirk), but also in England and Wales, are the most numerous and have a complicated structural history. Methodists have 200,000 worshippers weekly. Scotland's Episcopal church belongs to the Anglican communion but has fewer adherents than the Kirk. Other churches – Congregationalist, United Reform and others – can, like the Quakers, trace themselves back to the religious turmoil of the 17th century.

The distinctive neo-Byzantine façade of Westminster cathedral (not to be confused with the Anglican Westminster abbey), mother church of English Catholicism

In areas of some British cities there is a visible proliferation of far more recently created Pentecostal churches, often in makeshift buildings such as community halls, abandoned warehouses or bingo halls, but with buoyant congregations, with roots mainly in the black community. Their uninhibited experiential style is very different from the consciously measured and archaic formality prevalent in Church of England rituals. According to the London church census, while 300 churches closed in London in the period 2005-2012, 1,000 were opened: two-thirds of those that opened were Pentecostal black majority churches and a third catered for a particular language or ethnic group (such as Polish Lutheran or Ghanaian Seventh-Day Adventists). According to this report, in 2012 one quarter of all English churchgoers were in London; nearly one in five black Londoners went to church each week, two-thirds of them to Pentecostal churches.

The prevalent indifference to religion among the native-born white British population contrasts with Northern Ireland where the historic Catholic/Protestant divide is embedded in national identity. The percentage of the population reporting as Protestant or Catholic is much higher than in Britain. The Free Presbyterian Church of Ulster is perhaps the closest in belief and practice to the more enthusiastic evangelical churches of the USA. It originated in 1951 to resist what it perceived as growing liberalism, focusing instead on preaching and the exposition of sacred texts; its charismatic founder, the Revd Ian Paisley, entered politics and rose to be first minister (see chapter 5).

The Church of Ireland, a member of the Anglican communion, embraces both Northern Ireland and the Republic, though its 250,000 Northern Ireland members outnumber those in the Republic by two to one. Irish Catholics North and South also belong to one church although in their case the majority are in the Republic. Both communions have archbishoprics in Armagh (in the North) and Dublin. Each archbishop of Armagh has the primacy, being designated 'primate of all Ireland' whereas the archbishops of Dublin are primates of Ireland alone.

Beyond Christianity

As a result of post-war immigration, Christianity has non-Christian rivals for the first time in one and a half millennia. While nearly half of the foreign-born population in England and Wales identified in the 2011 census as Christian (48 per cent), a fifth identified as Muslim (19 per cent), and around 14 per cent had no religion. It is noticeable that foreign-born Muslims and Hindus (but not Sikhs) outnumber the UK-born adherents of those faiths. The Muslim share of the whole UK population is close to 5 per cent, the Hindu 1.5 per cent. Counting the number of places of worship is one way of assessing the strength of religions, and there are almost 1,700 mosques and 150 temples. But other faiths may not share Christianity's sense of sacred space. The number of synagogues is not an accurate guide to the number of British Jews, many of whom do not attend or even regard themselves as of the Jewish faith.

Schools may be a better reflection of relative strengths than places of worship. What are now termed 'faith schools' include a very large number of non-Christian establishments. Faith schools may vary in structure ('voluntary aided', 'free', academies) but all are associated with a particular religion. They are mostly run like other state schools and have to follow the national curriculum except for religious studies, where they are free to teach only their own religion. Membership of the relevant faith is a legitimate admission criterion and staffing policies may also differ.

In all, 34 per cent of state schools in England and 14 per cent in Wales have a religious character. This peculiar British compromise potentially will have a great impact on the future of belief. In 2014 Department for Educa-

Christianity has non-Christian rivals for the first time in one and a half millennia

tion guidance promoted 'fundamental British values', calling on faith schools to 'encourage respect for democracy' while nurturing students' spiritual, moral, social and cultural development. They must learn 'the difference between the law of the land and religious law', upholding the former. Schools were urged to promote 'individual liberty, mutual respect and tolerance of those with different faiths and beliefs', enabling students to 'acquire a broad general knowledge of and respect for public institutions and services in England.' They should 'further tolerance and harmony between different cultural traditions by enabling students to acquire appreciation of and respect for their own and other cultures.' Pupils must understand that 'the freedom to choose and hold other faiths and beliefs is protected in law' and that other people 'having different faiths or beliefs to oneself (or having none) should be accepted and tolerated, and should not be the cause of prejudicial or discriminatory behaviour.' Yet a bedrock of faith schools is an act of 'collective worship', explicitly acknowledged by government as a way of ensuring pupils' spiritual, moral, social and cultural development. The advice concludes uneasily that schools or individuals need not 'promote teachings, be-

The London Central Mosque, Regent's Park; London is said to have more mosques than any city outside the Islamic world

liefs or opinions' they do not hold but may not promote discrimination on the basis of belief, opinion or background.

The transition from 'voluntary aided' to 'faith' schools spans the shift to a multicultural UK. Yet in this sector the Church of England still dominates, educating about one million children in its 4,600 schools: one-quarter of all primary schools and one in 16 secondaries. With Catholic schools numbering 2,000, the two big churches predominate. The 2011 census identified around 15 million people who had been to a Church of England school, a figure likely to reflect English society before it felt the impact of mass immigration. Until 1997 all voluntary aided schools were Christian or Jewish: the first state-aided Muslim school opened that year, but only a few have opened since. There are also many confessional private schools which to stay open must pass an Ofsted inspection (see next chapter). Jewish schools have existed since Jews were allowed back into England (1655); independent Muslim schools have been opening since 1979 but reliable figures for their reach are elusive. Ofsted has intervened in Muslim schools, both state and private, and also in private Christian schools. In 2014 creationism taught as science was banned from academies and free schools.

The number of foreign-born Muslims almost doubled between 2001 and 2011

It can be hard to separate religious from national identity or even from colour. Religious identity increases in complexity the further we enquire. The census report states that over nine in ten Christians in England and Wales were white and the same proportion were born in the UK. Moreover the majority of people with no religion were white (93 per cent) and born in the UK (93%) and these numbers have increased since 2001. Muslims, the next most numerous, were more ethnically diverse. Two-thirds were from an Asian background and just over half were born outside the UK. The number of foreign-born Muslims almost doubled between 2001 and 2011. There is every reason to expect further rapid growth of the Muslim faith since so many of its adherents are young. While there are no official figures for conversions, one academic estimate puts those joining Islam at 100,000.

Apart from faith

The UK is home to some famously assertive atheists such as Richard Dawkins and A.C. Grayling, but they are not alone. In 2011 one-quarter of the England and Wales population professed no religion at all, a sharp increase of ten percentage points from ten years earlier. The proportion shunning Christian ceremony is greater still. Even some less sure of their total unbelief hold there should be a total separation of church and state. This 'disestablishmentarianism' can be found even among members of the Church of England. Figures in public life are under little, if any pressure to make a show of Christian faith, though some – such as former prime minister David Cameron – occasionally choose to do so.

Militant atheism – as opposed to agnosticism or simple indifference – is not common in Britain but it has its exponents, not least Richard Dawkins

However, while the number of formal adherents of religion has declined, thanks to the decay of faith in the majority population, the cultural and political significance of religion in a multicultural Britain has arguably increased. It is no accident that, as a recent analysis has shown, the queen's annual Christmas message to the nation has shown an increase in references to faith and religion since the millennium, after years of decline in the twentieth century.

Marriage has been waning since 1972. Increasing numbers of people delay it; couples choose to cohabit rather than marry, sometimes as precursor to marriage but sometimes as an alternative. Civil marriage ceremonies in 2013 accounted for 72 per cent of the whole, their share increasing steadily since they first exceeded religious ceremonies in 1976. More than eight in ten civil marriages took place in premises licensed for the purpose (hotels, historic buildings and stately homes), 14 per cent in register offices. When marriages do occur, 42 per cent of them end in divorce. Same-sex unions have further altered the landscape to the detriment of the churches. With marriage barred to them for years, many same-sex couples opted for the only solemnisation available – the civil partnership. But with the introduction of same-sex marriage in 2014, civil partmerships went into steep decline. Neither Anglican nor Catholic churches will marry same-sex couples. Christian marriages and funerals have declined even further than church attendance. Almost half of births occur outside marriage or civil partnership. Many babies have cohabiting parents – over the last decade over 60 per cent of all births registered outside marriage or civil partnership each year have been to a cohabiting couple. Fewer than one in eight births in 2014 was marked by a Church of England baptism or thanksgiving service. And Church of England funerals fell by 29 per cent over the same period to just under one-third.

14.   Not just Eton and Oxford

For centuries the provision of education was undertaken under the auspices of the church, wealthy benefactors and charities, as well as a plethora of profit-seeking providers of varying repute. Indeed the literacy and numeracy of a significant proportion of the population is one of the factors that enabled Britain to lead the way in the industrial and scientific revolutions from the middle 18th century.

From the 19th century governments intervened in education, prescribing standards as awareness of the country's faltering competitiveness set in. For much of the 20th century the cumulative, if slow, effect was to promote universalism. This increased the cost to the state and so education

The schoolroom in Stratford-upon-Avon where William Shakespeare is said to have studied

policy has always been politically contested. Political disputes are often resolved by compromise and so UK education policy is full of exceptions. Not the least of these is that the systems in the different countries of the UK vary considerably, for reasons of history and current devolved policy: much of what follows in this chapter is focused on the situation in England, where the great majority of the population live.

In the 21st century, the state is more present than ever but it now promotes diversity of provision. What has not changed is the extent to which educational performance is read as an index of national

Though the state now   achievement. Though the state now
wants to let go it also   wants to let go it also wants results, and
wants results   this has led over time to prescribing
                                  what is taught in schools. Today's pro-
gramme of study for schools includes a national curriculum, religious and sex education. Schools must teach religious education
though parents may still withdraw their children and pupils may
withdraw themselves at 18. Local councils determine the religious
education syllabus, but faith schools (see previous chapter) and
academies (below) can set their own. Sex and relationship education is compulsory from 11 and involves teaching reproduction,
sexuality and sexual health. It does not promote any particular sexual orientation.

Raising standards

The English national curriculum, introduced in 1988, sets out
programmes of study and attainment targets. It is a set of subjects
and standards used by primary and secondary schools so children
learn the same things. It covers what subjects are taught and the
standards children should reach in each subject. It must be taught
by all local authority maintained schools (i.e. state schools) in England: the minority nations set their own curricula. Although the majority of secondary schools in England now operate as academies
(see below) and are therefore free to set their own curriculum, in
most cases they do in practice model their teaching closely on the
national curriculum.

Key stage 1 is for ages five to seven (years 1-2); key stage 2 is for
ages seven to 11 (years 3-6); key stage 3 is for ages 11-14 (years 7-9);
and key stage 4 is for ages 14-16 (years 10-11). Key stage 5 for ages
16-19 (years 12-13) does not have prescribed study. The core curriculum consists of English, mathematics, science and physical education.
Other subjects figure on the curriculum, but their degree of prominence varies across the school career. These include art and design,
citizenship, design and technology, geography, history, information
and communication technology, modern foreign languages and
music. Periodically, subject controversies arise. Thus the teaching of

history attracted the attention of those wishing to stress chronology and an Anglo-centric approach; low take-up of modern foreign languages is always (impotently) lamented; inadequate skills in digital technology are deplored. It is not surprising then that the national curriculum is periodically overhauled, most recently in 2014.

State interventions first began in pursuit of common minimum standards. The instrument for improvement is the school inspection. These began in Victorian times, broadened in scope as anxiety grew about the country's comparative technical performance, and today cover all schools. In the maintained (i.e. state) sector they are the responsibility of the Office for Standards in Education, Children's Services and Skills (Ofsted) which 'regulates and inspects to achieve excellence in the care of children and young people, and in education and skills for learners of all ages'.

For the maintained sector Ofsted has four broad categories of schools. Those found 'outstanding' at their most recent inspection are normally exempt from future routine inspection. A school recently judged 'good' will receive a short (one-day) inspection every 3 years. A school judged to require 'improvement' will normally be re-inspected after 2 years. A school judged 'inadequate' has serious weaknesses and will be re-inspected within 24 months. In the worst cases 'special measures' are imposed. Schools are informed of an inspection – which generally will last for two whole days – only at lunchtime on the previous teaching day. For the fee-paying sector, the Independent Schools Inspectorate (ISI) performs a similar role to Ofsted, inspecting more than 1,200 schools affiliated to the Independent Schools Council (ISC), private further education colleges and English as a foreign language schools in England and Wales. ISI's inspectorial status is validated by the Department for Education (DfE), the sponsoring government department. Ofsted also inspects private schools falling outside the ISI remit. Its reports are the definitive verdict on teaching quality in schools.

Primary education takes children to the age of 11 at which point children move on to secondary education, which is on a different site and usually in a much bigger school. In recent figures Ofsted considered 77 per cent of primary schools either 'good' or 'outstanding', leaving 23 per cent 'requiring improvement' or 'inadequate'. Ofsted found only 57 per cent of secondary schools 'good' or 'outstanding' while 43 per cent were 'inadequate' or 'require improvement'. 24 local authority areas had less than 60 per cent of their secondary schools judged to be 'good' or 'outstanding' and of these 17 were in the North and Midlands.

Outside the formal inspection system, Ofsted has also expressed concern to government about the quality of unregistered schools. While home schooling is legal in the UK, it believes that establishments outside the inspection system are proliferating and many fall short of safety, qualifications and curriculum standards. Paradoxically, while parents may be fined for taking their children out of maintained schools during term-time even for short breaks, they may freely withdraw their children altogether from any type of formal education, under the guise of home schooling, without any form of inspection or regulation whatsoever. Dark corners exist into which even the state does not look.

The span of state education

The state is involved in the education of some children from the age of two. Extensive and growing (but expensive) pre-school provision has been boosted by successive governments wishing to facilitate the entry of young mothers into the labour market. Local authorities must provide 570 hours of early education places lasting 38 weeks of the year for children from certain disadvantaged homes. At three all children receive the same until after their fifth birthday, when compulsory schooling begins. Thereafter children must attend school until the end of the school year in which they become 16. Many continue their studies and a large number head for higher education. What follows refers to three stages of education: primary (to age 11), secondary (to 16) and tertiary (16 or 18 onwards). State provision dominates schooling, though there are variations between the nations: 93 per cent attend state schools in England, 96 per cent in Scotland.

For many years, pupil progress through the curriculum was measured at the various 'key stages' in Standard Assessment Tests (SATs). These were first introduced in the 1980s and have largely evolved, especially for younger pupils, into teacher assessments. In England, pupils face SATs in Year 2 (at 7) and Year 6 (at 11). In the public mind there is a strong association of tests at 11 with selection and allocation of pupils either to an academic or a non-academic stream. This reflects the once universal, but now largely defunct, '11+' exam: those who passed it entered one of the country's universally available grammar schools. Across most of England only mixed ability and unselective secondary schools now exist, but some of the home counties around London have retained the 11+ and grammar schools. Altogether about five per cent of state-funded secondary schools still select.

At 16, all pupils sit the subject-based GCSE exam. Performance varies sharply by gender and race as the figures for achieving five GCSEs (including English and mathematics) at A*- C grades illustrate. Almost 62 per cent of girls reach this level, a gap of at least ten percentage points over boys. Nearly 75 per cent of Chinese pupils achieve it, almost 18 percentage points above the national average. By contrast, pupils from a black background are 3.4 percentage points below the national average. White British boys from poorer backgrounds are greatly adrift. By 2020 all pupils will sit a new examination – the Ebacc – which sits on top of GCSE performance. The Ebacc is made up of English, mathematics, history or geography, the sciences and a language. In a classic illustration of how the DfE incentivises compliance with the policy of the day, schools that do not offer the Ebacc will not be eligible for consideration as 'outstanding' by Ofsted.

In the English state-funded system the most significant changes of recent years have been to the management and status of the schools themselves. Until recently, the maintained secondary sector consisted almost entirely of comprehensive (i.e. non-selective) schools, with a few grammars surviving, under direct local authority (council) control. In the 2010s, however, government has strongly encouraged the creation or conversion of existing schools into so-called academies: these academies have a high degree of independence, being outside the direct control of local authorities while remaining the ultimate responsibility of the DfE and being funded by central government.

By 2016, more than three in five of England's secondary schools had become academies

The idea of devolving powers to individual schools began under the previous Labour government in an effort to improve the performance of failing schools, especially in inner city areas, and was initially on a limited scale. The impact was widely considered to be positive in raising standards. In May 2010, when the Conservative-led coalition government came into office there were still only 203 academy schools. The spread of the academy system since then has been spectacular, more particularly in the secondary sector where schools are much bigger and budgets and opportunities correspondingly greater than in the primary sector. By 2016, more than three in five of England's 3,381 state-funded secondary schools had become academies, though only one in seven of the 16,766 state-funded primary schools. Academies on the English model do not exist in Scotland, Wales and Northern Ireland (though, rather confusingly, some Scottish schools are and always have been called academies).

Elected councils were once the strategic bodies ruling much of education, but successive structural shifts have drained their power: to the central state itself and to individual schools. Numbers of academies are now being run as chains, effectively private businesses dependent on the public purse. Some academies are sponsored by business interests, faith groups or even other schools, bringing a wide variety of influences to bear: particularly significant, and at times controversial, is the involvement of faith organisations in setting the curriculum and ethos of schools where they are involved.

This has been a remarkable change in a very short space

An academy school: Heartlands High in north London; 45 per cent of pupils do not have English as their first language but the school has above the national average for 5 A*-C grades at GCSE

of time, variously interpreted as freeing up schools to innovate and compete with each other; as over-commercialising education and leading to a salary bonanza for some involved in running these new enterprises; and as allowing the intrusion into mainstream education of religious sects. Whatever the merits of academies, it is clear that secondary education, in particular, is once again becoming increasingly diverse as the trend to a uniform system in the decades after 1945 is reversed. However, while the management of state schools is becoming more independent and devolved, the funding of pupils remains the responsibility of the state: as yet, academies cannot further sharpen competition by charging for their services, though they do compete for the most promising pupils, in some cases recruiting over increasingly wide territories.

Independent schools

What is an independent school? According to the UK government website 'academies are publicly funded independent schools', so on that basis the majority of pupils in English secondary schools are now attending independent schools. However, in common parlance and thinking, genuinely independent schools are outside both local and central government control and above all funding. They are self-reliant, determine their own priorities and control their own admissions, curriculum and discipline. They are largely financed by the fees that parents pay and also in some cases by endowments.

But, to confuse easy definitions further, genuinely independent schools are also often referred to indiscriminately either as 'private' or 'public' schools, despite the meanings of the two words being polar opposites. The concept of the public school, which distinguished them from private schools (sometimes of highly dubious quality) run by their owners for profit, was encapsulated in the Public Schools Act of 1868 which gave seven schools independence from the regulation of the state or the established church. These were Charterhouse, Eton College, Harrow School, Rugby School, Shrewsbury School, Westminster School, and Winchester College. To this day it is such boarding schools, recruiting students from all parts of the world and not just restricted geographical localities, that are popularly thought of as public schools.

The effort to create a universal system of education after 1945 faced the difficulty that a system was not being created out of nothing. Many English secondary schools were of old foundation, with some grammar schools dating from the Middle Ages, and they operated under a great diversity of provisions for funding and governance. From 1945 until the 1970s a large bloc of around 200 schools, mainly long-established, large and locally prestigious day grammar schools or else Catholic schools, operated on a semi-autonomous 'mixed economy' basis with their costs paid for by a combination of public funding and a proportion of fee-paying pupils; however, this 'direct grant' tier was abolished by the Labour government in 1975 as part of the drive to create a fully comprehensive system, sharpening the distinction between the state and independent sectors. These schools were then either fully absorbed into the independent sector or (especially in the case of the weaker Catholic schools) merged into the comprehensive system or closed. The former group includes many prestigious schools, most famously Manchester Grammar School.

In the independent sector as a whole average fees are £4,200 per term (boarders £9,500), but there is great variation and many schools also offer scholarships and bursaries. The 580,000 pupils who attend are mostly in secondary education.   The ISC believes one in eight adult Britons spent some time at an independent school. One-fifth are single-sex institutions, unusual in the state sector, and nearly half make some provision for boarders. The very favourable pupil/teaching staff ratio is below11:1.

Many independent schools have charitable status which confers important tax reliefs. In return the law requires them to demonstrate 'public benefit'. Some private establishments do this automatically, inspired by faith to work with local people, but government pressure has spread the habit. Over 93 per cent of ISC schools claim to participate in 'meaningful and worthwhile partnerships', either with state schools or the wider community; but of course they exist primarily to serve their own pupils. In 2011-2012, nearly two-thirds entered higher education compared to a little over half of those from state-funded schools and colleges. Five per cent attended Oxford or Cambridge and

Eton College: most renowned of all schools, with a galaxy of famous former pupils. Among writers alone its alumni include Percy Bysshe Shelley, Henry Fielding, Aldous Huxley, Anthony Powell, George Orwell and Ian Fleming

38 per cent other Russell Group universities (see below); state-educated alumni managed 1 per cent and 11 per cent respectively. This degree of access to prestigious British universities also makes fee-paying schools globally popular. Little wonder they are heavily internationalised with more than five per cent of pupils non-British.

Independent schools vary greatly in prestige, size and resources. One group stands out: the 277 members of the Headmasters' and Headmistresses' Conference (HMC) that take well over 200,000 pupils and include both the traditional boarding public schools and major day grammar schools operating outside the state system. One in five students attending the UK's top ten universities comes from these schools; more than nine in ten pupils reach higher education, a track record unmatched either by state schools or other independents. HMC holds that its member schools are distinguished by a commitment to the benefits of a holistic educational experience: academic excellence coupled with a strong emphasis on pastoral care and exceptional co-curricular opportunities. The widespread availability of boarding supports these aims.

At the pinnacle of the independent sector, Eton College (single sex alma mater of 19 prime ministers including four since World War II – and butt of anti-toff badinage) has £345 million of assets and a £297 million endowment fund. Its annual fees are £36,000. It too feels the need to demonstrate public benefit, educating 70 of its 1300 pupils for free and granting bursaries to over 20 per cent of them. Boys at Eton (and its almost equally famous, though traditionally far less academic brother Harrow, alma mater of Winston Churchill) may be identified by their distinctive uniforms as well as their career prospects. Other notable HMC members are Winchester College, Charterhouse, Rugby, Westminster, Marlborough College, Dulwich

College, St Paul's Boys' and Wellington College. British public life is studded with alumni and alumnae of these schools. Not only the quality of the education on offer, but top university access and assimilation into networks predetermine their life-chances.

Public school boys are famously self-confident: Harold Macmillan (prime minister, 1957-1963) with nine Old Etonians in his cabinet, boasted it was three times better than that of Clement Attlee (1945-1951) with only three. Yet they also face opposition, as when a Conservative backbencher denounced the two most powerful politicians in the land, David Cameron (prime minister, Eton) and George Osborne (Chancellor of the Exchequer, St Paul's) as 'two posh boys who don't know the price of milk'. Perhaps in response, new (and mainly state-educated) prime minister Theresa May appointed a cabinet that was 70 per cent state educated, the lowest proportion of privately educated ministers since Attlee. Among them was the first ever comprehensive school educated secretary of state for education.

At the opposite end of the spectrum from Eton in the independent sector is a long tail of minor institutions, some of them small boarding schools with limited academic pretensions, others religious schools operating at the margins of the educational system. Such schools are easily eclipsed in terms of university entry and exam results by many state schools. Where parents enrol their children in such schools it can be for reasons other than expectation of a better formal academic education than in the state sector: the belief they will have better pastoral care; make better social contacts; be subject to more (or less) rigorous discipline; be more firmly schooled in ethical and religious principles; or have better opportunities in fields such as sport or music. The diversification of provision by academies in the state-financed system may in time come to offer a challenge to such schools.

16-18 year olds

The UK's 382 further education (FE) colleges take about 60 per cent of 16-18 year olds, of whom about one-third of a million are pursuing apprenticeships. However, it is precisely the quality and

the quality and relevance of apprenticeships ... causes British employers greatest concern

relevance of apprenticeships which causes British employers greatest concern. In her *Review of vocational education: the Wolf report* (2011) Professor Alison Wolf argued that school league tables (which rank schools by GCSE performance) operated as 'perverse incentives' whereby students were steered to qualifications unhelpful to their work or higher education prospects. Recommending a clear distinction between the academic and vocational paths in schools, she commented that:

> 'In England … "staying on" at school is now so normal that it hardly counts as a decision. Well over 90% of 16-year-olds continue education or formal training after their GCSEs, well in advance of it being made compulsory a few years from now.'

The Ebacc was one government response to her findings.

What happens to those not on the degree path? The Wolf report severely criticised the efficacy of arrangements for school-leavers not staying on. Government has clarified the usefulness of certain GCSE subjects to a technical career and renewed the content of apprenticeships. Only a shrinking minority now leave school at 16. Nevertheless, demand for apprenticeships outstrips supply by a factor of ten and great concern about their quality persists.

Only a shrinking minority now leave school at 16

Most of those staying on to study (either at school in 'sixth forms' or FE colleges) will at 18 sit another nationwide subject-based exam, the A-level. This either enhances employment prospects or confers entry into higher education. It is much more specialised than GCSE: typically, students only take either three or four subjects. The overall pass rate is above 98 per cent. Girls continue to get the best results, with four in five obtaining grades A* to C, compared with three in four for boys, though the gap between top-performing girls and boys has narrowed. 2016 saw a further decline in entries to modern languages, with the numbers taking French falling below 10,000 for the first time.

Higher education

UK universities have great global prestige. They include 20 of the 40 most internationalised institutions (on several measures) in the world. Three are in the top ten of the THES World University rankings, 34 feature in the top 200, 74 in the top 800; only US universities are more globally attractive and their lead over the UK is declining. In 2015 the Higher Education Policy Institute identified 55 current world leaders (presidents, prime ministers, monarchs) from 51 countries who had experienced UK higher education. It has powerful brands such as 'Oxbridge'. Ministers boast that in higher education, the UK is a superpower.

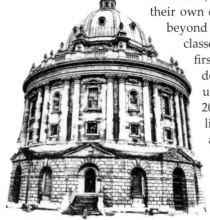

Of course, UK universities primarily serve their own country. Access extended much beyond the professional and business classes only in the 1960s when for the first time the total number of students passed 50,000. Thereafter universities grew rapidly: by 2014-2015, there were almost 2.25 million students (including over half a million postgraduates). From 2016 school-leavers began applying for the first time to an uncapped UK university sector and the numbers gaining university places rose to the highest ever, powered by a widening gap between females and males and confirming a shift towards traditional subjects like Maths and English.

The Radcliffe Camera, at the heart of Oxford University's colleges

Higher education is largely publicly funded. According to Universities UK there are 159 higher education providers in receipt of public funds (14 in Scotland, nine in Wales and two in Northern Ireland). This however counts the University of London as one despite its 13 constituent colleges, which include Imperial College, King's College, University College London and the London School of Economics (LSE) – prestigious bodies virtually operating as universities in their own right. By the same reckoning, the country has but one private institution, the University of Buckingham.

Despite public funding and the frequent interventions of politicians in issues such as access for under-represented groups, some universities, Oxbridge above all, zealously resist state interference and have large private foundations which make it easier for them. Oxford regards its 36 colleges as 'independent, self-governing and financially autonomous'. With them it has combined endowment assets approaching £4.9 billion. Cambridge (31 colleges) has combined funds of £3.7 billion. These are, however, the only two British universities with endowments above £1 billion; in the USA there are 60. The federal character of the USA with its 50 state university systems also offers opportunity for locally-inspired private funding, sometimes inspired by religious motives. The history of UK universities suggests that once they ceased to be clerical institutions they struggled to escape state influence.

Until the 19th century there were just two universities in England, Oxford and Cambridge, whereas there were four in Scotland with its far smaller population. Things only changed with the establishment of the University of London (1836) which at first mimicked Oxbridge in being entirely a male institution, only admitting women from 1878. Oxbridge itself remained under an often suffocating clerical domination which continued, in only slowly weakening form, into the 20th

Until the 19th century there were just two universities in England

century. The burgeoning industrial cities of Victorian England, however, all soon housed colleges and these in time achieved university status too: Birmingham (1900), Liverpool and Manchester (1903), Leeds (1904), Sheffield (1905), Bristol (1909).

These 'redbrick' universities are the UK's most prestigious after Oxbridge: they combine with it to exert influence as the 'Russell Group'. Over time, British governments became more determined to encourage diversity. In 2015 barely 10 per cent of white British boys from the most disadvantaged backgrounds went to university. They were five times less likely to get there than the most advantaged white boys. The far higher participation rates for other boys were: boys of black Caribbean heritage (20%), boys of Indian heritage (50%), and boys of Chinese heritage (60%). The government-backed Social Mobility Commission found in 2016 that 'the university population does not reflect wider society', though it acknowledged that young people from 'low participation areas' were 60% more likely to attend in 2014 than in 2006.

At mid-20th century the UK's universities were small and few in number. Britons with degrees were exceptional. How, then, were numbers driven up? First by opening new universities to accommodate baby boomers coming of age in the 1960s; then in the 1980s by liberalising access to university charter status, an opportunity swiftly seized by colleges of advanced technology and polytechnics. In the early 21st century it was overt government policy to drive up student numbers towards 50 per cent of the age cohort (a target now abandoned) and the cap controlling expansion at existing universities was removed.

The number of universities is also set to grow further. Five private companies (one a for-profit organisation) now give degrees and government is considering liberalising the process whereby new providers secure their own degree-awarding powers and university title. The extent of further expansion depends on student demand: in 2015 a government minister reported that 'almost 60% of graduates are in non-graduate jobs' (though they were generally thought more employable than non-graduates). The OECD has monitored the astonishing impact of university expansion on society. In 2000, 29% of 25-34 year olds had degrees; by 2014 it was 49% (the US moved from 38% to 42% over the same period). Above all this reflects great success in attracting women, who in 2013 made up 56% of graduates.

Anglia Ruskin University: it grew out of the modestly sized Cambridge College of Arts and Technology to a huge institution with 40,000 students

This vast expansion forced a re-evaluation of student finance. In the 1960s students entered university fee-free and with a means-tested maintenance grant: they graduated free of debt. The grant alone survives, and then only for students from families with low household income. In 2001 tuition fees were introduced up to a maximum (in practice a fixed charge) of £3,000. This was raised to £9,000 in 2009. From 2017-2018 universities assessed as having 'high teaching standards' will be allowed to increase fees in line with inflation.

Tuition fees remain politically controversial. In a purely competitive system, many UK universities would command a much higher fee than an inflation-adjusted £9,000; there is little doubt that tuition costs greatly exceed it, especially at Oxbridge where the staff/student ratio is generous. Naturally there are powerful market and financial pressures on the government to raise, or even abolish the ceiling. Other powerful forces, as well as students, resist any further increase on hardship grounds. There is no clear evidence that higher fees deter enrolment: undergraduate numbers faltered with the £9,000 cap but growth soon resumed. OECD figures show that UK students funded 19 per cent of higher education costs, well above the EU average (14 per cent) but dwarfed by the USA (46 per cent).

Students generally pay their fees via a state-backed loan at low interest rates. It is repaid after graduation but only after earnings pass a threshold. One factor in the failure thus far of student fees to deter university applicants is the fact that this is loan money, rather than money coming out of the student's or parents' pocket, and for many students the time when they will have to repay it seems far away. Critics of the system have suggested that much of this debt may never be repaid and will have to be written off.

A particularly happy initiative by the state was the creation of the Open University by the Labour government in 1969: the world's first successful distance teaching university, with a mission to be open to people, places, methods and ideas, providing high-quality university education to all. With over 200,000 students it is a world leader in the design, content and delivery of supported open learning. No other British university can match it for diversity of intake,

Logo of the Open University: familiar to many because of the OU's involvement since its creation in quality educational TV programmes

whether measured by class or ethnicity, yet it also scores high for the quality of the university experience. Its own Massive Open Online Courses (MOOC) arm Futurelearn launched its first courses in 2013 with over three million enrolled and 85 university and cultural partners. It is too soon to say whether MOOCs, a relatively recent development, will deliver quality at scale to match the OU achievement.

15.   Culture for all

The arts shape perceptions of the UK. A random list of figures evoking the country's cultural identity might include Hugh Grant, Shakespeare and Milton, Adele, Dr Who, Patrick Stewart, Sherlock Holmes, Judi Dench, the Brontë sisters, Oliver Twist, Damien Hirst, Alice in Wonderland, Byron and Shelley, Coldplay, Chaucer, James Bond, the cast of *Downton Abbey* and the audience and performers at the Last Night of the Proms. Any such list summons up not just our contemporaries but a cavalcade of figures from the past, both real and imagined: contemporary Britain may surprise – even disappoint – the visitor who hopes to find traces of the England of Shakespeare or Dickens at every corner. But that said, there is no doubt that the UK offers a uniquely accessible centuries-old wealth of cultural heritage in an age when English is the lingua franca and global travel and communication has never been easier.

This relatively small country has long had great cultural weight. Until recently this would have been explained mainly by the long-standing strength in depth of British stage acting; the high output of quality fiction; and the worldwide appeal of its popular music. However the last two decades have also seen a revival of film-making; a massive renewal programme at galleries and museums; great strides in architecture and design; the eruption of a home-grown fashion industry, and more besides.

John Maynard Keynes: the founder of Keynesian economics was also a patron of the arts and the first chairman of the Arts Council

Until the mid-20th century support for the arts was essentially a private matter: 'high culture' was largely monopolised by the rich. But the end of

World War II ushered in a government committed to building a 'New Jerusalem' and under the influence of J.M. Keynes in arts policy. In quick succession came the establishment of the Arts Council (1946, heir to a wartime Council for the Encouragement of Music and the Arts, aiming to mobilise Britain's culture for victory), with Keynes as chairman; the return of the national collection of paintings to the National Gallery; the founding of the Institute of Contemporary Arts (ICA, not a museum of modern art but a focus for artists working across a range of forms); and the setting up of the Third Programme (now Radio 3) for the cultural (primarily musical) output of the BBC. Soon a national theatre company was formed at the Old Vic.

the end of World War II ushered in a government committed to building a 'New Jerusalem'

In the following decades, state subsidy steadily built a new mass public for the arts. Significant state support continues but now in the dismal context of squeezed public finances and amid conflict over regional imbalances. This grim and disputatious setting frequently compels the arts to justify themselves in financial terms. Grants and National Lottery money, administered by the Department for Culture, Media and Sport (DCMS) now exceed £680 million per annum. The government's Culture White Paper of March 2016, the first of its kind in more than half a century, based much of its case on the contribution of the arts to UK global standing and the economy rather than on the intrinsic value of public exposure to and participation in the arts – the animating impulse of the 'New Jerusalem' era.

The 'creative economy' accounts for over 8 per cent of the total British economy and is worth £133 billion per annum. During a period (2007-2014) when the economy as a whole was in the doldrums, this sector powered ahead. And the span of activities with quantifiable creativity is large and growing: the computer games industry alone employed 24,000 people in 2014. Of course, such officially-derived statistics take the broadest possible definition of the creative arts: advertising and marketing; architecture; crafts; design (product, graphic and fashion); film, TV, radio, video and photography; IT software and computer services; publishing; museums, galleries and libraries; music, performing and visual arts. What follows in this chapter concentrates on a more traditional understanding of the creative realm: stage, film and TV, literature, art (painting and sculpture), museums and music.

The stage

Stage performance in the British Isles has a long history, stretching back perhaps one thousand years to the village green performances of 'mummers' or travelling players. In medieval England there were passion or 'morality' plays expounding Christian ethics. 16th century London made of the stage a new popular entertainment to replace bear-baiting and other amusements. It evolved, nourished by centuries of playwrights and above all William Shakespeare. Productions of his 38 plays still fill theatres nationwide, endlessly reworked in search of new meaning: a female King Lear, a black Henry V. The school curriculum of all UK countries has always embraced stage plays. Children grow up theatre-aware: an outing to see a performance of that year's 'set' Shakespeare (i.e. prescribed for GCSE or A-level examination) is a feature of the school year. Thus a virtuous circle sustains interest in acting as a professional or amateur activity but also nurtures a wider public interest in the stage, bringing with it a steady financial stream from audiences. Little wonder the UK also has a wide network of performing arts schools.

It is estimated that over 6,600 productions were staged in 2014. UK Theatre believes that more tickets are sold for the theatre than for football's English Premier League, English Football League and Scottish Premiership combined, generating £1 billion of annual box office sales. London may be the centre, but all around the country big and small theatres abound, some subsidised. These are purpose-built auditoria whose foundation dates indicate how theatre is woven into local history. The best known among them include the Birmingham Rep (1913), the Bristol Old Vic (1766, the longest continuously-running theatre in the UK), the Chichester Festival Theatre (1962), the Crucible (Sheffield, 1971), the Theatre Royal

Newcastle (1788), the Nottingham Playhouse (1948), the Theatre Royal Bath (from 1705 on a variety of sites and since 1805 on its present one) and the West Yorkshire Playhouse (1970) in Leeds.

The number of performance spaces in London defies accurate counting. *The London Stage* says that the West End (see below) has 45 theatres (plus another nine nearby projecting 'West End values'). Then there are 70 'off West End' or 'fringe' theatres. To these numbers must be added a variety of more-or-less improbable venues, mostly not purpose-built, where plays may be staged, including the back rooms of pubs, gym halls, libraries and the open air. And, finally, there are the great subsidised spaces of the National Theatre and the Barbican.

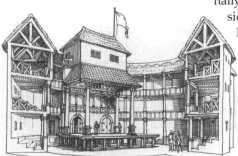

The cult of Shakespeare was the 18th century achievement of David Garrick, first actor-manager in a line of succession running through John Kemble, Edmund Kean, Henry Irving, Donald Wolfit and Laurence Olivier to Kenneth

The reconstructed Globe theatre on London's South Bank, the brainchild of American actor and director Sam Wanamaker

Branagh in our own day. Each toured the kingdom bringing Shakespeare to the masses. Today, England hosts a flourishing Shakespeare industry. Its two most visible statements are the Royal Shakespeare Memorial Theatre at Stratford-upon-Avon, home to the Royal Shakespeare Company (RSC), and Shakespeare's Globe, a scholarly re-creation of a Jacobean theatre at Bankside on the South Bank of the Thames. Stratford-upon-Avon, the Midland town of the Bard of Avon's birth and death, owes its fame to the enterprising Garrick and today's Shakespeare Memorial Trust: the RSC keeps three performing spaces in the town. Many companies across the country expect to perform Shakespeare every so often in the normal course of events. Since there are few sizeable towns without theatres (though many lack residential companies) access to live performed Shakespeare is unproblematic. In the 21st century the willingness of British actors of star TV or film status to return to the stage created a new young audience for those lucky enough to obtain tickets. For the rest live relays to cinemas offered mass access to Benedict Cumberbatch as Hamlet, David Tennant as Richard II, Ian McKellen as Lear, Patrick Stewart as Antony.

The UK also has a (Royal) National Theatre (RNT), inevitably located in London. The company was founded in 1963, but its century-long quest for a home culminated in 1976 in Denys Lasdun's three contrasting auditoria on London's South Bank. Since then it has offered a varied repertoire of unfailing excellence, staging Shakespeare, British playwrights of all periods, international theatre in translation and a steady stream of new work. In 2014-2015 it staged 25 productions: 3,380 performances in the UK and internationally, requiring 628 actors and musicians. A number of RNT productions have been exported, both to the West End and New York's Broadway; some (*The Madness of King George*, *The History Boys*, both by regular RNT playwright Alan Bennett) have become films. The RNT is a pinnacle of subsidised theatre with lavishly-equipped stages, attracting actors of the first rank and unafraid to bring contemporary controversy to the stage.

David Tennant as King Lear: he is known to an even wider audience as the tenth Doctor Who

Though equally unafraid, the National Theatre of Scotland offers a contrasting model: a theatre without walls, building-free but committed to touring every part of the country. A new Glasgow headquarters is projected for the company featuring a large rehearsal space, room for technical and costume production and community drama – but it intends to stay on the move. There is growing concern about regional imbalance given the high concentration of major performing venues in London whose 20 best-funded theatres receive more than £1 million annually from government.

The great public theatres should not obscure Britain's thriving commercial theatre. In London this is known (in reference to the popular name for the entertainment heart of the capital) as the West

Cameron Mackintosh and Andrew Lloyd Webber ... have transformed this tired location into the creative seat for musicals that have toured the globe

End, where a collection of ageing theatres – most of them were built in late Victorian or Edwardian times – remains in business. After a period when these stages saw little experimentation new plays may again be seen there. The West End has also benefited from overspill

productions from the subsidised theatre: *One Man, Two Governors*; *War Horse*; *Matilda*; and *Cats*, a notable popular triumph for the RSC. Two inspired entrepreneurs – Cameron Mackintosh and Andrew Lloyd Webber (also a composer) – have transformed this tired location into the creative seat for musicals that have toured the globe: *Cats*; *Les Misérables*; *Miss Saigon*; *The Phantom of the Opera*, not to mention periodic revivals of *Oliver!* and *Mary Poppins*. These productions play many venues: press reports suggested the most successful ones (*Phantom* and '*Les Mis*') took receipts 'more than twice' those of *Avatar*, the highest-grossing film in Hollywood history.

In the 20th century British-born or raised actors most usually had to be seen as Americans, or at least passably mid-Atlantic, to succeed in Hollywood: Charlie Chaplin (helped by the universality of the silent screen), Bob Hope, Cary Grant, Audrey Hepburn, Anthony Hopkins, Gary Oldman. A feature of the 21st century is the wide renown of many British stage actors gained from screen or TV roles. One explanation is the revival of British film; another is the extraordinary success of the BBC, ITV and Channel 4 television channels (for public service broadcasters, see chapter 17) in period or other drama. This in turn has turbo-charged theatre attendances as new-minted stars return to their first love, the stage. The later careers of Ian McKellen, Patrick Stewart and Judi Dench, and the recent careers of Anna Friel and Benedict Cumberbatch all illustrate this trajectory. While many British TV or stage actors (Hugh Laurie, Damien Lewis) will still impersonate Americans if required, there is now the contrary phenomenon, the US actor who pretends to be English (Johnny Depp, Gwyneth Paltrow, Meryl Streep, Renee Zellweger)!

Film and TV

Oxford Economics found that UK film contributes over £4.6 billion to GDP and supports over 117,000 jobs. This Cinderella of the British arts is starting to flourish, boosted by domestic creativity and tax breaks. It claims to generate ten per cent of tourism tax revenues. The UK has always been a significant market for English language film but Hollywood (for which it is a European gateway) gained a stranglehold at the birth of film and the British have never been able to compete. Home-grown talent (directors Charlie Chaplin and Alfred Hitchcock, actors Cary Grant, Basil Rathbone, Ronald Colman, Rex Harrison and Anthony Hopkins) naturally gravitated to Hollywood. Ineffably British films such as the James Bond or Harry Potter series are, to a considerable extent, US productions.

Hollywood ... gained a stranglehold at the birth of film and the British have never been able to compete

The English language, a huge advantage in most cultural and economic spheres, has been a major drawback in film. However, US film-goers' taste has boosted the screen careers of grizzled British thesps, whose practiced vowels embody a popular idea of villainy: Alan Rickman, Jeremy Irons and Maggie Smith. The UK, more orientated towards markets, less *dirigiste,* has not followed France in insisting on *une exception culturelle* to ensure that the home industry would not be obliterated. (For a period in the 1920s and 1930s, however, cinemas were required to show a quota of British-made films to protect the domestic industry: the result was an output of mainly low-budget dross, so-called 'quota quickies', avoided by the film-going public, who much preferred the American product.)

Even with state protection absent, recent years have brought a considerable revival. Its components are a boom in independent output, assisted by the willingness of major public sector broadcasters to co-fund productions (*Truly, Madly, Deeply*; *Four Weddings and a Funeral*; *The King's Speech*; *Philomena*) and strong technical expertise – the UK is world leader in digital graphics. They have helped London host the third busiest production industry in the world nourished by abundant technical skills, a bottomless reservoir of actors, copious screenwriting talent and countless telegenic locations. There is extensive crossover from TV to film, with major channels all involved in making films they later network, often in collaboration with European public service broadcasters. 'High-end television relief' (a tax break introduced to stop big culturally-British productions moving offshore) has assisted nearly 100 programmes since 2013. In 2001, Ofcom (the communications regulator) reported that there were around 500 UK television production companies, most of them small producers. By 2014, only 230 small producers had at least one programme broadcast by the main public service broadcasters. Major US media groups (NBC Universal and Warner Brothers) had acquired many UK production companies: seven of the ten largest are now owned by giant foreign media corporations. And despite London's inevitable preeminence the strength of independent film-making outside the capital is striking: Liverpool hosts the Film Arts and Creative Centre, the UK's only exhibition and performance space dedicated to film, video and digital art.

Independent production in television has some defence via two main regulations. First, at least 25 per cent of public service broadcasters' non-news programmes must be produced by independent producers. Second, the broadcasters must develop codes of practice setting out the principles that apply when agreeing contract terms with independent producers. Under both these rules, a qualifying independent producer cannot be more than 25 per cent owned by any company which also owns a UK broadcaster. The argument against cultural protectionism is that it fosters complacency and conservatism. Left to survive in the marketplace, UK public service broadcasters have constantly invented reality formats that have been Americanised: *Idol* (*American Idol*), *X-Factor*, *The Apprentice*, *Strictly Come Dancing* (*Dancing with the Stars*), *Big Brother*, *The Great British Bake-off* (*The American Baking Competition*) and *Masterchef*.

House of Cards, while not a reality show, might fall into the same category. Exportable successes that have survived in their own format include *Downton Abbey*, *Peppa Pig*, *Top Gear* and *Who Wants To Be A Millionaire?*

Literature

In some ways the experience of fiction publishing parallels that of film, fighting for space and integrity in a world language it shares with the American behemoth. Most of the famed British fiction publishers (Macmillan, Penguin) have been swallowed by American-dominated conglomerates and are now imprints. However, poetry, always a British publishing strength still thrives: Faber & Faber continues independently with twelve Nobel laureates and six Booker Prize winners on its list. Recent decades have brought many small independent publishing firms to the fore. One of them (Bloomsbury) showed its ability to pick a winner by publishing the many-times rejected J. K. Rowling: the first Harry Potter book was published in 1997 and within a decade, shattering world records for the fastest-selling books in history, the series had sold more than 400 million units. The Independent Publishers' Guild, with a membership of small and medium-sized publishers in all genres, claims its highest-ever membership of 600 while the total number of publishers exceeds 2,200. The London International Book Fair, held each spring, has become a major international show and deal-making centre for the publishing industry, second only to the autumn book fair held in Frankfurt (Germany).

British fiction-writing rests on a tradition of centuries. In the field of children's literature alone, writers such as Lewis Carroll, Beatrix Potter, Enid Blyton and Roald Dahl are known around the world. It does not require a flight to Hollywood (or indeed a screenplay) to suc-

Agatha Christie (1890-1976), the world's best-selling fiction author of the 20th century

ceed, though many books have been successfully translated to the big screen. Of all the world's authors writing since the start of the 20th century, the most successful and by a wide margin, in terms of copies sold, is the English crime fiction writer Agatha Christie – whose characters such as Miss Marple and Hercule Poirot have also featured in innumerable TV and film adaptations.

British publishing is supported by an enduring tradition of reading physical books, sales of which passed £3 billion in 2014, though digital books have since 2010 eclipsed hardbacks as the second most popular format (behind paperbacks). Before Allen Lane created the Penguin imprint in 1935, the paperback format was associated mainly with sensationalist pulp fiction: he transformed its image, winning a vast readership for affordable high-quality fiction and non-fiction alike. An attachment to physical books sharply differentiates the UK and US home fiction markets: the bulk of sales of blockbusters like the individual Harry Potter titles or *Fifty Shades of Grey*, were in that format. The strength of the theatre also means that play scripts are continuously in print. A vast amount of fiction – short stories as well as novels – appears annually. Television, and especially public service broadcasting, has likewise fed a wide non-scholarly market for history, biography, travel and other serious subjects alongside the ghost-written celebrity memoirs which tend to dominate the Christmas bestseller list.

Oxford University Press (OUP) and Cambridge University Press (CUP), capitalising on the branding provided by the university names and enjoyment of the tax advantages conferred by charitable

Oxford University Press ... is the largest university press in the world

status, are major global players in non-fiction publishing. Both are technically departments of their universities. CUP, founded in 1534, is regarded as the oldest still existing publishing house in the world. OUP is the largest university press in the world. It began its international operations when it opened a branch in New York in 1896, and then further branches which traced the reach of of empire: Canada (1904), Australia (1908), India (1912), and Southern Africa (1914). Now it has offices in more than 50 countries and publishes its mainly academic and educational titles in 40 different languages.

Literary prizes illustrate the contradictions of book creating and selling. The Booker Prize undoubtedly brought contemporary British fiction to a wider audience from its inception in 1969. For almost half a century it considered writers from the UK, the Commonwealth, Ireland or Zimbabwe. From 2014, what is now the Man Booker considered any novel originally written in English and published in the UK in the year of the prize, regardless of the nationality of their author. This step assisted the global reach of the prize itself but by opening the competition to American authors, blurred the original focus on home grown fiction. Booker itself saw the move more in terms of celebrating the versatility of English. Other prizes such as the Women's Prize for Fiction (formerly the Orange Prize) for a novel written in English that demonstrates 'excellence, originality and accessibility', the Man Booker International (for an entire oeuvre) and the newer Folio Prize were already global in reach.

Prizes expand the reputation even of an established author. In 2012 Hilary Mantel won both the Man Booker and Costa Book Award for her historical novel, *Bring Up the Bodies*. Such trophies – especially when accompanied by the Oscar-like publicity that attends the Man Booker – tend to turbo-charge sales. The Daily Telegraph newspaper compiled a list of the 25 most lucrative awards, headed by the £85,000 International IMPAC Dublin Literary Award, the largest prize for a single novel published in English, nominated by public libraries and so presumably reflecting popular taste. The Samuel Johnson Prize (soon to be renamed) rewards writing in English by any nationality about current affairs, history, politics, science, sport, travel, biography, autobiography and the arts: winners such as Helen MacDonald soon saw booming international sales. Poets have the T.S. Eliot and Forward Prizes; home-grown short story writers the BBC National Short Story Award. The oldest of all is Edinburgh University's James Tait Black Prize, founded in 1919, for the best biography, work of fiction and drama in English, Scots or Gaelic. An 'Independent Foreign Fiction' prize rewards writer and translator of the best work by a living author translated into English and published in the UK.

While the state interferes little in the creative process, many UK writers have held university academic posts: in fiction, J. R. R. Tolkien, Anita Brookner, Rose Tremain; in poetry W. H. Auden, C.S. Lewis, Andrew Motion. Norfolk's University of East Anglia School of Literature, Drama and Creative Writing was founded by novelists Angus Wilson and Malcolm Bradbury. Its alumni include Tracey Chevalier, Ian McEwan and Kazuo Ishiguro. Copyright, which applies from 70 years after an author's death, also secures certain reproduction rights and in their lifetime authors have library lending rights.

C. S. Lewis, the author of The Chronicles of Narnia and The Screwtape Letters, was with J.R.R. Tolkien (The Hobbit, The Lord of the Rings) a member of an Oxford literary group known as 'The Inklings'

Art

Britain's 21st century in art promises to match an astonishing 20th. British sculpture, through its two foremost exponents Barbara Hepworth and Henry Moore, has a worldwide reputation. But until World War I painting seemed characterised by insularity and unresponsiveness to continental trends which publications like *The Englishness of English Art* sought to explain. Achievement, patronage and market grew rapidly from the 1950s – the era of Francis Bacon and Lucien Freud – helped by the internationalisation of modern art. By the late 20th century, British artists, often graduating outside mainstream schools, figured ever more strongly. Some, such as Damien Hirst and Tracey Emin, were commercially attuned 'Young British Artists' (YBAs). Their entrepreneurial approach chimed with the taste of wealthy patrons (Charles Saatchi, Jay Jopling) who founded their own contemporary galleries. A recent survey numbered 35 such venues, often in non-traditional locations. In 2015 Hirst went one further, opening his own London gallery.

In the Mayfair area of London traditional galleries/auction rooms (Sotheby's, Bonham's, Christie's) continue to thrive. Mayfair is principal home to the London fine art market, which accounts for almost 20 per cent of world sales and is the third largest market after China

the London fine art market is the third largest market after China and the USA

and the USA. Open to the less affluent are London's renowned public art museums, all recently expanded in scale. Some of these giant institutions benefited when artists strongly featured in their permanent collection were reappraised. Such has been the happy trajectory of the reputations of J.M.W. Turner and Samuel Palmer (held in depth by Tate Britain). The Tate has established spaces in St Ives (Cornwall) – an area with strong painting and sculptural associations – and Liverpool. But the gallery most in synch with the growth of interest in modern and contemporary art is the vast Tate Modern, opened in 2000 in a converted power station to become the most visited modern art gallery in the world. Vexing questions such as 'what is art?' have been swept away by a flood of apparently untroubled visitors. In 2016, a striking 200ft-high extension opened: in its cavernous interior, over half the solo displays were by women artists.

Major galleries like the two London Tates and the National Gallery now skilfully market 'blockbuster' exhibitions (for which they charge entrance fees at international rates) but their permanent collections are open to the public without an entrance fee. The National Gallery, which pioneered free entry to galleries in the 19th century, remains the country's premier art museum, a repository of international art. The adjacent National Portrait Gallery provides a visual tour of British history and culture through its leading figures. Scotland also has both a National Gallery and a National Portrait Gallery but they are comparatively modest in scale.

England's traditional regional galleries often showcase regional art: the Walker (Liverpool); the Whitworth (Manchester); the Birm-

The neo-Classical façade of the Walker Art Gallery in Liverpool, advertised as 'the national gallery of the North'

ingham Museum and Art Gallery. Provincial galleries of modern art such as Nottingham Contemporary, the Turner Contemporary (Margate), the Arnolfini (Bristol) or the Edinburgh Gallery of Modern Art have an international scope. Beyond doubt the national scheme has stimulated cultural visits and the visiting public has become more diverse. Yet all major art institutions have needed to embrace commercialism, hosting cafes and shops that sell replicas of their exhibits and branded goods. While no reliable estimate has been made of the contribution from these ancillary activities it certainly offsets declining support from the Exchequer.

While an undoubted socio-cultural success the national scheme does not address the disparity of financial clout between the UK's major art museums and their lavishly-endowed equivalents in the United States. To mitigate the impact of this unequal contest, the Acceptance in Lieu (AIL) scheme enables taxpayers to transfer important works of art and other heritage objects into public ownership to defray inheritance tax, or one of its earlier forms. The taxpayer is given the full open market value of the item, which is then allocated to a public museum, archive or library. In 2014-2015, 29 cases – including a wide range of works of art worth almost £40 million – were accepted for the nation in lieu. Exceptionally the UK government also intervenes to prevent paintings of significance from leaving the country, usually by giving public money to support a special appeals fund. Certain cultural objects above 50 years old may be barred from export because they have more than financial value. Such 'national treasures' are retained at home if closely connected with UK history and national life or of outstanding aesthetic importance, or with outstanding significance for the study of some particular branch of art, learning or history. Twelve cases were deferred from export under these 'Waverley criteria' in 2014-2015, in the hope that they would be sold to a UK owner.

Museums

An unkind observation was once made that the UK's preoccupation with its past indicated it needed a curator rather than a prime minister. The very large number of museums – ranging from great national collections to small local and often highly specialised collections run by charities, special interest groups or enthusiasts – almost seems to validate the observation. The national museum accreditation scheme, run by Arts Council England and partner bodies in Wales, Scotland and Northern Ireland, has more than 1,700 museums participating. Annual visits to the member museums of the scheme are now close to 40 million, having risen 158 per cent since the scheme was established in 1988.

Like the national art galleries, the national museums are publicly-funded and provide free access to their permanent collections. The British Museum enjoys the greatest global reputation, assisted by the longevity and breadth of its collection and the enterprise of successive directors, notably the recently-departed Neil McGre-

The reading room of the British Museum: among its many famous regular users was Karl Marx

gor. Like the Louvre in Paris, the Smithsonian in Washington and the Pergamon in Berlin, the British Museum was conceivable only in an imperial country or one with a reach far beyond its own borders. The collection began with 71,000 objects collected by the physician, naturalist and collector Sir Hans Sloane (1660–1753). Founded on Sloane's death it was the first national public museum

the British Museum was conceivable only in an imperial country

in the world, immediately granting free admission to all 'studious and curious persons'. Its permanent collection of over 8 million objects draws on every continent to illustrate and document the story of human culture from its beginnings to the present: it regards itself as a repository for the cultures of the world which happens to be located in London. Such are its grounds for declining to restore to Athens the 'Elgin Marbles', part of the Parthenon frieze. Among its other possessions are the 2nd century

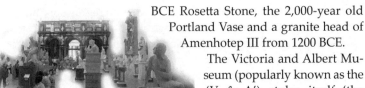

BCE Rosetta Stone, the 2,000-year old Portland Vase and a granite head of Amenhotep III from 1200 BCE.

The Victoria and Albert Museum (popularly known as the 'V & A') styles itself 'the world's greatest museum of art and design'. Established in 1852, it was inspired by

One of the 145 galleries (with 8 miles of corridors) of the Victoria and Albert Museum

the Great Exhibition of the previous year, its founding principles to make works of art available to all, to educate working people and to inspire British designers and manufacturers. The V & A nestles in a quarter of London that also hosts the National Science Museum ('striving to be the best place in the world for people to enjoy science') and the Natural History Museum. The Science Museum also grew out of the Great Exhibition. It was and is a global statement of the country's industrial achievement, subject-matter for the tableaux that inaugurated the 2012 Olympics. The Natural History Museum is home to life and earth science specimens, 70 million items in botany, entomology, mineralogy, palaeontology and zoology. Some of its collections have historical as well as scientific value, for they include specimens collected by Darwin, among others. The corner of Kensington housing these three is sometimes known affectionately as 'Albertopolis' after Queen Victoria's consort and their 19th century inspiration. Its eminence was underlined in 2016 with the opening of a new Design Museum nearby.

The Imperial War Museum (IWM) covers conflicts involving Britain and the Commonwealth after 1914. It has five museums outside its giant south London flagship: IWM North in Manchester; IWM Duxford near Cambridge; the Churchill War Rooms in Whitehall, London; and HMS *Belfast*, a warship moored on the Thames. The National Maritime Museum (in Greenwich, London) is the largest of its kind in the world, boasting a vast collection spanning artworks, maps and charts and nautical memorabilia. Outside London, Bradford's National Media Museum (recently stripped of some of its photographic collection), the National Railway Museum (York, with a sister outpost at Shildon, County Durham, the first national museum of the North East), and the Museum of Science and Industry (Manchester) are all part of the Science Museums Group. National Museums Liverpool has seven separate sites including the International Slavery Museum, the Merseyside Maritime Museum and the Museum of Liverpool. The National Museum of the Royal Navy Museums and Historic Ships, logically based in the Royal Naval Dockyard, Portsmouth (Hampshire) groups nine museums mostly nearby.

Music

British popular music might have been expected to suffer, like film, from sharing a common language with the USA. And certainly, popular crooners until the 1960s commonly sang in affected American accents – until everything changed with the arrival of the Beatles and the Rolling Stones. Other bands followed in every generation: Cream; Pink Floyd; Duran, Duran; Culture Club; Oasis; the Spice Girls; Coldplay and One Direction. While the tide has ebbed and flowed since the 1960s British popular music has never returned to its former obscurity. It has even invented genres such as Garage and Grime while the British impact on electronic music has been great. All this musical output reaches huge audiences in the home, and at the many music festivals, most famously Glastonbury.

Of the 10 all-time biggest-selling rock bands, five are British: the Rolling Stones, Queen, Pink Floyd, Led Zeppelin and – in first place – The Beatles. Nor is it just groups. The death of David Bowie refocused the career of this several-times-reinvented artiste, perhaps more innovative in fashion than in song. Amy Winehouse rapidly became a global star before her early death. Adele's album *25* (published, exceptionally, on an independent label) sold eight million copies in the USA alone in 2015 – runner-up Sam Smith sold three million

Mick Jagger and Keith Richards: the face of rock n' roll for more than half a century

– and topped iTunes charts in 110 countries. This matters, for while the UK music market is the fourth-largest in the world – its biggest selling LP of the 21st century has been Adele's *21* at 4.75 million – not much is left of British popular music publishing. Since 1956, the Ivor Novello Awards, given by the British Academy of Songwriters, Composers and Authors, have attempted to redress the balance by honouring song with a British or Irish contribution of at least one third. Popular music of any provenance benefits from BBC Radio One and its vast monthly audience close to 45 million.

After World War II, British classical music thrived, assisted by the continued vigour of two composers. Ralph Vaughan Williams saw the encouragement of native and folk culture as part of his remit, composed nine symphonies during a long life and arranged the hymnal of the Church of England. Benjamin Britten, a figure of European stature, was the first major English composer of opera since the 17th century. A benign cultural setting spans BBC Radio 3, a free 24-hour classical music station with a mission to explain (and its commercial rival, Classic FM); the BBC Proms, claimed to be the largest classical music festival in the world; and 44 cathedral choirs that sometimes perform liturgically, plus countless other choirs both professional and amateur. All cities and not a few towns host classical concerts. Not all have dedicated venues but thousands of parish and other churches willingly become concert halls and derive useful secondary income thereby. There are many major performing spaces, though concerns about the acoustic quality of the two premier London locations (the Barbican and the Royal Festival Hall) have led to the announcement of a huge new venue in the City.

The young Benjamin Britten
(1913-1976)

There are at least 175 professional orchestras (the BBC alone has five, as well as two professional choirs) as well as numberless amateur ensembles. The country's music schools and academies turn out a large number of performers with a high quotient of stars: bass baritone Bryn Terfel, violinist Tasmin Little, soprano Lucy Crowe, mezzo-soprano Sarah Connolly, and conductor Sir Simon Rattle. This wide range of talent has stimulated composers who for the first time include large numbers of women: Judith Bingham, Judith Weir, Elizabeth Maconchy, as well as James MacMillan and Harrison Birtwhistle. The old gibe 'England (sic) is a land without music' has never been more inappropriate.

There are at least 175 professional orchestras ... as well as numberless amateur ensembles

The role of the state

The Department for Culture, Media & Sport, the DCMS, defines its role as making Britain 'the world's most creative and exciting place to live, visit and do business', a goal that neatly marries the search for prosperity and support for the arts for their own sake. It claims 78 per cent of the adult population engages in the arts but only 51 per cent attend museums. In the arts, as in sport (next chapter) and heritage (final chapter) the National Lottery has for twenty years provided an important financial windfall. But lottery income flows from the whole country and should impose its own pressure to spread the largesse evenly.

Arts Council England (ACE: mission 'great art and culture for everyone') plans in 2015-2018 to invest £1.1 billion from government and £0.7 billion from the National Lottery on promoting the arts. ACE is a non-departmental body of the DCMS and has national counterparts (the Arts Council of Wales, Creative Scotland, the Arts Council of Northern Ireland) that are similarly funded. ACE is the latest incarnation of the post-war Arts Council with a 'national portfolio' of 663 financially-supported organisations. Sensitive to accusations of being London-centric it has pushed up the share of grants-in-aid going outside the capital to 60 per cent and of Lottery funding to 70 per cent. Yet there is an underlying difficulty in doing this be-

the National Lottery has for twenty years provided an important financial windfall

cause of London's great concentration of significant cultural institutions, numbering 250 out of the 663.

The European City of Culture was inaugurated in 1985 under
the auspices of the European Community 'to put cities at the heart
of cultural life across Europe'. Glasgow was the winner in 1990 and
today claims to have 30,000 working in the creative industries partly
as a result. In 2008 Liverpool became the second UK city to be designated: it is thought to have attracted almost ten million additional
visitors as a result. Mindful of the benefit to Liverpool, government
inaugurated its own scheme in 2010 – the National City of Culture,
a quadrennial award. Derry/Londonderry (2013) was the first re-
cipient and was succeeded by Hull in 2017. Being a city of culture
does not directly bring state money though in practice the arts councils do invest in trying to ensure a lasting local legacy.

16.   Playing the game

Britain has parented an unusually large number of sports. Cricket, rugby, golf and football among others all originated in, and were exported from, the United Kingdom.

The peculiar global distribution of many games was a result of the British empire, as Britain's soldiers, administrators, engineers, missionaries and prospectors carried their sporting enthusiasms with them. The distribution of cricket and rugby to this day largely follows the boundaries of empire, though rugby remained confined to the white empire and commonwealth whereas cricket was taken up by other races. Golf was spread

The peculiar global distribution of many games was a result of the British empire

first by British colonists from its roots in Scotland; its global status was acknowledged when it became an Olympic sport at Rio 2016. Football was likewise a British export, but in its case more by way of trade than empire, its first carriers to Latin America the British navvies who in the 19th century built Argentina's railways. Even where a game was not invented by the British they left their mark: the rules of tennis, a French invention, were codified by 19th century British Indian Army officers. And, while baseball and American football are not British sports, baseball is merely a more sophisticated version of a type of game brought over by 18th century English colonists, while American football emerged in the latter half of the 19th century as a college sport evolved mainly from rugby.

The prominence of sport in British life in its turn also carries an echo of its imperial and military history. The battle of Waterloo, the Duke of Wellington famously declared, was 'won on the playing fields of Eton'. The English public school tradition of 'games', competitive activity thought to promote team spirit, rules observance

and personal discipline was an article of faith among the administrators of empire. 'Wearing the badge with pride' is an expression
used today that transfers to the field of sport older ideas about loyalty to the flag or the regimental colours. When the England football
team fails, the patriotism and moral fibre of the players is questioned quite as much as their actual abilities, as if to say that 11 true
Englishmen should be a match for 11 of any other nation.

Success on the sports field has likewise come to be a substitute of
sorts for the loss of empire. Great store is set by national achievement:
victory in the 1966 football World Cup is still commemorated as if it
had been Waterloo or Trafalgar. However, scratch the surface and it
can be seen that the way in which 'national' is defined varies from
sport to sport and very much reflects the complex tensions between
the different constituent nations explored in other chapters of this
book. We shall look in more detail at that issue as this chapter unfolds.

One measure of UK sporting prowess can be found in the all-time
Olympic medals table where it lies fourth behind three bigger countries (the USA, the USSR/Russia and Germany). The 2012 London
Olympics (65 medals, 29 golds) were a triumph for a unified country
competing as 'Great Britain and
Northern Ireland'; at the Glasgow
(2014) Commonwealth Games,
where the constituent nations com-
peted separately, England topped
the gold medals table (Scotland
came fourth, Wales 13th and Northern Ireland 15th). The Rio
Olympics in 2016 saw the best ever away performance by Great
Britain and Northern Ireland (67 medals, 27 golds). Remarkably the
national team ('Team GB') moved into second place for medals, overtaking China. It was a handsome return for UK Sport, the overseeing
body that had pumped £350 million into preparations since 2012.

The Rio Olympics in 2016 saw the best ever away performance ... second place, overtaking China

How can the popularity of the various sports be measured? Participation is of course one measure. Ranked by individual activity
in England, swimming is the most popular sport, followed by athletics and cycling. But most people see such activities as a way of
keeping fit rather than as a sport. Hockey and ice-hockey, basketball
and netball, athletics, archery, boxing, kick-boxing and wrestling

are among countless competitive physical games on offer and all of them have their enthusiasts. From time to time the home countries produce champions in them but they have not become entrenched in the national consciousness as part of the 'British way of life'. In what follows we look more closely at five sports which in their different ways each say something distinctive about the character of Britain and its people.

Horse racing

'A day at the races' has been an excursion since the 18th century and it has retained its popularity into the

> *'A day at the races' has been an excursion since the 18th century*

modern era despite the proliferation of other amusements on offer. In 2016, measured by attendances, horse racing was Britain's second most popular sport, beaten only by football. Many perhaps attend simply to bet on the results rather than for love of the sport per se; and most who visit a racecourse have never sat on a horse. Nonetheless it has shaped a certain image of Britain and has a distinctive place in the culture.

Horse racing is at one and the same time both the most classless and class conscious of all British sports. Classless in the sense that those who follow it are not confined to any one demographic. Class-conscious in that it has its well-understood and timeless hierarchies. Horse racing is traditionally known as the 'sport of kings' and it has certainly been a particular enthusiasm of both the present queen and her mother before her. 'Royal Ascot' is one of the pinnacles of the social calendar when ladies still sport absurdly spectacular hats in a segregated enclosure. But all classes converge at races. The 'Epsom Derby' – whose raucous jostling together of every sort and condition of humanity is celebrated in William Powell Frith's 1850s painting 'The Derby Day',

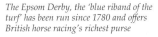

The Epsom Derby, the 'blue riband of the turf' has been run since 1780 and offers British horse racing's richest purse

on display at Tate Britain – though diminished from its former glory remains a big day out for many Londoners. Likewise the Cheltenham Gold Cup attracts seemingly half of Ireland and the (steeplechase) Aintree Grand National half of Liverpool and beyond. There can be few adult Britons who, even if they have never bet on anything else, have not joined an office or works sweepstake on the result of the Grand National.

Golf

Golf first appeared in 15th century Scotland where its popularity became such that it had to be banned to prevent it interfering with military training. St Andrew's, on the Scottish east coast, probably laid out the first 18-hole course in 1764, preparing the way for the modern game – though the first rules seem to have been set down in Edinburgh some 20 years earlier. The first English club followed in 1766. St Andrew's remains the world's most famous club, hosting 12 courses. Since 1860, the British Open has been played at celebrated Scottish locations like Royal Troon, Turnberry, Gleneagles and Carnoustie. Indeed, seven of the 14 British Open host courses are in Scotland (and one in Northern Ireland), a balance that reflects the game's ancestry. The Open is the oldest championship in professional golf, awarding the coveted Claret Jug since 1873.

An estimated 3.5 million Britons play, though their numbers are thought to be in decline. Golf requires a great deal of land: the green belts surrounding every city (see final chapter) are studded with golf courses, which in the case of London occupy more than 7 per cent of the entire

A 1920s poster for the home of golf

green belt. In Scotland most courses are open to anyone for a one-off charge (even the world famous Old Course at St Andrew's – though that is not cheap) but in England courses are usually run by member-ship clubs, of varying degrees of exclusivity. However cut-down ver-sions of the game, such as 9-hole 'chip and putt' courses, open to all, are found in many parts of England, especially beside the seaside.

The competitive game is highly organised. England Golf is at the apex of a county-based competitive system for amateurs. Scottish Golf functions similarly, and says it represents 607 golf clubs with a total membership of over 220,000. The organisation of profes-sional golf dates from the creation of the Professional Golfers' As-sociation in 1901. Today, the various Masters showcase individual achievement. After a long fallow period the UK regularly produces top players, and from all four home nations.

Rugby

The origins of rugby are by legend attributed to a famous early 19th century breach of football rules at the English public school of that name: one player picked up the ball and ran with it. As it grew in popularity, rugby spawned two socially distinct variants. 'Rugby union' – the leading form, and often just called rugby – was until the late 20th century a resolutely amateur game, regarding profession-alism with distaste and, except in Wales, played mainly by the middle classes. 'Rugby league', the other form of the game, originated in the 1890s as a breakaway from the Rugby Football Union by clubs in the industrial areas of the North that wished to introduce remuneration for their working class players. These clubs also went on to modify the rules to make the sport more open and faster and in 1922 the Northern Union changed its name to the Rugby Football League.

In both variants national sides play 'test' series against other rugby-playing countries. Rugby union long retained an insular perspective. England first played Scotland in the 1870s and from this developed, erratically, a limited international forum: the Five (later Six) Nations tournament (of the 'home countries' plus France and Italy). Each na-tion plays all the others and if it wins all its games is said to have com-pleted a 'grand slam': such feats are rare.

William Webb Ellis

In 1823 Rugby School pupil William Webb Ellis picks up the ball and runs: the sport's founding legend

Other than France, the most successful rugby-playing countries outside the British Isles (including Ireland) were all part of the British empire: Australia, New Zealand and South Africa. The sport is little known in much of the world. The absence of a global competition for rugby union was only put right in 1987 by the creation of a Rugby World Cup but once it was established it rapidly gained a popular following. In 1995-1996 the game finally became professional, first in the northern hemisphere, then in the southern.

Rugby league, played from the start by professionals, found the transition to a genuinely international sport much easier. The Imperial Rugby League Board was formed in 1927 by Britain, Australia and New Zealand and a Rugby League World Cup was inaugurated in 1954: it will next be contested in 2019. Today's Rugby League International Federation (RLIF) has 15 full members and the game is played under its rules in 35 countries, including much of Europe, though the number of participants in most countries is few.

The UK nations support rugby union unevenly. Wales has 23.5 registered players per thousand population, far ahead of Scotland (9.1) and England (6.2). Wales is the one home nation where rugby has universal appeal and can be considered the premier sport – a status matched elsewhere in the world only in New Zealand. Wales, despite the country's small size were winners of the 2005, 2008 and 2012 grand slams and back-to-back Six Nations titles for the first time in 34 years in 2013. Wales is preeminently the land of song (see chapter 6) and the sound of Welsh supporters in full voice when the national team plays at home is among the world's more memorable sporting experiences. Within England interest is unevenly distributed, being generally greater in the South and West than North and East, and especially where professional football provides less competition: of the 12 clubs in the current English Premiership, several are in modest-sized places such as Bath, Exeter, Northampton, Worcester and Gloucester which have never had major football clubs, while outside London the biggest cities are unrepresented. Club rugby grounds are in consequence proportionately much smaller than football grounds, though the English national ground (Twickenham) is the second biggest sports stadium (after Wembley) in London.

Interest in rugby league is low in the minority UK nations while in the English regions it remains predominantly Northern, primarily in Lancashire and Yorkshire. Again there is a bias towards smaller towns and cities such as Wakefield, St Helen's, Halifax and Widnes. Despite this being a Northern sport, the Rugby League Challenge Cup final, the premier event of the season, is staged in London: not at rugby union's Twickenham, but at Wembley. Such is the community base of the sport that cup final days have traditionally emptied these smaller competing towns of much of their population in a mass exodus to London. Of major English cities, only Hull has more rugby than football supporters.

Wales is the one home nation where rugby ... can be considered the premier sport

Football

The English Football Association (FA) was founded in 1863 and became the sport's authority, codifying its rules, and establishing the FA Cup, first played for in the 1871-1872 season. However, while football would soon become identified as the 'game of the working man', its first organised competitions reflected a different base: the early FA Cup finals were contested by amateur and military sides, with the Old Etonians featuring in six of the contests. The FA recognised professionalism in 1885 and only professional clubs won the FA Cup from that point on.

The English Football League was formed by professional clubs, initially all from the North and Midlands, in 1888. Thereafter the Football Association (based in London) and the Football League (based in Lancashire) co-existed in an uneasy balance of powers, with the FA responsible for rules, the administration of the game as a whole and the national side and the Football League for the professional divisions. Such remained the case until the formation of the English Premier League (the Premiership that replaced the old Football League Division One) in the early 1990s, which created a new elite from the top professional clubs. The Football League continues to exist, for lower division clubs. In Scotland the story was similar: the Scottish Football Association was founded in 1873 and the Scottish Football League in 1890. A Scottish Premier League was created in 1998 but it failed to replicate the success of the English Premier League it was set up to imitate and merged back with the Scottish Football League in 2013.

After the establishment of the English professional league (consolidated into four divisions) in the late nineteenth century, Saturday afternoon attendances ('gates') gradually grew ever bigger, spurred by fierce local loyalty and the rising capacity of grounds. Most fans stood (in 'stands' or open terraces) with minimal facilities and every big city had its major club or clubs in the First Division, with the smaller towns providing the clubs for the lower divisions. The most famous stand at a British football ground remains Liverpool's 'Kop' (a diminutive of Spion Kop, site of a British army defeat in the Boer War).

During the 1950s and 1960s, geographical and social mobility slowly began to dissolve local identities and the social solidarity of the stands. In the 1970s and 1980s a series of disasters due in varying ways to poor safety standards and culminating in the Hillsborough disaster (1989) laid bare the creaking infrastructure of Britain's ageing football grounds. Meanwhile, football gained an unenviable reputation for hooliganism which deterred many from going to matches. By the 1980s average attendances had dropped sharply, further exacerbated by hard times in many industrial working class communities, the major base of club support: many grounds were often half-empty. Legislation after Hillsborough forced extensive change on the footballing authorities, above all the introduction of all-seater stadia. Those responsible for running football had feared such change would mean only greater costs and that higher ticket prices would drive away fans. In fact, the opposite happened: the arrival of better facilities and the upgraded image of the Premier League meant ever higher prices went hand in hand with ever bigger and better behaved crowds.

a series of disasters ... laid bare the creaking infrastructure of Britain's ageing football grounds

At the same time, further enriching football, BBC and ITV (the free-to-view commercial channel) were pushed aside by the seemingly limitless resources of subscription-only sports channels covering live matches by satellite. The four-division structure of the English professional game was shaken up; while there had always been a gradient between the old Division 1 and Divisions 2, 3 and 4, the Premiership began to operate on a different plane. The big clubs marketed their identities, selling team strips, renaming their grounds, printing players' shirts with their sponsors' logos; the biggest, especially Manchester United became international brands with more supporters in Asia than at home. The Premiership sucked in talent from other countries, to the extent that only a minority of players were now English. The rewards available to players escalated: by the 2013-2014 season even the lowest paying Premiership club, Crystal Palace, paid an average annual salary of £1 million to first-team squad members and Manchester City paid five times that rate. It was a remarkable change in the professional game: only in the 1960s had English players broken through a £20-a-week wage ceiling imposed by Football League clubs and established their right to move club when contracts ended.

At one time, other than for the occasional mid-week fixture, all league matches kicked off at 3pm on a Saturday afternoon; now, TV schedules dictate and big games are staggered to maximise the number of games that can be watched live on TV. Actual spectators occupying seats at the ground have become less important for the Premiership clubs, except for creating atmosphere. In 2009-2010 Premiership clubs derived 26 per cent of their income from gate receipts; just four years later it was down to 19 per cent. The 2016-17 TV deal – worth over £8 billion with world broadcast rights included – looks set to depress this share further.

Not that paying supporters get off lightly: the 2015-2016 season saw protests at Liverpool and other Premiership clubs against inflated season ticket prices. And yet there is no shortage of paying customers. Manchester United, the club with the biggest ground, invariably play in front a capacity crowd of more than 75,000 – twice their average attendance back at the end of the 1980s. All the top clubs routinely fill their grounds for every match and all have recently increased their ground capacity or have building works in progress to do so. Meanwhile any semblance of local ownership has fast been disappearing. Premiership clubs have fallen into the hands of Russian oligarchs, Asian billionaires and American sports consortia. Less wealthy foreign purchasers have been quick to acquire clubs in the lower divisions.

Football's 10 richest clubs (2015-2016 season), by revenue (Deloitte)

1	Manchester United (England), £515.3m.
2=	Barcelona (Spain), £463.8m.
2=	Real Madrid (Spain), £463.8m.
4	Bayern Munich (Germany), £442.7m.
5	Manchester City (England), £392.6m.
6	PSG (Paris St Germain) (France), £389.6m.
7	Arsenal (England), £350.4 m.
8	Chelsea (England), £334.6m.
9	Liverpool (England), £302m.
10	Juventus (Italy), £225.1 m.

All major European football nations underwent a version of this process, but the most dazzlingly moneyed trajectory was in England. In the 2015-2016 season, according to figures compiled by Deloitte, five of the world's 10 teams with the biggest revenues were English, with Manchester United in first place. In the decade to 2014-2015 transfer spending by Premier League clubs grew by about 350 per cent to £835 million and total transfer fees in 2015-2016 exceeded £1 billion for the first time. With success a purchasable commodity, competition became oligopolistic. In the first 15 years of the 21st century, the Premiership was won only by Manchester United, Manchester City, Arsenal and Chelsea, all now among the world's 10 richest clubs.

The rude disruption of this sequence in 2016 by unfancied Leicester City seemed a temporary reassertion of traditional local identity. In the 20th century English football had been famed for its mobility: few clubs were permanent fixtures in the top division. The legacy of that mobility is that the lower divisions include numerous clubs that have in the past won the top division; indeed the lower divisions currently include two former European Cup winners (Nottingham Forest and Aston Villa), a fall in fortunes unimaginable in most continental leagues. The memory of past glories – even if handed down from father to son – and the hope of future triumphs has been a glue holding together hometown football loyalties but these are under pressure from the seductive lure of the now seemingly entrenched power of the biggest clubs.

The global prestige of the top Premiership clubs contrasts starkly with the fate of the England national team

The global prestige of the top Premiership clubs contrasts starkly with the fate of the England national team. For decades the FA forbade participation in international competitions, permitting England only to play 'friendlies'. This fed illusions of invincibility, later to be cruelly dispelled; deluding itself about standards, the FA preferred a 'home nations' contest: only in 1950 did England enter the finals of the World Cup (founded 1930). Its solitary victory (at home in 1966) harshly illuminates its usually mediocre performance. England has never won or even reached the final of the European Championship and was eliminated in 2016 by tiny Iceland. The notably poor record over recent years has been attributed to the financial success of the Premiership, where only 31 per cent of players are eligible for the national side. English club sides also once disdained European competition, echoing the self-imposed isolation of the national side. Clubs might play 'in Europe' but only in 'friendlies'. Once they entered real competitions a dispiriting gulf in class was disclosed. It took until 1968 for Manchester United to become the first English club to lift the European Cup (today the Champions' League), but that however was a turning point. Twelve English victories followed in the period to 2012, with Liverpool taking the trophy on no fewer than five occasions.

Sir Alex Ferguson, Scottish manager of Manchester United from 1986-2013: at one point the English Premier League had more Scottish than English managers

The decline of Scottish football, once a proud junior brother to football in England, has been all too apparent in recent decades. Glasgow Celtic were the first British club to win the European Cup (in 1967); furthermore an endless succession of Scottish players starred in English league sides in that era. Now, however, the Scottish domestic league is distinctly second rate in European terms and outside observers find it drearily predictable: there have only been two winners (Celtic and Rangers) of its top division since 1985. Scotland has not got past the qualifying round for the World Cup since 1998. Top English teams now source their players from all over the world, and rarely from Scotland. Even the long line of Scottish managers who rose to the first rank in English football (in recent years most notably Alex Ferguson at Manchester United) has been displaced by coaches from European countries. The main Welsh teams – Cardiff, Swansea and Wrexham – play in the English leagues but there has never been a significant team from the industrial valleys of South Wales, where rugby has ruled.

Cricket

Cricket, once undisputed as England's summer game (football was played in autumn, winter and spring) famously baffles Americans and continental Europeans. Much confusion arises from the large number of rules, whose custodians are still based in London at Lord's cricket ground – an echo of centralised imperial administration. Lord's contrives confusingly to be at one and the same time the headquarters of world cricket, the county ground of Middlesex, and the premises of the private and exclusive Marylebone Cricket Club (the MCC). Visitors to Lord's will encounter MCC members dressed in loud blazers, panamas and striped ties worn for the nonce – another echo, this time of public school uniform.

Class and status distinction persisted long and hard in cricket: 'gentlemen' were amateurs of independent means who played for sheer love of the game; but for 'players' (those often of working-class origin) it constituted their livelihood. Until the 1950s county and England teams were invariably captained by gentlemen amateurs, whom players were required to address as 'Mr': social mobility and the loss of prime status by the England team eventually did for that. Even so, attempts to prevent the emergence of a market in players persisted. English cricketers seeking to boost their income in the 'close' (winter) season by appearing in Australia's Sheffield Shield were punished. Other more

Until the 1950s county and England teams were invariably captained by gentlemen amateurs

curious discriminations also existed. Before 1992 Yorkshire, England's premier county club, fielded only those born within its boundaries, a rule fabled to have doomed many heavily pregnant wives of cricket fans to a last-minute dash by road or rail.

The game itself turns on three 'unities': time, runs (scored by batsmen who run between two sets of sticks known as stumps which are topped by horizontal 'bails'), and wickets (meaning dismissals of batsmen whose spells at the crease may end in various ways, termed 'getting out'). Batsmen score their runs by facing (and hitting) a ball – hard and encased in hand-stitched leather – which is 'bowled' (in prescribed fashion) in series of six, known as an 'over'. On no other sport, unless it be tennis, has the impact of a unique scoring system been so great. A batsman may be dismissed in nine different ways; there are four possible outcomes of a match; a side may 'declare' its first (of two) 'innings' (i.e. cease to bat) if it thinks it has scored enough runs. As new forms of cricket are developed to please television audiences and technology in-

'Old Father Time' removes the bails from the stumps – signifying close of play – on a weather vane at Lord's

trudes, so the rules become yet more elaborate. Cricket has its own vocabulary, exceeding even football in its quotient of metaphor. One should always 'play the game' (act fairly) even while 'batting on a sticky wicket' (a difficult pitch) and thus forced 'onto the back foot' (the defensive). An English gentleman can do no other. If he cheats, it is 'not cricket' – or perhaps he is no gentleman. The apparently leisurely pace (even county games have a four-day schedule) of this famously literary game has attracted outstanding prose stylists such as Neville Cardus and John Arlott. Perhaps this is why the BBC, having lost its television rights, retained a mass radio following for its 'ball-by-ball' Test coverage.

In contrast to football, the acme of achievement is with the international side and not with its component clubs. Participation in the top tier (the County Championship, now arranged in two leagues) is selective, including certain English counties plus Glamorgan in Wales; others play each other in the discouragingly-named 'Minor Counties' competition. From Lord's an elaborate fixture list of international matches (test matches) is devised that pits cricketing nations against each other in the summers of northern and southern hemispheres. Five days are allotted in which to achieve a test match result. This 18th century pace allows ample time for fortunes to swing to and fro and it is considered by purists to be the finest form of cricket. However, for more than half a century the national and international games have experimented with new formats limited either by time or the number of balls bowled. All are designed to produce a result within one day, generate prodigious feats by the players, create great excitement and attract large crowds.

Cricket has played an important social role in every country where it has a mass audience. In the West Indies it helped to fuse a regional and national consciousness, for the growing success of its national (or rather multi-national) side demonstrated that white supremacy was a myth. In South Africa the prowess of the national team was long a virile symbol of apartheid though later it came to ex-

The most famous trophy in cricket: a small urn containing the 'ashes of English cricket' (a burnt bail) and commemorating England's first test match defeat by Australia

emplify racial harmony. Australia's ability to beat England – from the very beginning of international cricket – accelerated its transition from colonial to dominion status, building a national identity. India, the most populous cricket-playing country, is now the greatest force in reshaping the world game and host to the most lucrative competition – the Indian Premier League (IPL). The most famous international clash is between England and Australia (who compete for 'the Ashes' – which are literally that: a small urn of ashes).

Cricket in England does not express national identity as it does in Australia, India or the West Indies: Scyld Berry has argued it is truly communitarian only in the three northerly counties of Lancashire, Yorkshire and Nottinghamshire. While test cricket is as popular as ever in England, this is sport for consumption: the days when boys could reliably be seen with bat and ball on scraps of waste ground or in parks have largely gone. Even in the Afro-Caribbean community, fervent cricket-followers in the first generation or two of arrivals in Britain, cricket among the young has largely given way to the lure of football and basketball. There are, however, many teams made up of players of Indian or Pakistani heritage; thus the wheel has turned full circle and cricket has been returned from the places it was exported to.

The Olympics in London and Rio

The success of London's bid to host the 2012 Olympics is thought to have owed much to its focus on 'legacy'. Its character was shaped by two of the conflicting pressures upon the planners: to be able to justify the burden on the public purse and to create world-class venues on a brownfield site. As we have seen, these Games were tremendously successful in PR, participative and national sporting terms. When Team GB surpassed itself at Rio '16, it invited scrutiny of the ruthless approach of UK Sport. Before both Games it had set medal targets for each competing sport, unsentimentally biasing spending away from team competitions with fewer medals to offer. Cycling, rowing and gymnastics greatly benefited, but basketball, a popular sport among urban youngsters did not.

What was the lasting imprint of the London Olympics? Its built legacy is visible around the Olympic Park in a previously run-down area of the capital (see chapter 8). 'Leaving a legacy for sport in the UK', another stated aim, has however turned out to be elusive. It is claimed that 15.5 million adults now play sport at least once a week, 1.4 million more than in 2005-2006. However, most adults – 58 per cent – still do not play any sport at all and the real level of activity of most of the reported 15.5 million may well be doubted. Of course international prowess in a particular sport does not necessarily mean that the population as a whole has other than a passive interest. The British Cycling Association aimed to make the country No.1 in cycling, achieved its goal at the London Olympics, and retained it at Rio '16. But while there has certainly been a steady annual rise in cycling, bike use by the general population lags far behind some other parts of Western Europe. Perhaps people would rather watch: when England hosted the early stages of the 2014 Tour de France, nearly five million people turned up.

Sport and national identity

The status of the national sides varies across sports, and is complicated by great and at times extraordinary inconsistency of national representation. In world terms this is remarkable: for other countries, whether it is the USA, France, Germany or Italy there is but one 'national' team. In this respect, UK sport reflects the peculiarly confused history of this often 'disunited' kingdom.

Thus in football, England, Scotland, Northern Ireland and Wales all compete separately: in the 2016 European Championship finals all but Scotland were represented. No other country has more than one team competing in international football, something which has at times caused resentment among other nations. However, the lack of a UK team has also come at a cost, as many of the finest players from the home nations – from George Best (Northern Ireland) in the 1960s, to Kenny Dalglish (Scotland) in the 1970s and 1980s to Gareth Bale (Wales) in the present day – have been unavailable to combine with players from the strongest national squad, England. Scotland's erstwhile annual clashes with England in home internationals were affairs of real passion: football was the first mass arena in which the flag of St Andrew (a diagonal white cross on a blue background – often dubbed the Saltire) emerged as the Scottish national flag (as opposed to the more monarchical Scottish lion). Support for the England side has been variously symbolised but has crystallised on the emblem of St George (a red cross on a white background), the English national flag: the nationalism is more diluted among the majority of English supporters, but the same emblem of St George is also used by right-wing English nationalist groups.

The identity-tinged hooliganism at England v. Scotland matches and the Troubles in Northern Ireland (which had led to the abandonment of the 1980-1981 competition) were factors in the final ending of the home internationals football championships after the 1983-1984 season. While Scotland's identity in distinction to England was at issue in the home internationals, within Scotland itself identity conflicts also exist: fans attending matches between the country's two top teams, Glasgow Rangers and Celtic have traditionally indicated their sectarian loyalties by waving national flags: the union flag for Rangers and the Republic of Ireland tricolour for Celtic.

While football in Northern Ireland has inevitably been affected by sectarianism, relative to the bitterness of the conflict within the province as a whole football has often seemed a force for inter-communal harmony. A province originally created to secure a Protestant identity turns out a football team that plays in green, a traditionally nationalist colour and – remarkably – one also favoured by the Republic of Ireland team.

Conflicts about national identity can be especially visceral in football but they also have their reflection in other sports. There was irritation among the loyalist community in Northern Ireland at the branding of the UK Olympic squad as 'Team GB', implicitly excluding the province. In fact 21 of the province's 29 athletes chose to compete as part of 'Team Ireland' and the UK parent body has long been the 'British Olympic Association'.

National identity in rugby union has been generally benignly expressed but not the less intense. England, Scotland and Wales all compete separately in international competitions but a single team represents the entire island of Ireland. Conflicts have arisen over flags and anthems over the decades. However, at the last two World

Cups the Ireland team came onto the pitch with both the Irish tri-colour and the flag of Ulster. As well as the national teams, the 'British and Irish Lions', including players from all the countries of the British Isles, is a formation used to tour the countries of the south-ern hemisphere.

In cricket, conflicting national identities have rarely been an issue as the game has been largely confined to England. Curiously, while the Yorkshire county club long insisted on Yorkshire birth for its play-ers, the England side has always been something of an open house, with innumerable players born in all corners of the empire and com-monwealth, from Indian princes to exiles from apartheid South Africa. There is no Welsh national cricket team; the occasional Welsh-man has played for England. There is a Scotland side, but cricket in Scotland arouses little passion other than among the rather few who play it, and a Scotsman captained England in the 1970s; there is also an all-Ireland team, but cricket in Ireland is likewise very much a mi-nority enthusiasm.

In more individualist sports such as tennis or golf, identity has also been less of an issue. However, Andy Murray's rise to tennis stardom stirred controversy: when he won the Wimbledon men's champi-onships in 2013, becoming the first player from these islands to do so since the 1930s, it was disputed whether his victory could be claimed for Britain or for Scotland. In the men's international tennis competi-tion, the Davis Cup, Scotland, Wales and England compete together as Great Britain; the Ireland Davis Cup side represents both Northern Ire-land and the Republic, though Northern Ire-land players also have the option of playing for Great Britain.

In golf, the international team contest is the Ryder Cup: this was formerly contested be-tween Great Britain and Ireland on the one hand and the USA on the other. In 1979, how-ever, the contest having become embarrass-ingly unequal, the format was changed to Europe versus the USA – one case where British sportsmen compete for Europe.

Andy Murray – Scottish or British, or both?

17.   The news media

Britain's news media present an unfamiliar landscape to many visitors. There are nine national daily newspapers. From the north of Scotland to the south-west of England – over 800 miles – the same range is on offer, a collateral benefit for a population living entirely in one time zone. A large number of weekly regional, national and local papers also still appears though the number of local dailies is shrinking. Elsewhere in print is a lively part-publications industry with new titles constantly being introduced, some exits and ever-improving design standards. These two sectors illustrate a relatively robust home market in news on paper. Print empires are large, but no one media group dominates and under current competition rules it is not clear that one ever could. As the 2011 phone-hacking scandal (see below) revealed, the various media groups not only jealously watch each other; they are also very capable of seeing off government attempts to interfere with what they construe as freedom of the press. In its wake, the Independent Press Standards Organisation (IPSO) replaced the Press Complaints Commission (PCC) as the independent regulator of the newspaper and magazine industry.

But if news in print arrives via the market, broadcast news does not. Radio is highly regulated and operates under licence: the giant British Broadcasting Corporation (BBC) towers over the national and the regional landscape. Television is dominated by public service broadcasters enjoined by Ofcom, the official regulator, 'to deal with a wide range of subjects; cater for the widest possible range of audiences – across different times of day and through different types of programme; and maintain high standards of programme-making'.

The designated public service broadcasters are the BBC, Channel

4 Corporation (C4C), the Channel 3 licensees – ITV, STV and UTV
– and Channel 5. BBC Alba and S4C provide Gaelic and Welsh-lan-
guage channels. All BBC services come under the heading of public
service broadcasting but only the main channels of the others fall
into this category. Public money flows overwhelmingly to the BBC
(and a small amount to
Channel 4); the other public
service broadcaster (PSB)
channels derive their income
from advertisers. All operate
under the weight of PSB expectations.

**broadcasting is subject to a
high degree of regulation
unfamiliar to a visitor from
the United States**

It is the looming presence of the BBC that gives television and
radio a further distinctive twist. It is the nation's broadcaster of
choice and a time-hallowed funding system partly insulates it from
market forces through a levy on every household or other place
with equipment able to receive broadcasts. It is state regulated but
not controlled by the government, an important distinction explained below. TV (and radio) broadcasting is subject to a high degree of regulation unfamiliar to a visitor from the United States.
This does not cause concern among the wider public which is accustomed to public service broadcasting. Those not watching PSB
channels are most likely to receive them via satellite, followed by
Freeview with cable far behind.

Public service broadcasting

Since 2003 public service broadcasting has been defined by law
as informing our understanding of the world; stimulating knowledge and learning; reflecting UK cultural identity; and representing
diversity and alternative viewpoints. This attempt to situate public
service broadcasting in a contemporary cultural landscape continues and updates a long-standing tradition: the BBC itself, almost
from its inception, had a mission 'to inform, to educate, and to en-
tertain'.

As a monopoly provider in its early decades the BBC set the
tone for broadcasting (radio, then television) as a whole. By the

time a commercial station had arrived (1955 for television, the 1960s for radio) listening and viewing habits were – to a considerable extent – set. It is true that the share of viewers' time won by the non-public service broadcasting channels is rising incrementally: Ofcom found it had passed 29 per cent by 2014, an advance of about one per cent annually over the preceding decade. But the more remarkable figure is that public service broadcasting channels still held 71 per cent of all viewing at that date. Their continued strength may reflect a recently-acquired ability to offer on-demand viewing, neutralising an advantage once confined to cable- and satellite-delivered channels.

What do viewers want? The most watched programme genres on the five main PSB channels in 2014 were entertainment (19.4 per cent of viewing), news (12.6 per cent) and sport (11.4 per cent), but there is evidence that viewers consciously discriminate between channels. Notably, news viewing on public service broadcasting channels represents 95 per cent of the whole, perhaps a signal of trust in the BBC current affairs operation, given its dominance. Two in three UK adults rate such news broadcasting 'trustworthy'. Again the bedrock of this is the reputation of the BBC: when asked 'of all news sources, which one source are you most likely to turn to if you want impartial news coverage?' 53 per cent nominated it. The figure for Sky News was 8 per cent.

The BBC

In September 2015 BBC director-general Tony Hall reviewed his organisation's prospects after years of austerity. It was a sombre moment for an organisation ap-

The original Broadcasting House: much expanded, it is the headquarters of the BBC in Portland Place in London

proaching its 90th birthday as a public corporation. The BBC exists under royal charter (renewed in 2017) and functions double-headedly. It has an executive structure under a director-general who provides editorial and creative leadership, managing the operational delivery of services. It also has a supervisory trust that sets strategic objectives, issuing a licence to each service stating expectations and spending limits. This sets the BBC's editorial standards and above all protects the BBC's independence. Yet the Trust (which has taken different forms during the BBC's history) has been unable – or unwilling – to defend a number of directors-general against government pressure. Nor has it emerged well from revelations

about the predatory activities of Jimmy Savile and other personalities now known to have been paedophiles who from the 1960s thrived in its permissive work environment. An inquiry produced a blistering report on their activities: it led the BBC executive immediately to review its policies and procedures on child protection, complaints, whistleblowing, and investigations – and to commit to independent audit and publication.

Commemorative plaque at the Alexandra Palace in north London, the first home of television

The BBC began in 1922 as a private company with a radio monopoly. As such it was the natural vehicle to develop TV, achieving a global first with the first high-definition broadcast in 1936. For years a publicly-funded BBC was axiomatic. Under its first and long-serving director-general John (later Lord) Reith it established an arms-length relationship with government while building a reputation for high-minded broadcasting. Not until 1955 did national commercial television begin. By the 1960s most British homes had a TV set receiving signals via a roof-based aerial. That decade brought a second BBC channel (BBC 2) and in 1982 came a further public service commercial channel (Channel 4). Then channels began to multiply. Satellite, followed by cable broadcasting stimulated this growth but the real acceleration came after the turn of the century from digitalisation. The two BBC television channels became nine; many households have free access to dozens of channels; on cable and satellite there are hundreds more. Despite this proliferation, the 2015 Conservative government, in the course of an otherwise highly critical inquiry, found 'the BBC is reaching a wide audience within the UK … almost all adults in the UK use BBC services each week, giving (it) a central place in people's lives'. *Since virtually every household in the country funds the BBC … it must cater for all tastes* This prominence also extends to radio: with ten national radio stations and 40 local ones the BBC is if anything even more dominant than it is in TV.

Controversy exists as to how – or whether – the BBC is to continue as a universal provider. It currently spends 60 per cent of its income on TV, 16 per cent on radio and 5 per cent on online. Since virtually every household in the country funds the BBC through a licence fee (see below), it must cater for all tastes. It aims to provide quality output in every programming genre – something that should not be confused with high culture output: the BBC must programme top-notch quizzes and reality TV as well. If universal funding ceased this imperative would be removed. At present the BBC, which carries no advertising but has guaranteed forseeable income, can – indeed must – programme content of an elevated tone that does not command wide viewing or listening: in this and other respects it has to meet standards set by parliament rather than chase ratings. Yet though it has lost its monopoly and many advantages, it thrives. Its audience reach in TV is 82 per cent of the UK population, in radio 65 per cent, online 50 per cent: taking all three together, 97 per cent of the UK adult population uses it weekly. On average, people spend over 18 hours a week watching or listening to its output.

The TV licence, which is only used for the benefit of the BBC (other than a small amount allocated to the Welsh Channel S4C), has existed as a levy on anyone with a TV set since 1946. It is not an option to seek exemption by claiming never to watch BBC programmes; technically it does not apply to households only with radio but it does apply to those without TVs but able to watch TV programmes on other electronic media. The TV licence is vigorously policed and enforced: TV detection vans patrol the streets tracking down non-compliant households. Magistrates courts have the issuing of fines for evaders as a major element of their workload: three or four thousand such cases are heard by magistrates each week, which critics have argued clogs up the courts.

The licence was relatively uncontroversial in the days when the BBC was one of only two main providers (with ITV) but with the proliferation of other subscription and advertising-funded channels it has become more politically problematic and every funding review is now a cause of argument. The standard licence fee paid by most has been frozen since 2010: thus its real value has been eroded by inflation, albeit at modest rates, and the BBC has struggled to keep up with its commercial challengers. The expansion of some services has required the reduction or closure of others: a BBC 3 television channel, catering specifically for the 16 to 34 age range, was launched in 2003 but to reduce costs in 2016 switched to an online-only service, with a near 50 per cent budget cut. A BBC 4 television channel, launched shortly before BBC3 and targeting a somewhat older demographic, has survived thus far, helped by the popularity of its often very low-budget but nonetheless well-regarded documentaries and foreign-language imports.

A straitened corporation has cut senior salaries and severance packages and stepped up its efforts to obtain a commercial return for its output: American and European viewers of costume dramas have enjoyed the result. In the United States imitation of BBC products has sometimes been the sincerest form of flattery with reformated versions of BBC hits like *House of Cards* and *The Office*. In the UK, where costume dramas are also popular, polling suggests that the public is still willing to pay the licence fee as the means of funding the BBC, though not

The BBC is easily the largest public service broadcaster in the Western world

by a large margin: 48 per cent back it, compared with 29 per cent favouring advertising and 20 per cent for subscription. However, the BBC also remains deeply entrenched in and strongly supported by wide swathes of influential opinion in British public life instinctively resistant to the wholesale 'Americanisation' of British culture.

The BBC's Northern base, MediaCity at Salford Quays, Greater Manchester. ITV's North West regional franchise, Granada, also operates from there

Thus this public service broadcaster is likely to remain for the foreseeable future the dominant provider, existing under royal charter, the very opposite of a market model driven by audiences alone.

The BBC is easily the largest public service broadcaster in the Western world, dwarfing even the giant companies of France, Germany and Italy: by contrast PSB in the United States scores highly for trust but is dwarfed by the major networks. The BBC's own 'public purposes' capture what public service broadcasting means: sustaining citizenship and civil society; promoting education and learning; stimulating creativity and cultural excellence; representing the UK, its nations, regions and communities; bringing the UK to the world and the world to the UK; delivering to the public the benefit of emerging communications technologies and services. Even without embellishment this list suggests that if there is a British identity, the BBC aspires to be part of it. But does it succeed?

Some 74 per cent of UK viewers rated BBC 1 highly for its nations/regional news content in 2015. However, when this is broken down by nations a rather different picture emerges. The proportion of people in each nation who think the BBC is good at representing their life in news and current affairs content is an unimpressive 61 per cent in England and Northern Ireland; worse, it dips to 55 per cent in Wales and to 48 per cent in Scotland. Much dissatisfaction was expressed with the BBC's coverage during and after Scotland's 2014 independence referendum. Undoubtedly it has made an effort to shift activity out of London. It has invested in Scotland and opened MediaCityUK in 2011. This Salford (Greater Manchester) base produces thousands of hours of television, radio (major programmes like *Woman's Hour*) and online content: 2,700 staff work in departments including Children's, Learning, Radio 5 live, Sport, Radio Manchester, Breakfast, Religion & Ethics, the BBC Philharmonic, some R & D, Drama and Comedy). By volume, over 30 per cent of output now originates in Salford. Beyond the BBC, the gross share of productions majority-sourced outside London by public service broadcasters has broadly grown since 2011, though in the case of Channels 3 and 4 it seems to have reached a plateau.

Is there any other media organisation that would have broadcast such a no-holds-barred interrogation of its top executive?

Trust is vital for the BBC, but the quest for broadcasting integrity can be painful as a 2012 interview with director-general (DG) George Entwhistle illustrated. It was conducted by John Humphrys – known for his abrasive style – on Radio 4's *Today Programme*, the BBC's flagship current affairs radio vehicle. The occasion was a recent BBC2 *Newsnight* broadcast that had wrongly implicated a former senior politician in a child sex abuse scandal. *Newsnight's* reputation had already been tarnished by its suppression of an investigative report into the paedophile activities of Jimmy Savile. Humphrys forensically interrogated the recently-appointed Entwhistle who bore ultimately responsibility for the programme. The hapless DG, unable to mount a persuasive defence, was embarrassingly exposed: within 24 hours of the interview he had resigned. Is there any other media organisation that would have broadcast such a no-holds-barred interrogation of its top executive by a member of its own staff and with such devastating effect? Yet this is not an exceptional case.

The BBC has a huge online presence with the success of its iPlayer (allowing on-demand viewing). The weekly UK reach of its website rose from under four million to nearly 25 million in 2002-2014. Nearly seven million listen on radio or online to the *Today Pro-*

gramme; audiences for the radio soap *The Archers* nudge five million. Website success may be a collateral benefit of the public trust the BBC enjoys as broadcaster: it can be hard to find an authoritative voice on the web. The BBC's reputation is also high outside the UK. It has global reach, with 2015's weekly international news audiences of 283 million, up from 233 million in just nine years. The combined (TV, radio and online) weekly global audience was 308 million. BBC World Service – its highly respected global radio news arm – is claimed to reach about 300 million, one-third of them in Africa, with its single biggest audience being the USA (30 million). While such figures may give a somewhat exaggerated sense of the BBC's real global influence, the BBC is certainly often cited as a first port of call by those wanting independent information about their own country, especially where alternative sources are few.

The press

Visitors can hardly fail to notice that daily newspaper reading remains a national habit. It is certainly long-standing: the first daily appeared in 1702. The Belfast News Letter (founded 1737) is the world's oldest surviving daily newspaper. A recent government survey found a majority read a daily newspaper at least three times a week, usually The Sun, Mail or local daily newspapers.

Newspapers ('the papers') are highly visible in every corner shop. Unlike the USA, the whole country wakes up at roughly the same time; when it retires, late night current affairs shows preview the next morning's press. Relatively small internal distances create the effect – perhaps the illusion – of a nationwide common experience, a benign environment for genuinely national dailies. On behalf of publishers the News Media Association is upbeat:

> 'the UK has one of the strongest and most diverse newspaper markets in the world. Its ability to inform, entertain and hold power to account is unmatched. It reaches more people today than ever across its print, online, mobile and social platforms. Newspapers are the powerhouse for news provision in the UK, investing two-thirds of the total spent on original news content, setting the political and social agenda and feeding other news outlets'.

This claim is under severe test, however. During 2011-2015 the newspaper industry was rocked by what became known as the 'phone-hacking' scandal. Phone hacking was a technique used by journalists to listen to people's mobile voicemail: a murky undergrowth of corrupt police-press relations was revealed to lie beneath sensational tabloid 'kiss'n tell' journalism. Former News of the World editor Andy Coulson (who had become official spokesman for the prime minister) was found guilty of conspiracy to hack phones though News International chief executive Rebekah Brooks

the newspaper industry was rocked by what became known as the 'phone-hacking' scandal

was cleared along with four other defendants. Allegations that News International journalists were involved in hacking people's phones for information led to the closure of the 168-year-old title in 2011 and a trial reportedly costing up to £100 million. Though News International titles were the principal target of investigations, other papers including the Daily Mirror were implicated. The row over phone-hacking led to the establishment of a committee of inquiry under Sir Brian Leveson, parliamentary inquiries and the launch of three lengthy police investigations.

While the news remains national, technical advances allow growing regional and sub-national differentiation. This has long been true of sports coverage where titles have to address local loyalties, prominently featuring local teams. With editorial ever more physically separate from production this trend may grow and reflect shifting identities and loyalties. However newpapers face severe financial challenges: the profits big media groups derive from publishing are falling and so is hard copy advertising revenue. Digital access largely explains this decline: free newspapers are most popular among young people, suggesting the buying habit is on the wane, and ever more people take their news, some of it fake, from internet sources of whose reliability and journalistic standards they know nothing. Against this, however, is the fact that today as for several decades most people follow the news by watching the BBC, ITV and (to a lesser extent) Channel 4 news bulletins. The BBC evening News at Ten alone has an average audience of 4.9 million, far more than any newspaper.

Reflecting the pressures on the industry, Britain's ten national daily papers were reduced to nine in March 2016 when The Independent ended its 30-year print life, retreating to online only: its daily sale had dropped to a mere 67,000. But most dailies face difficulties. Their gross market is shrinking, and some research suggests that the multiple of readers to sales, once more than 3:1, is dropping too. The Sun leads the tabloid pack (they prefer to be known as 'compacts') with a 2016 daily circulation of 1.78 million. The Daily Mail comes close behind. The Daily Mirror now sells but 800,000 copies per day – when it was at its peak as Britain's biggest paper in the 1960s it sold five million. The Daily Star is even worse off with below 500,000 sales; the Daily Express, the biggest post-war rival to the Daily Mirror till the end of the 1960s, sells even fewer.

The 'qualities' (once known as the 'broadsheets') have also shown a downward if more nuanced trend. The Daily Telegraph, traditionally favoured by middle class supporters of the Conservative Party, lost nearly a third of its circulation between 2010 and 2016 alone, down to 472,000. The Times, however, has for a few years been fairly stable at close to 400,000; and although historically by far the most famous British newspaper overseas, its contemporary circulation is actually well above the level it had in most of the 20th century (before the coming of Margaret Thatcher), when it was widely regarded as a stuffy newspaper solely for those who considered themselves part of the establishment.

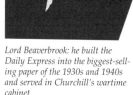

Lord Beaverbrook: he built the Daily Express into the biggest-selling paper of the 1930s and 1940s and served in Churchill's wartime cabinet

The print Financial Times has lost ground badly over the last few years, selling fewer than half the copies it managed in its glory days of the Tony Blair premiership (1997-2007), years of economic boom which it preeminently chronicled, selling more than 400,000 a day: it nonetheless still sells more

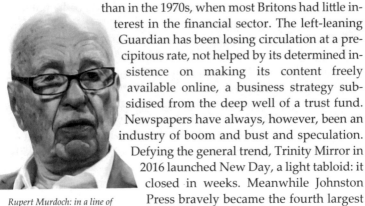

than in the 1970s, when most Britons had little interest in the financial sector. The left-leaning Guardian has been losing circulation at a precipitous rate, not helped by its determined insistence on making its content freely available online, a business strategy subsidised from the deep well of a trust fund. Newspapers have always, however, been an industry of boom and bust and speculation. Defying the general trend, Trinity Mirror in 2016 launched New Day, a light tabloid: it closed in weeks. Meanwhile Johnston Press bravely became the fourth largest UK publisher by purchasing the i (a pop version of the Independent). All dailies try to keep their readers hooked by publishing Sunday versions of themselves, though the sales of these Sundays have not escaped the downward trend.

Rupert Murdoch: in a line of press barons stretching back for more than a century

British newspapers have always had their share of proprietors who sought to translate their wealth and the reading public they brought with them into political influence. The Harmsworth brothers, Alfred and Harold, founders of the Daily

'It's The Sun Wot Won It' boasted the front page headline of The Sun

Mail (1896) and Daily Mirror (1903) walked tall during the era of William Randolph Hearst in the USA and were duly ennobled as Viscount Northcliffe (Alfred) and Viscount Rothermere (Harold). Even their influence was eclipsed by the Canadian-born Max Aitken, elevated to the peerage as Lord Beaverbrook, the proprietor of The Daily Express who became a close ally of Winston Churchill. Later still came other famous proprietors – Robert Maxwell, Conrad Black and the Barclay brothers. Most successful of all in our own times is the Australian Rupert Murdoch, whose interests span the globe. His business empire includes both The Times and The Sun newspapers.

The 'press barons' have always both troubled and fascinated political leaders: one pre-war prime minister compared them to harlots; Tony Blair got too close to Rupert Murdoch for the liking of most in his own Labour Party; David Cameron won the 2010 and 2015 elections with much of the the press on his side, but lost the 2016 EU referendum when most of it opposed him. Yet the real influence of newspapers in shaping opinion has always been an open question. 'It's The Sun Wot Won It' boasted the front page headline of The Sun after the Conservatives unexpectedly won the 1992 general election. However, newspapers follow their readers – their paying customers after all – quite as much as the other way round: at the next general election, in 1997, The Sun saw the way the tide was flowing and got on board behind Labour, which won by a landslide. For the great majority of the population, the most significant source of information about politics and current affairs is, as it has been for decades, the BBC and ITV, and if they read the opinion pieces in a daily newspaper it is because they serve to confirm and comfort the opinions they already had – which is why they bought that particular newspaper in the first place.

Nor has the influence of proprietors over editors ever been consistently demonstrated: whatever the temptations, most proprietors have tended to be wary of intruding onto the editorial floor, except where their own immediate financial interests were concerned. Nonetheless the degree of concentration of the press in a few hands has always been a contentious issue. Nowadays The Times and The Sun are owned as part of a complex global media empire; The Express and the Star are owned by Northern & Shell which also owns Channel 5; the Daily Mail, the Evening Standard (a London free paper), and the Metro (another London free paper) are owned by Associated Press. Single-owned titles are the Telegraph (Telegraph Media Group), the Financial Times (Nikkei, the Japanese media group), the Daily Mirror (Trinity Mirror, which also holds extensive regional dailies), and The Guardian (the non-commercial Scott Trust).

The demise of titles published outside London but having some UK-wide reach or reputation was completed in 1959 when The Manchester Guardian became The Guardian, its editor moving to London soon after. But at the national/provincial level a distinctive voice has survived. A Scottish press always co-existed with British titles and it has resisted London's lures: the Glasgow-based Daily Record (and Scottish Mail), and Herald (once the Glasgow Herald), the Edinburgh-based Scotsman, Aberdeen's Press & Journal, Dundee's Courier and Sunday Post. Yet circulation is also being lost in Scotland, both to the UK titles (which anticipated devolution by inserting 'Scottish' ahead of their name on the masthead) and to on-line. In Wales Cardiff hosts Trinity Mirror's Western Daily Mail which tends to reflect the interests of the capital, Cardiff, where news is made. Its East and West editions help it against the Swansea-based South Wales Evening Post. Northern Ireland has not only its own party system but its own constellation of papers: the Belfast Telegraph (and its sister the Sunday Life) has the biggest circulation followed by the Irish News and the Ulster (formerly the Belfast) Newsletter. Newspaper readership, like most things in the province, tends to divide on sectarian lines.

As we have seen in earlier chapters, the sense of English regional identity, certainly when it comes to interest in local politics, is rather dilute and, reflecting that, the English provincial press is entirely

the English provincial press is entirely overshadowed by the London dailies

overshadowed by the London dailies, with circulations measured only in the tens of thousands even for the most successful titles. The regional press has its own oligopolistic structure: the Yorkshire Post is owned by Johnston Press; Trinity Mirror owns the Manchester Evening News, Bristol Post, Liverpool Echo and Nottingham Post. The biggest-selling – perhaps surprisingly located in the relatively modest Midlands city of Wolverhampton – is the Express & Star, closely followed by the Manchester Evening News and the Liverpool Echo. Other locally important titles include the Newcastle Evening Chronicle and the Leicester Mercury. In London itself the Standard functions both as a local and a late-edition national daily: it is now a freesheet, living on advertising alone.

Faced with an existential challenge from the digital world, all national titles launched websites and there is some evidence that this will sustain them. Some papers' websites are simply each day's paper online, though constantly updated; others such as the Daily

Mail's Mail Online offer a racier read. Some (The Times, Financial Times) charge for online but most remain free; The Sun has taken down its paywall. The Mail clearly leads the pack in terms of its digital following and the Guardian finds consolation in its alarming financial state from its undoubtedly large serious international readership. One global league table of news websites puts the Daily Mail in 8th place, the Guardian in 10th and the BBC in 13th. Whether website visitors – especially the young – will continue to go to 'name' websites for their news is another matter, as is the long-term financial viability and editorial integrity of models so dependent on 'click-bait' advertising.

Given that all titles sell into one national market, they must differentiate themselves from each other by politics, social interest and format. Only two of the nine surviving national print dailies are reliably left-of-centre: the Guardian and the Daily Mirror. The others are all to a greater or lesser degree Eurosceptic, critical of immigration, in favour of free markets. The newspapers also differentiate socially: just a glance at each title will quickly reveal its appeal to 'AB' readers or to 'C1s and C2s'. This suggests one way of classifying Britain's titles: broadly speaking the tabloids offer large headlines and small articles, 'qualities' the reverse. This however is a less reliable distinction than it was since The Times (once the newspaper of record) and the Mail shifted from broadsheet to tabloid size and The Guardian adopted a unique format, the 'Berliner'. For all their vaunted sensationalism, UK tabloids are not comparable to US supermarket tabloids. They are openly partisan yet they still cover all the main serious news stories of the day. Each distinguishes itself from its rivals not by content so much as presentation.

UK tabloids are not comparable to US supermarket tabloids ... they still cover all the main serious news stories of the day

In-depth coverage of current affairs is also provided by the country's long-established political weeklies: The Spectator (established in 1828 and claiming to be the oldest continuously published magazine in the English language), The Economist (founded 1843, once edited by Walter Bagehot) and The New Statesman (founded in

1913). The fortnightly Private Eye, a satirical magazine focused on politics and with a strong investigative edge is the best political seller of all. But political content does not command general taste: generally, weeklies reflect consumer preferences. Of the top ten by circulation, four are supermarket magazines and three are TV listings publications. This makes them sensitive to shifting patterns: 'lads' mags' featuring (in their own words) 'the pursuit of sex, drink, football and less serious matters' were once best-sellers. Now they have mostly ceased publication, unable to compete with superior online products.

18.   From the cradle to the grave

The National Health Service (NHS) would probably make most people's list of top ten characteristically British institutions, bracketed with parliament, the BBC and the monarchy. It is younger than them, but old enough to have sheltered an entire generation to retirement age. For them, it is a unifying factor generalising the transmission of health care to almost the whole population. Such are folk memories of pre-NHS Britain – such indeed was the reality – that popular attachment to health care free at the point of use is fierce. Politicians of both parties have responded with hypothecated taxes to fund it, raising national insurance payments (2002) and legislating a sugar tax (2016). Yet health care is costly, ever more so in real terms, and governments seek economies. When, as is frequent, there are clashes between health practitioners and the government, the claim that 'privatisation' is planned is the most dangerous and urgent for politicians to defuse. Any extension of private health care provision is quickly attacked as a step on the road to care being paid for by the patient.

But if the idea of the NHS is politically secure, the continuity of its name and principles is deceptive. Its organisation, funding and reach have all changed

the claim that 'privatisation' is planned is the most dangerous and urgent for politicians to defuse

and not just once. It was never entirely national: there are significant variations in health care experience across the UK, and private health provision was never eliminated. The legitimate span of its activity shifts constantly. Towering above all else is its sheer cost. It is the second largest item in public spending, exceeded only by the welfare budget (and in some respects difficult to distinguish from it). At its 1948 launch, the NHS had a £437 million budget (roughly £9 billion today); the budget for the 2015-2016 financial year was around £115.4 billion. This is partly explained by a population that has grown by a third, but crucially the NHS does things undreamt-of in 1948: it bears the weight of widening public expectation. Yet the same public also funds it through taxes and taxation is never popular. With privatisation ruled out and health care demand spiralling, 21st century governments have turned to radical and structural reform to deliver savings.

The lifetime of the NHS bridges the transition of the population from scarcity to affluence. Today the UK health profile is that of a mainly prosperous urbanised country where 74 per cent of adults rate their health as 'good' or 'very good'. Life expectancy at birth has risen by three years every decade for a century. The average male lifespan is now 79, for females it is 83. The diseases that thrived on poverty are largely history: 84 per cent of all deaths are caused by non-communicable conditions; intentional and unintentional injuries only 4 per cent. Yet higher living standards bring their own ailments, and in some respects UK health care shows up badly. Heart disease, the single most important killer, accounts for almost one in five deaths: premature death from it is almost the highest in Western Europe. Mortality from respiratory diseases and cancer (28 per cent of the whole) shares this unenviable distinction. While smoking has fallen sharply, its legacy persists: male deaths from oesophageal cancer are Western Europe's highest, and second highest for women. The UK also records some of the highest rates of excess weight in Western Europe and rates of Type-2 diabetes are rising alarmingly.

Before the NHS

Popular attachment to the NHS feeds on memory, including folk memory, of earlier health care. Before 1948, provision was a patchwork quilt of voluntary agency, charitable and religious institutions with few national services. Hospitals and doctors charged. The most cost-efficient dental treatment was extraction: it eliminated future maintenance costs. Official concern about the health of the populace stretched back half a century to recruiters appalled at the

unfitness of many volunteers for the Boer War
(1899-1902). Official inquiries between the
world wars only confirmed that proper
health care provision was unaffordable
for most people and often done without. But as the Second World War ap-
proached, government anticipated mass
casualties from bombing raids, and re-
sorted to interventions like the National
Blood Service (1938). The unprecedented scale of wartime regulation of
civilian life accustomed the population
to intensive national organisation by
the state. By the time the war ended
belief in a national scheme, though not
entirely universal, was widespread. The
1942 Beveridge report, laying out plans
for a comprehensive system of social in-

*William Beveridge: health and wel-
fare from 'the cradle to the grave'*

surance that would provide security 'from the cradle to the grave', including a national health
service, was heralded as a blueprint for a
better post-war Britain. It provided the
basis for the establishment of the NHS by
the post-war Labour government.

Nevertheless, the NHS launched in
1948 by health minister Aneurin Bevan
did not have to take the form that it did.
Systems aspiring to be universal had existed
elsewhere in Europe, but this was the first
provision of completely free health care on
the basis of citizenship rather than the
payment of fees or insurance premi-
ums. The new service was based on
three core principles: that it meet the

*Aneurin (Nye) Bevan, Labour politician
from the South Wales valleys and
founder of the National Health Service
in the 1940s.*

needs of everyone; that it be free at
the point of delivery; that it be based
on clinical need, not ability to pay.

Consistent with these principles there were no charges anywhere in the service. To assemble a genuinely national service, Bevan cleverly absorbed all providers within a public framework, leaving family doctors (general practitioners or GPs) independent but staffing its gates. Access to the system came via referral from GPs (initially its most vehement opponents), a feature unchanged during the many reorganisations that followed.

NHS principles

One core NHS value was ruptured as early as 1952 to meet the costs of the Korean War. Savings for this were found by the introduction of prescription charges at one shilling (there were 20 shillings in £1). A flat rate of £1 for ordinary dental treatment was also brought in. Free prescriptions were restored in 1965, but only for three years before succumbing to new austerity measures. They have increased steadily since then and now contribute to NHS England at twice their former rate; in Scotland and in Wales, in contrast, they have been abolished, a cost which is borne mainly by English taxpayers. Even in England, they remain a flat rate charge: they do not vary with the cost of the drug, be it paracetamol or beta blocker. This breach of the free-of-charge principle is mitigated not only by the flat rate but by the great number of exemptions from the charge: the over-60s and the under-16s; 16-18 year olds in full-time education; pregnant and recent mothers; those with certain specified medical conditions; the severely physically disabled; disabled war pension recipients; NHS in-patients; and the recipients – or partners of recipients – of certain state benefits.

Excepting prescription charges, all NHS services remain free at the point of use

Excepting prescription charges, all NHS services remain free at the point of use including GP visits, hospitalisation and accident and emergency (A & E). The NHS adheres to other core principles by remaining clinically-driven and extensive, if not quite comprehensive. The NHS has never quite achieved universality of scope. Early on optical and dental treatment were treated separately: those resisting the 1952 charges railed against paying for 'false teeth and spectacles' (a slogan revealing how poorly-equipped were many post-war mouths), but over time their separation from the mainstream grew. Dental care is available 'on the NHS' (if it can be found) but patients pay at an itemised rate set by the Service. Optical care has long been largely in private hands.

A second contested boundary is that between health and social care. The tendency over recent decades has been to define the latter as a separate problem. However many, especially the older infirm, end up in NHS hospitals because of lack of care at home rather than any real clinical need, forcing the NHS to foot the bill. This is a problem that is escalating in line with the unrelenting rise in the number of old people living by themselves or with other old people too incapacitated to help them. Finally, a third area with blurred edges is palliative care: NHS hospices exist but are outnumbered by those in private or charitable hands.

Exceptions at the periphery cannot obscure the NHS's achievement in raising standards and expectations: far from being a backstop service for the poor, the NHS has been for decades the principal instrument for achieving landmark health improvements. The list is astonishing: mass polio and diphtheria vaccinations for under-15s (1958); organ transplants (from 1960); the contraceptive pill (by prescription for married women, 1961, universally in stages 1967-1974); hip replacements (1962), abortion (up to 28 weeks from 1967, now 24 weeks); heart transplants and fertility treatment (1968); IVF (1978); child bone marrow transplants (1979); MRIs and keyhole surgery (1980s); first AIDS health campaign (1986); the first liver, heart and lung transplant (1987); free breast screening for the over-50s (1988); the organ donor register (1994); NHS walk-in centres (2000); gene therapy (2002); bowel screening and meningitis vaccination for babies (2006); HPV vaccination for teenage girls (2008); the first hand transplant (2012). This trajectory – which includes global firsts – expresses the centrality of the NHS to greater longevity, falling mortality and a rising quality of life.

Put simply, the NHS has done ever more, steadily moving into areas beyond the imagining of its founders. Incurable conditions became operable; therapeutic efficacy widened; technical advances turned long hospital stays into short ones; prolonged operations sped up. A population growing accustomed to a rising standard of living and universal access imposed expectations and NHS staff wanted to respond. But more demand and activity swelled the budget, and this is the stuff of sensitive political differences when the population largely depends on socialised health care. Unsurprisingly, governments compelled to raise taxes or borrow to fund health began to demand greater efficiency. This spurred major structural changes in 1990, 2002, 2004 and 2011. In each the common element was a desire to emulate market behaviour within an essentially public service. But the public were not only concerned with savings and waste. They observed – or experienced – the impact of winter crises in the NHS and epidemics, and demanded improved performance. Periodically, fluctuating waiting lists have provoked public scandal. 2009 brought an emergency national inoculation campaign against swine flu. Now the influenza vaccine ('flu jab', annually changed to combat evolving strains) is given free on the NHS as an annual injection to those at risk: certain adults, toddlers and infants, all of 65 and over. The public expectation is that the NHS will do more and more but national resources are constrained.

the NHS has done ever more, steadily moving into areas beyond the imagining of its founders

Since privatisation is unacceptable, the 21st century solution has been imposition of a system of performance targets. Patients have a legal right to start non-emergency NHS consultant-led treatment within 18 weeks of referral by their GP, unless it is clinically appropriate to wait longer. In the case of suspected cancer there should be only a one month wait from diagnosis to first definitive treatment and not more than a two-month wait from urgent GP referral to first definitive treatment. Patients in A & E (entirely an NHS activity) should be seen within four hours of arrival, and so on. Monthly and quarterly statistics track NHS performance by area and provider against these and other targets, and these statistics are published with the intention of

Since privatisation is unacceptable, the 21st century solution has been ... performance targets

spurring better performance and promoting patient empowerment. Performance against target can reach 95 per cent or better but can also fall to the mid-80s. Targets are becoming more sophisticated, already embracing departmental performance and scheduled eventually to cover the record of individual surgeons.

Two changes led by the NHS have had an especial impact upon women. The extension of the right to free contraception in the late 1960s was not without controversy but quickly became unchallenged in the 1970s. Its social impact seems to have been greatest on women aged under 25. Buoyed by rapidly rising prosperity in the 1950s and 1960s there was a high rate of creation of young families which also had little access to reliable contraception: when the number of live births to women under 25 peaked in 1968 at 378,021 (England & Wales figures), it represented a remarkable 46.1 per cent of all births in that year. Thereafter the proportion of births to such younger women declined steadily. By 2013 there were only 148,855 births to women under 25, representing but 21.3 per cent of the total and little more than the numbers born to women 35 and over. The ability to choose when to give birth has certainly contributed to behavioural change: 94 per cent of women born in 1941 were married at 35 but only 60 per cent of women born in 1973 had married by that age.

Abortion is not a matter of partisan controversy in the UK. Opposition remains but its only success has been to restrict legal terminations after 24 weeks: 92 per cent of terminations are carried out before 13 weeks' gestation in any case. About 190,000 are carried out annually, 98 per cent of them funded by the NHS, though two-thirds were contracted out to the independent sector. However, the UK is far from united in this respect. The 1967 Abortion Act never embraced Northern Ireland: there a (pre-partition) law of 1861 still criminalises mothers seeking terminations. This is still not a partisan issue within the province but only because it has tended to be something on which influential voices on both sides of the sectarian divide have found common cause. Lack of access to terminations has had a huge impact on the lives of young women both north and south of the Irish border. Of 5,500 abortions annually for women resident outside England and Wales, over two-thirds were for

women from the Irish Republic and 15 per cent came from Northern Ireland.

The NHS today

The NHS is very large, treating one million patients every 36
hours. It is a famously large employer of 1.6 million, reputedly the
fifth largest employer in the world, after the US Defence Department, McDonalds, Walmart and the Chinese People's Liberation
Army. In 2014 it had 150,273 doctors,
377,191 qualified nursing staff, 155,960 **The NHS is ...**
qualified scientific, therapeutic and techni- **reputedly the fifth**
cal staff and 37,078 managers. Such num- **largest employer in**
bers may suggest a rigid monolith but it is **the world**
not so. First, the NHS is devolved to a considerable degree: each UK nation has its own service. Second, the
devolved administrations themselves are highly disaggregated,
principally into 'trusts' (clusters of health providers). And the NHS
since 1990 has operated with an 'internal market' configured to
have some parts of it 'purchasing' and others 'providing' health
care services. While structures and terminology have changed several times over the last quarter-century, the fundamental distinction
between purchasers and providers has endured.

England is the largest NHS national component. It emerged from
the 2013 reorganisation with the Department of Health (DH, embracing 23 agencies and public bodies) providing strategic leadership and funding for both health and social care. NHS England is
an independent body, at arm's length from government, whose
main role is to improve health outcomes. It in turn oversees clinical
commissioning groups (CCGs). CCGs are statutory clinically-led
NHS bodies which plan and commission local health care services.
They spend 60 per cent of the NHS budget, commissioning most
secondary care services including planned hospital care, rehabili-
tative care, urgent and emergency care (including out-of-hours),
most community health services, and mental health and learning
disability services. Since CCGs operate within the internal market,
they can commission any service provider that meets NHS stan-

dards and costs. These may be NHS hospitals, social enterprises, charities or private sector providers. Both NHS England and CCGs are legally obliged to involve patients, carers and the public in their commissioning decisions.

How efficient is it?

The success of a health care system can be measured in various ways. Based on the allocation of national resources the UK is a low spender: it manages to provide for the health of its population relatively cheaply. According to the OECD, expenditure on public and private health care in the UK in 2013 amounted to 8.5 per cent of GDP, ranking it 13th among 15 OECD countries in Western Europe, where most countries have various forms of social insurance-based schemes. Major European countries such as Germany and France with largely or partly insurance-based systems were spending around 11 per cent. The USA, with a largely private system just before the intro-duction of Affordable Health Care, exceeded 17 per cent. However, gross spending is not the only indicator. Thus, NHS England has fewer physicians or hospital beds per thousand inhabitants than most comparable Western European countries, perhaps implying more efficient turnaround of patients – or that patients are less likely to be treated properly or are sent home without as long to recover. In 2016 the NHS became embroiled in a prolonged and bitter dispute with junior doctors over 7-day working, suggesting productivity gains might have hit a ceil-

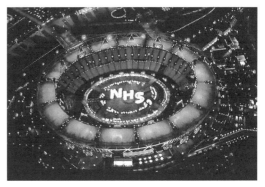

Celebration of the NHS at the London Olympic Games opening ceremony – but it meant nothing to most foreign viewers

ing at least with that notoriously overstretched element of the NHS workforce.

Another way to score the effectiveness of the health care system is by outcomes. In 2014 the US-based Commonwealth Fund compared the performance of eleven health care systems: Australia, Canada, France, Germany, the Netherlands, New Zealand, Norway, Sweden, Switzerland, the United Kingdom, and the United States. It ranked the UK first overall and first across a whole host of categories encompassing quality care (effective, safe, coordinated and patient-centred), access (cost-related problems) and efficiency. However, in specific areas the NHS showed up less well. In mortality amenable to health care, it ranked ninth, in infant mortality eighth and it was ninth for healthy life expectancy at age 60. In the Fund's 'Healthy Lives' category, Britain was placed 10th, ahead only of the bottom-ranked United States.

Given the dependence of almost everyone in the UK on the NHS, another valid comparison might be standards of health. Here the evidence is also not encouraging. In England unhealthy lifestyles abound. According to Public Health England (established in 2013 to 'protect and improve the nation's health and wellbeing, and reduce health inequalities') 40 per cent of deaths are related to lifestyle, causing the NHS to spend £11 billion annually. Three-quarters of men and two-thirds of women aged 45-64 are overweight or obese; 5 per cent of the heaviest drinkers consume nearly one-third of all alcohol; eight million adults – almost one in five – smoke. In Scotland the picture is even worse: life expectancy for both men and women is the lowest in Western Europe, dragged down by the biggest city Glasgow, which has the unhealthiest population in the UK. Prevention and early detection of illness is not a strength of the NHS, which is skewed to late interventions in hospitals rather than proactive health education and sophisticated primary care. The knife-wielding surgeon remains the iconic figure of British health care and most facilities for primary care – in GP surgeries – are rudimentary. Late diagnosis is considered a major cause

In England unhealthy lifestyles abound ... in Scotland the picture is even worse

of the UK's poor record in combating many cancers and other conditions where early detection can be vital.

Medicines

Visitors requiring health treatment may encounter unfamiliar clinical judgements on the efficacy of medicines. The rate of consumption of common pharmaceutical products such as hypertension drugs, anti-cholesterols and anti-depressants is highly variable among OECD countries, though the UK is often at the high end of the spectrum. The UK is home to major pharmaceutical companies (see chapter 20). Globally such firms control a great deal of research into new medicines and expect to receive an income that covers the cost of this highly expensive activity – as well as advertising and paying dividends to shareholders. In socialised health care this poses a major financial challenge since the taxpayer, ultimately, pays. The NHS is one of the world's largest buyers of drugs, paying about £14 billion annually, the bulk of it for branded products. In a remarkable reversal of the market the National Institute for Health and Clinical Excellence (NICE) recommends the price that should be paid for a given drug: government then negotiates the actual price with the company. Drug firms deny charges that they spend more on advertising than on research, but faced with the market power of such a large buyer have had to acquiesce in price-capping for the gross NHS drugs bill.

NICE was founded in 1999. It aims to get the most cost-effective and clinically-effective drugs and treatments widely available on the NHS, to speed up the introduction of good value treatments and promote successful innovation by clinicians, pharmaceutical companies and the medical devices industry. It added public health guidance to its role in 2005. NICE guidance is produced by health care professionals, NHS staff, patients and carers, members of the academic world, and other members of the wider health care and public health community. It must be taken into full consideration by health and social care professionals and organisations when making clinical decisions but is not designed to replace their knowledge and skills. Periodically it comes to public notice in a negative way, for example when it declines to fund the prescribing of a new drug. At such times there can be harrowing conflicts over an individual patient's belief in the efficacy of the drug and official advice that it does not represent value for money to the NHS. Such conflicts are unknown under private health care. However, NICE's role should not be confused with the licensing function: a separate agency ensures that medicines, health care products and medical equipment are safe and do what they are supposed to do.

The private sector

In 2012 the NHS spent £123 billion while private health care spending totalled £24 billion. The government share of total health spending rose from 79 per cent in 2000 to 83 per cent in 2013, one of the highest levels among OECD countries, comparable to that in the robustly socialised systems of Denmark, Norway and Sweden. It is in strong contrast to the United States where government provides less than 50 per cent. UK personal health spending is below 10 per cent of total health spending and falling. Private health care can be expensive, and a measurable difference in outcomes between the private and public health care sectors has not been demonstrated. If the results are the same, the incentive to opt for private care diminishes. The similar outcomes are partly due to the sharing of staff and also to the blurring of private/public boundaries. Private hospitals account for only 40 per cent of the 550 establishments with private hospital beds, so most private surgical and recuperative treatment occurs in NHS hospitals.

One estimate puts the number of UK residents with private health insurance at 5 million, 7 per cent of the population. However, a recent poll suggested many more would take it out if they could afford it. The private sector itself believes that one in six Britons will 'go private' at some point in their life, whether with insurance or not. This might include many non-acute treatments: vasectomies, contraception, foot care. Nevertheless, in acute care the experience can vary greatly between the highly individuated treatment of a private patient and an NHS patient cared for by hospitals that –

inter alia - have not yet achieved full single-sex care. UK private care is moreover close to being an on-demand service. In the NHS by contrast, waiting lists are one of the means whereby care is rationed. The list of most popular private surgery treatments is revealing: cataract surgery is much the most common, followed by hernia repair, hip replacement, shoulder surgery and knee replacement. And of course private treatment prevails in optical and dental care.

In the NHS ... waiting lists are one of the means whereby care is rationed

Will the NHS survive?

It has been said that the NHS is the nearest thing the British have to a national religion. The public values it and sets boundaries to political interference. Three million use it every single week. But dissatisfaction is growing and there is cause for concern. There have been major scandals at NHS hospitals. The Mid-Staffordshire Foundation Hospital Trust was broken up in 2014 after inquiries had disclosed an appalling catalogue of wilful neglect and box-ticking, especially in the care of older patients. After a probe led by NHS England's medical director into sustained failings in care quality and treatment at 14 trusts, eleven (covering 16 acute hospitals) were placed in special measures. There have been other scandals – including some in private care – and there is plenty of personal experience of neglect or even actual negligence. While every incident harms a real individual their number only gains true perspective against the background of the sheer size of the NHS.

Even when the service works well there may be cause for complaint. Despite major building programmes during the 21st century there are many hospitals with poor or dated design. An in-patient can be confronted with a large and noisy ward, the opposite of a quiet space. More than two decades after government first called for their abolition mixed-sex wards persist. And a socialised system cannot be free of conflicts between clinical judgements and public opinion. The former may favour in-patient treatment at specialist regional centres of excellence, and indeed these may be more cost-effective. But local opinion can quickly mobilise in defence of a local facility. When it does, local politicians have little choice but to rally to the defence of 'their' hospital; those who do not have been punished by the electorate. In a private system this is a commercial decision where public opinion lacks leverage.

In 2015 alarming data about in-patients' weekend mortality rates led government to promote '7-day working', precipitating a dispute with hospital clinicians below consultant level. Thus policy and working practices inevitably collide. This conflict is compounded by the inevitable impact of financial austerity on a public health service. Hemmed in, the NHS naturally trades on the global reputation of such famous providers as Great Ormond Street Children's Hospital or Moorfields, the specialist eye hospital. The private patient income of NHS hospitals has grown steadily since 2012 when a change in the law permitted them to earn 49 per cent of their income this way. It is financially attractive, but resources are scarce. The beneficiaries are mainly non-UK residents: sophisticated accounting procedures are needed to ensure the taxpayer is not subsidising them. Money has been tight for a decade: the NHS chief executive believes it needs a huge cash transfusion, rising to £8 billion annually by 2020. As we have seen, this would still leave it modestly funded compared to health care based on social insurance elsewhere.

Great Ormond Street Children's Hospital: one of the big London teaching hospitals drawing many overseas patients

19.   The law of the land

English and Welsh law consists largely of statutes (acts of the Westminster parliament). There may be no codified constitution but judges interpret these statutes, asking such questions as 'what did parliament intend when it made this law?'. They may seek guidance from earlier court cases, and possibly other statutes, and then rule. This ruling itself then becomes law: it creates a precedent. Collectively precedents are known as common law. Scotland now has its own parliament, but had in any case never given up its distinct legal system. Its court system is similar to England's but with significant differences in criminal, property and family law.

UK law divides between criminal and civil. Criminal law is intended to punish wrongdoers for offences against society and, if they are convicted, fines or imprisonment follow. Famously, criminality has to be established 'beyond a reasonable doubt'. By contrast civil law regulates relationships between individuals: actions begin when individuals or organisations sue others. But civil courts differ from criminal courts in requiring a balance to be struck. The outcome is not punishment but redress: the defendant who loses is liable for damages or an injunction. The whole paraphernalia of UK justice has a distinctive look: it has lately wrestled with weak performance and declining public esteem and responded in part with structural change. Nowhere is this truer than in the interface of law and politics.

Government and the law

The apex of English law was long the lord chancellor, secretary to medieval kings. Over the centuries the lord chancellor added new roles: head of the judiciary in England, Wales and Northern Ireland; appointments to the judiciary; cabinet member bound by collective responsibility: speaker of the House of Lords. The lord chancellor was part of all three branches of government – the executive, legislature and judiciary, something that would have been anathema under the Ameri can constitution. The defence of the

'Sitting on the woolsack' in the House of the Lords: the lord chancellor sat on this symbol of England's wealth from wool from the 14th century to 2006; it is now taken by the speaker of the Lords

blurring of roles was that judiciary and executive thereby understood each other's legitimate objectives; past lord chancellors had moreover fiercely defended their judicial independence against parliamentary intrusion. The objection was that executive and political activity was preoccupying incumbents. While the judiciary asserted its independence, this was not visible in the lord chancellor: his broad portfolio obscured it.

A 2005 act of parliament stripped the lord chancellor both of the speakership and headship of the judiciary, passing judicial appointments to a new Judicial Appointments Commission (JAC). The new 'secretary of state for justice and lord chancellor' thus became an entirely executive position. With a judicial background no longer required, the first non-lawyer in four centuries could be appointed. While the justice secretary runs courts, prisons, probation services and attendance centres, two other justice ministers – the 'law officers', attorney general and solicitor general – independently advise government, examine over-lenient sentences and oversee prosecuting authorities.

Since the 1980s, the decision to prosecute no longer rests with the police. An investigating officer could not be relied on to make a fair prosecuting decision and police forces applied varying standards allowing weak cases to arrive in court, and resulting in many judge-directed acquittals. The independent Crown Prosecution

Service (CPS, 1986) is now the principal England and Wales prosecuting authority for criminal cases investigated mainly by the police, border or national crime agencies. Crown prosecutors proceed if there is enough evidence to provide a 'realistic prospect of conviction' against each defendant on each charge. They then decide whether a prosecution is in the public interest.

CPS prosecutions have, however, attracted their own controversy. By 2016, dropped crown court prosecutions in England and Wales neared one in eight; prosecutions resulting in convictions dipped below 80 per cent. Often the CPS offered 'no evidence' in abandoned prosecutions. Since defendants protesting their innocence spent months awaiting trial in such cases, the criminal justice pendulum seemed to have swung too far away from the accused.

In Scotland the Crown Office and Procurator Fiscal Service (COPFS) has an extensive role reaching from prosecutions to seizing criminal proceeds, establishing the cause of sudden, unexplained or suspicious deaths and investigating criminal conduct allegations against police officers. However, it remains a Scottish government department, under the 'lord advocate', its ministerial head and the government's principal legal adviser, whose deputy is the solicitor general for Scotland. Criminal prosecution decisions and investigation of deaths are taken independently and mostly taken locally by a 'procurator fiscal'. Yet the lord advocate must remain impartial. In 1988 Pan Am flight 103 exploded over Lockerbie (southern Scotland). Prolonged American and Scottish investigations led to a Libyan being charged and convicted of mass murder, receiving a minimum 27 years' sentence. But some bereaved relatives doubted his guilt and disbelieved official accounts, forcing an (unsuccessful) review. In 2009 the Scottish justice minister returned the prisoner to continue his sentence in Libya on compassionate grounds, even though the lord advocate maintained the rightness of the prosecution and argued that Scottish courts had vindicated it. The justice minister's decision, dismaying to the US government, was a political, not a legal one.

The police

Modern policing began in London with Sir Robert Peel's Metropolitan Police Act of 1829. This established a full-time, professional and centrally-organised police force under his political control as home secretary. New uniformed constables gradually displaced the

scattered 18th century parish forces and within thirty years were required everywhere by law. Policing began from the top but there was ever a tension between local accountability and central government's desire for control. Nineteenth century government sought to harmonise policing standards by establishing county constabularies each with a 'chief constable'. In the 20th century town forces merged with county constabularies reducing their numbers.

Postage stamp commemorating Sir Robert Peel (1788-1850): his police force were nicknamed 'peelers' or 'bobbies' (Bobby being a diminutive of Robert)

The 21st century instrument of local accountability in England and Wales is the directly-elected police and crime commissioner (PCC). The 41 PCCs appoint and monitor the chief constables while respecting their operational independence. They set police and crime objectives and each force's budget and precept (a supplement to local tax). Fewer than 15 per cent of voters took part in the 2012 PCC elections but the incumbents rapidly asserted themselves. When the South Yorkshire chief constable was suspended by his PCC following the inquest into the 1989 Hillsborough football disaster he became the fourth to suffer this once-rare fate. Yet PCCs themselves are not beyond reproach and have faced ten investigations into allegations against them. The 2016 elections saw a somewhat more encouraging 26 per cent turnout with roughly equal numbers of those elected being affiliated to the two main parties. There were only three independents.

Peel's police force were the first professionals, embodying a new model for maintaining order. Their general instructions stipulated their duties: pre-

Peel's police force were the first professionals ... a new model for maintaining order

venting crime and disorder (the previous alternative was draconian – using the military); recognising that policing requires public willingness to observe the law; understanding that public co-operation diminishes inversely with physical force and compulsion, therefore using it only as a last resort; constantly demonstrating impartiality; readily offering individual sacrifice to protect and preserve life; signalling that the police are part of the public, doing full time what every citizen must; avoiding even seeming to usurp the powers of the judiciary; knowing that the absence of crime and disorder, not the visible evidence of police action, is the mark of police efficiency. From these principles sprang many distinctive characteristics of the British police: their singular uniforms, and especially headgear; the designation 'officer' for all ranks that confers status; their tradition of not carrying firearms; above all the convention that policing must be by consent.

Whether this traditional model can be sustained in modern conditions is moot. Though most police across the country are unarmed at all times, more police carry firearms than ever before, especially in London – a direct response to the threat of terrorism. Where arms are carried they are emphatically made visible, as any user of major transport hubs will affirm. British policemen have always had weapons of a sort. He – there were no policewomen until after World War I – originally carried a truncheon and over time added others. But until recently the public rarely saw police with guns. Uniforms are also changing, with some kit appearing more and more American. But the habit of terming police as officers has gone global, and the application of public consent has been extended into the composition of the force itself via significant shifts in minority ethnic and female participation, unlocked in part by relaxing physical entry standards. Of 127,000 police officers, some 28 per cent are female and 5.5 per cent of minority ethnic background. The need to maintain public consent also drove reluctance to introduce severe measures of crowd control such as water cannon. In Northern Ireland the police for decades had a quasi-military role, though since the Good Friday agreement (see chapter 5) a heavy emphasis has been placed on non-sectarian policing by consent.

London, Peel's inaugural policing model, was always exceptional. The dual function of the Metropolitan Police ('the Met') is to provide local policing and to protect the capital. London's 32,000 serving police officers amount to some 25 per cent of all police officers in England and Wales, meaning the capital has a significantly higher proportion of police to population than the country as a whole. The Met is headed by a commissioner accountable to the Greater London Authority (GLA). While the mayor of London (see chapter 8) acts as PCC, more detailed monitoring rests with the GLA police and crime panel. Commissioners are joint mayoral-government appointments.

the capital has a significantly higher proportion of police to population than the country as a whole

Outside London county constabularies continue with their executive heads termed chief constables. These forces have tended to amalgamate with the formation of bigger local government units, and are now accountable to PCCs. While county constabularies are an emblem of policing by consent, they face strong centripetal pressure. 2013 saw the establishment of a National Crime Agency in England and Wales to tackle criminals posing the highest risk. Its divisions ('commands') cover organised crime, border policing, economic crime and child protection, the national cyber crime unit and specialist capability teams. Scotland suggests one possible future: its eight regional forces have been replaced by Police Scotland, whose 17,400 officers comprise the UK's second-largest force after the Met but patrol an area of over 28,000 square miles. Not all in Scotland have been happy with such centralisation, however.

Her Majesty's Inspectorate of Constabulary (HMIC) has origins as far back as 1856 and is responsible for inspecting police forces in England and Wales, Scotland having a parallel system. HMIC independently assesses all forces and policing from neighbourhood teams to serious crime and prevention of terrorism. It found English and Welsh police forces 'good' or 'outstanding' on almost three-quarters of its criteria in 2015. But the general respect in which the police were held has subsided: affectionate references to 'the bobby on the beat' are no longer much heard. Symptomatically, the current prime minister, Theresa May, as home secretary more than once admonished the police in abrasive terms that home secretaries in previous times would never have contemplated. A general decline in deference combines with new operational modes: if today's bobbies are visible on patrol it is often in high speed cars. Citizens complain that the police fail to investigate some routine crimes with any energy, allowing persistent offenders to flourish; the police cite workload and ever more demanding administrative procedures. Criticism of the police was also stoked by a series of high profile misdemeanours including the work of under-cover police officers infiltrating radical groups (1980s-on), the handling of the Stephen Lawrence murder (1992-on, see chapter 12), the Rotherham child abuse scandal (1997-2013), corrupt collusion with the press in the phone-hacking scandal (2011, chapter 17) and a disproportionate number of black men dying unexplained deaths in custody. Such events cost the police their power to investigate complaints against themselves: this has passed to an Independent Police Complaints Commission (IPCC) that sets the standards for police handling of an initial complaint and now monitors PCCs as well. Its two weaker predecessors were not independent.

As with assessing crime trends however (see below), the relationship between appearance and reality is not straightforward. Greater criticism of the police does not necessarily mean that the police have got worse: on the contrary. The benign image of the bobby in previous times is not always shared by those familiar with police methods in the past. They cite slovenly investigation of crimes, especially against the uninfluential; indifference to some crimes, such as abuse of children; casual and undisguised racism; aggressive forms of interrogation that could force 'confessions' even out of the innocent; the rolling up of unsolved crimes in charges against petty criminals in order to improve clear-up rates; the receipt of back-handers from the press in return for stories. In that respect much has improved: chief constables have driven top-down reform and sought to raise standards of education, training and practice. Police forces are now willing to investigate their own in a way that was once rare. Sentimentality and hypocrisy once characterised political and media discussion of the police; that is no longer the case. However the efforts of the senior ranks to create a police force that is efficient, fair and honest come in an environment of public scrutiny that highlights failures as much as achievement.

Crime and punishment

Statistical problems bedevil the accurate measurement of crime. Crime survey figures suggested the number of crimes in England and Wales fell sharply in 2015 to 6.4 million, largely the result of fewer thefts and less criminal damage. But the police, in contrast, recorded a 7 per cent increase in crime to 4.4 million. Improved recording of crime by the police may explain the increased incidence of violent – and notably sexual – offences, with many at their highest-ever level. By contrast, much fraud does not come to police attention so incidence can seem low even though there is substantial evidence that fraud, especially via the internet is at high levels; and banks have undoubtedly been complicit in disguising card fraud for fear of unsettling customers. Reported levels of crime can be a measure of attitudes towards particular crimes as much as their actual incidence. A generation ago women often failed to report rape for fear of being accused of having brought it on themselves; and child victims of sexual abuse who dared to come forward faced disbelief and perhaps harsh physical punishment.

But despite the difficulty in assessing crime levels, it can be said that in one important respect the UK is in general a safe and largely law-abiding country: there is a low risk of facing physical violence. UN statistics show that the homicide rate of 0.9 per 100,000 people is much the same as in other Western European countries such *the chance of a visitor from* as Spain and the Netherlands *abroad being murdered is* (0.7), Italy (0.8), Germany and *vanishingly low* Sweden (0.9), Ireland (1.1) and France (1.2). This compares with the figure of 3.9 for the USA. As most murders in the UK are committed by people closely related to the victim, the chance of a visitor from abroad being murdered is vanishingly low. Likewise while burglaries are relatively common, street robberies are not, at least in most places.

The death penalty (usually applied by hanging) was temporarily suspended in 1965, one year after the last execution and abolished four years later. One factor was increasing anxiety among jurors in murder cases about the consequences of handing down a guilty verdict: cases were publicised where later evidence showed the wrong man had been hanged. (Technically the death penalty remained available for a curious mix of offences until various dates as late as 1998, including treason, setting fire to a naval dockyard, and piracy with violence, though no one was ever executed under these extensions.) Parliament regularly debated calls for restoration until 1997, but demands to 'bring back hanging' faded away as public opinion, for many years strongly at odds with what parliament had decided, came in time to approve of what parliament had done – a striking illustration of the point made in earlier chapters that the UK has by long tradition been a representative, parliamentary democracy not one governed by referenda, a principle much undermined in recent years.

The aims of a prison sentence have always been seen as threefold: to punish offenders, to prevent them from committing other crimes, and to reform and rehabilitate them. However the emphasis given to the three different elements has varied greatly over time, in response in part to criminological research but more often to public opinion and the vagaries of politics. However, one fact stands out: the number of people in prison is more than twice what it was in the early 1990s (and eight or nine times the level of the 1930s) despite there having been no such dramatic increase in criminality. More people are jailed, sentences are longer, and the range of offences for which people are incarcerated is wide, including many offences, such as in relation to drugs, where the only real victim is the offender. In 2016 there were over 95,000 in UK prisons – 20,000 more than in France, with a similar population, and 30,000 more than in Germany, with a population more than a quarter larger.

Michael Howard: as home secretary in 1993 he famously declared that 'prison works': prisoner numbers have since doubled

Public opinion – mediated via politicians and a salacious press – has undoubtedly contributed to severe sentencing, partly by restricting the freedom of the judiciary to impose more lenient sentences. Being tough on crime is always a good headline for a politician and it can sometimes be used for cynical advantage. A number of offences lead to a minimum fixed-term custodial sentence in any case and an independent Sentencing Council issues guidelines which the courts must follow unless it is in the interests of justice not to do so. The attorney general even has powers – in very serious cases – to review inappropriately low crown court sentences. In imposing a sentence judges must weigh the seriousness of the crime, harm to the victim, the offender's level of blame, their criminal record, their personal circumstances and whether they have pleaded guilty.

As prisoner numbers have risen, the pressure on prisons (133 in England and Wales; 15 in Scotland) has likewise increased. Her Majesty's Inspectorate of Prisons for England and Wales (HMIP) has issued a series of damning reports on the country's ageing prison estate. Prisons built in Victorian times to Victorian standards – a time when millions lived in cramped and squalid condtions – are packed with numbers of prisoners far beyond what the Victorians themselves intended. Some institutions with exceptionally primitive facilities are scheduled to close and nine new establishments are promised, but new buildings will not alter the prison regime itself. Many of the incarcerated are held on remand, including those charged with a serious crime, convicted of a serious crime in the past, unlikely to attend court, likely to commit another crime while on bail and previous bail offenders. While punishment and 'keeping criminals off the streets' are achieved, the third goal of reform and rehabilitation has fallen away as a shrinking prison workforce has struggled to cope with a rising (and increasingly discontented) prison

Reading Gaol, where Oscar Wilde was incarcerated in the 1890s. It closed as a prison in 2013

population. More than a quarter of all convicted of crimes reoffend but the proportion rises to almost half of those recently released from prison.

Lawyers

The costume drama of an English trial, especially in London's famous Central Criminal Court (the 'Old Bailey'), is famous: the judge in full bottom wig (100 per cent horsehair and completely hand-made over about three months), flowing black, scarlet or violet robes and regalia; counsel (trial lawyers) in less ornate but still florid barrister wigs with black gown and white tie-on bands (collarettes for lady barristers). A 2008 savings-driven reform put paid to much of this: many judges now shun wigs, wing collars and bands, especially in civil and family proceedings, preferring a new civil robe though circuit judges may still appear in traditional gowns minus the rest. But barristers, given the chance to dispense with their wigs, elected to keep them, and a judge may yet cut a colourful figure in a senior court; even in other courts he will still be distinguished by a brilliant sash.

The costume drama of an English trial ... is famous

England and Wales have two categories of lawyer. Barristers are specialist legal advisers and court room advocates: independent, objective and trained to advise clients on the strengths and weaknesses of their case. Their specialist knowledge in and out of court can make a substantial difference to the outcome; even when civil cases are settled by negotiations out of court, a barrister may still be involved. A limited number of senior and able barristers become queen's counsel (QCs), eligible to prosecute for the crown; they are said to 'take silk' because QCs may wear black silk court gowns. They are instructed only in very serious or complex cases. Most senior judges

English judges confer

are former QCs. In Scotland barristers are styled advocates and their Faculty of Advocates, like the English Bar Council, is independent of the state. They may also progress to QC.

QCs seem stubbornly white and male: out of about 1,600, only 250 are female and barely 100 are from minority ethnic groups. Given the normal pattern of progression to the judiciary this is relevant to the composition of the bench. However, the numbers 'called to the bar' (becoming eligible to represent a client in court) now show male/female parity and the ethnic minority proportion is rising fast. Since some will become QCs the situation should change. There are over 12,000 barristers in self-employed practice in England and Wales, covering all aspects of the law, some retained by government or industry. Employed or self-employed, the bar remains predominantly a referral profession, with barristers usually 'instructed' by solicitors.

Solicitors – the lawyers on the high street – provide general legal support and advice to clients and, if a case is to go to a senior court, will typically brief the barrister who acts there. Solicitors see themselves as confidential advisers with direct client contact about property transactions, wills, and relationship breakdown; the legal side of commercial transactions; personal rights against public or private bodies; community support via legal aid work for those unable to pay. They represent clients personally in magistrates' courts, county courts and tribunals and exceptionally at the crown court, High Court, Court of Appeal or even the Supreme Court. The ability of citizens to gain access to the law has become a matter of controversy. Legal aid was established in 1949, but as society became more litigious so the legal aid budget increased incrementally. A 1999 act of parliament streamlined administration but failed to curb costs and so in 2013 entitlement to legal support (now administered by a legal aid agency) was withdrawn, except in very limited circumstances, for those involved in divorce, child contact, welfare benefits, employment, clinical negligence, and housing law cases.

The courts

For historical reasons the United Kingdom has several separate jurisdictions: one apiece for England and Wales, Scotland, and Northern Ireland. In most cases, the Supreme Court is now the final court of appeal for all civil cases, and criminal cases from England, Wales and Northern Ireland. It hears appeals over points of law, concentrates on cases of the greatest public and constitutional importance and maintains and develops a leading role in the common law world (i.e. those nations, including the USA, which still use it).

Below the Supreme Court are 500 courts and tribunals. English and Welsh criminal cases start in a magistrates' court without a jury. This level of court normally handles 'summary offences' – motoring, minor criminal damage, or being drunk and disorderly. Punishments available to magistrates include up to six months' imprisonment, fines up to £5,000, or a community sentence. Substantial crime (burglary, drugs) may also start at magistrates'

The Royal Courts of Justice in the Strand, London, seat of the High Court and Court of Appeal

court but the most serious crimes (murder, rape, robbery) will be passed up to the crown court: it is nominally referred to as one court though it sits in dozens of places across the country, the most famous being the Old Bailey, the Central Criminal Court of England & Wales which may hear particularly serious cases from all over the country. The crown court will normally have a jury – to determine guilt – and a judge to set the sentence. Crown court sentences range from community service to prison sentences including life. Appeals from the crown court may go to the High Court, the Court of Appeal and the Supreme Court. The High Court and the Court of Appeal of England & Wales are located at the Royal Courts of

Justice in London, though High Court proceedings are also heard at registries around the country. Civil cases can come before magistrates or the county court with appeals to the High Court and Court of Appeal.

Tribunals aim to provide a less costly and more responsive justice system, especially to consumers in debt or with other disputes, people involved in the adoption or protection of children, businesses in commercial disputes, individuals asserting their employment rights or challenging the decisions of government bodies and people affected by relationship breakdown. This system has its own structure for dealing with cases and appeals, though an occasional decision may also go to the Court of Appeal. Tribunals are active in all parts of the UK. Their range is wide, covering employment, immigration, criminal injuries, social security and child support, war pensions and armed forces compensation, victims and witnesses of crime.

At the apex of the legal system stands the Supreme Court. Its name invites comparison with the United States Supreme Court but

At the apex ... stands the Supreme Court, an entirely new institution

it is a very different institution, newly created and grafted onto a venerable legal system. Final right of appeal in UK law once rested with the lords appellate of the House of Lords (the 'law lords'), originating in a court that once advised the sovereign, passed laws and dispensed justice at the highest level. By the 21st century, these law lords had become a small group of very senior judges within the upper house. Now the Supreme Court, situated in the Middlesex Guildhall on Parliament Square, signals a complete and visible separation from parliament, underlines its independence and increases transparency of the relationship between parliament and the courts.

Entry to the (then) EEC in 1973 opened a controversial process of access for UK litigants to Community law. In time the law lords were partially eclipsed by the European Court of Justice (ECJ) as final court of appeal. The 1998 Human Rights Act brought the European Convention on Human Rights (ECHR) into UK law. Individuals may now challenge a public authority decision on rights grounds in a British court: previously, individuals had to approach the European Court of Human Rights in Strasbourg directly. A UK court must determine if existing legislation is compatible with the ECHR; if it cannot it will issue a 'declaration of incompatibility'. This places no legal obligation on parliament to amend or repeal legislation, but sends a clear message to legislators to change the law and make it compatible with human rights. The European Court of Human Rights is not part of the European Union and is unconnected with the ECJ.

Scotland has a supreme civil court, the Court of Session, that sits both as a court of first instance and a court of appeal. Scotland's equivalent of magistrates' courts is justice of the peace (JP) courts. A JP is a lay magistrate, appointed from within the local community and trained in criminal law and procedure to try less serious summary crimes: speeding, careless driving and breach of the peace. Most cases move up to Scotland's sheriff courts unless they are sufficiently serious to go straight to the Court of Session. In criminal cases a jury sits, but in civil cases the judge sits alone.

Judges and juries

For more than three centuries, judges have been appointed on the expectation that they will function freely, exercising their judicial powers without interference from litigants, the state, the media or powerful individuals or organisations. Theory requires judges to make their decisions on the basis of the facts of the case and the law alone. Apart from the jury (if there is one) no-one else hears the entire proceedings of any single trial; no-one is better qualified to comment on their legal implications. By convention politicians do not comment concurrently on court proceedings; attempts to persuade the press to be equally self-disciplined have been less successful. Judges are appointed by the Judicial Appointments Commission (JAC); they serve until the age of 70 and cannot be removed while on good behaviour, a device to maintain and strengthen judicial independence. Taking appointments away from the lord chancellor rendered an opaque process transparent, for the JAC visibly selects on merit, through open competition, from

MAGNA CARTA, 1215 ~ FOUNDATION OF LIBERTY

Postage stamp celebrating Magna Carta, signed at Runnymede, near Windsor in 1215: it influenced the American constitution

the widest range of eligible candidates in English and Welsh courts and tribunals, as well as for some tribunals with jurisdiction in Scotland or Northern Ireland.

Magna Carta (1215), a sort of charter of fundamental rights forced from King John by his barons, famously declared:

> 'No free man shall be seized or imprisoned, or stripped of his rights or possessions, or outlawed or exiled; nor will we proceed with force against him except by the lawful judgement of his equals or by the law of the land. To no one will we sell, to no one deny or delay right or justice.'

This ancient charter, though framed for very different times and purposes, has always been cited as the first codification of basic English freedoms, not least the right to a trial by jury. Each year, nearly 180,000 English and Welsh citizens aged 18 to 75 undertake jury service for ten or more working days, their names drawn randomly from the electoral register. The first women jurors sat in 1919, once they could vote, illustrating the strong linkage of citizenship to duties under the criminal justice system.

English juries played a remarkable role in defending individual rights against the executive

Some accounts date juries to Anglo-Saxon practice before 1066. After that, and certainly following Magna Carta, their distinct function was to resolve points of law. While a noble might be tried 'by his peers' the right of commoners to demand it emerges only in the 17th century, by which time other forms of determining guilt (trial by ordeal, trial by combat) had lapsed. After this English juries played a remarkable role in defending individual rights against the executive. Acquittal of the 'Seven Bishops' (1688) in a libel trial precipitated the Glorious Revolution; the throwing out of treason charges against Hardy, Horne Tooke and Thelwall (1794) checked Pittite repression for a while. In 2013 the attorney-general remarked: 'The right of the jury to return the verdict it collectively believes is the true one is inalienable ... do we want a legal system in which the jury can return a verdict which seems to us to fly in the face of the evidence? My answer is yes...'

For centuries juries were required to bring in a unanimous verdict to secure a conviction but in England and Wales majority verdicts of 10 to 2 are now allowed (and in Scottish criminal cases, where there are juries of 15, only a simple majority is required). Juries generally sit only in criminal cases. Certain kinds of inquests (deaths in police or prison custody, railway or air accidents, workplace deaths) require the coroner to sit with a jury and it decides the verdict. Such were the inquests into the deaths of Princess Diana (2008) and of 96 Liverpool fans at Hillsborough football ground (2016) which returned a verdict of unlawful killing. Serious trials without juries are rare but complex fraud trials may dispense with them if tampering is feared, and Northern Ireland saw over 300 non-jury trials a year (in 'Diplock' courts) during the emergency for fear of witness intimidation by paramilitaries.

Public inquiries

The judiciary impinges on public consciousness in one other way. Recent decades witnessed a number of high-profile public inquiries into miscarriages of justice or malfeasance by agencies of the state, each chaired by an experienced and senior judge.

Such inquiries can take several forms. One is the independent judicial inquiry such as the Denning inquiry into the 1960s Profumo affair, the Scott inquiry into arms-for-Iraq (1992) and Lord Hutton's inquiry (2004) into the circumstances surrounding the apparent suicide of a weapons scientist during the Iraq War. But such bodies lack the powers to require witnesses to give evidence on oath: by contrast, a tribunal of inquiry with full judicial powers offers the advantage that justice is more likely to be 'seen to be done'. However, the Vassall tribunal (1963) – concerning a naval espionage scandal – led to journalists being called as witnesses and two of them being jailed for refusing to reveal their sources. In 1972, the government rapidly announced an inquiry under Lord Chief Justice

Widgery into the shootings on 'Bloody Sunday' (see chapter 5). It exonerated the army and suggested many victims had been handling weapons, polarising opinion further. After prolonged pressure a fresh (Saville) public tribunal of inquiry was conceded. It took no less than 12 years to lay responsibility on the army. The Chilcott inquiry provides a further variant: a committee of privy counsellors. Set up in 2009 it took seven years to consider the run-up to, military action in and aftermath of conflict in Iraq (see chapter 10).

20.   Science superpower

Science and engineering suffuse UK history: it has for centuries been an inventive country. Science originally meant physical science: the study of inanimate natural objects through physics, chemistry, astronomy; in modern times some of the most dramatic advances are being made in life sciences (the study of living organisms – biology, botany, zoology, biochemistry). The 17th century beginnings of the Royal Society and the openness of Cambridge University to experiment in the natural sciences helped power the scientific revolution, as did the availability of finance for industrial innovation; the agricultural and industrial revolutions that were the result shaped not only Britain's course but that of the modern world. Such achievements established a remarkable tradition of scientific inquiry that outlived loss of premier industrial status and broke fresh ground in the new sciences of the 20th and 21st centuries. A government minister put it well: 'Britain has been a science superpower since the dawn of the Enlightenment'. An appendix at the end of this chapter provides a list illustrating the diversity of British inventions.

The strength of the UK university sector in science cannot be disputed. The 16 per cent share of science majors among graduates is double that of the United States (and indeed the OECD average); no fewer than one-third progress to doctoral level. The UK ranks second only to the USA for the quality of its scientific research institutions and fourth for university-industry collaboration. It came third in the 2016 Global Innovation Index published by INSEAD and the World Intellectual Property Organization (behind Switzerland and Sweden and ahead of the USA in fourth place).

'Britain has been a science superpower since the dawn of the Enlightenment'

The 2016 Brain Prize was won for the first time by an entirely UK team of neuroscientists. Earlier British winners included geneticist Karen Steel (King's College London, for work on deafness) and Trevor Robbins (Cambridge, psychology). In 2014 the new Breakthrough Prize (labelled the world's biggest science award) went to five mathematicians, two of them British. UK winners of the Nobel Prize, perhaps the most prestigious of all science awards, include 80 in physics, chemistry, physiology or medicine – more than any country except the USA. A 2015 British Council analysis of Nobel Prize winners revealed that 38 per cent of laureates who had studied abroad, had done so in the UK – more than in any other country.

The UK undoubtedly still punches above its weight in science and innovation. Yet the country has long been seen as much poorer at converting ideas into successful large-scale applications. Few sectors illustrate this enduring weakness better than computers. In 1983 UK ownership of personal computers (at one in ten homes) was the highest in the world and there were several home-based manufacturers including Sinclair Research. By 2016, however, few Britons used home-produced hardware or software: software originated in the USA was run on computers built in Asia. Similarly, despite government support, no strong new UK biotechnology companies have emerged to compete on a global scale (though the country remains home to two well-established national champions). There have been many start-ups, but they tend quickly to fall into the hands of predatory multi-nationals.

Scientific breakthoughs are made in the UK, but their further development ... has often left these shores

This has been seen across many sectors for many years. Scientific breakthoughs are made in the UK, but their further development, especially their industrial application, has often left these shores. Because of the size of its economy, the UK is in absolute terms a major investor in R&D, ranked 8th in the world. However, the level of investment in R&D lags behind comparable advanced economies and has long done so, with cumulative effects. According to the Office for National Statistics (ONS), total R&D expenditure in the UK in 2014 represented 1.67 per cent of gross domestic product (GDP). This was below the EU average. On this measure Britain ranked well behind the Scandinavian countries (at around 3 per cent) and the other two major EU economies, Germany and France, and was for the most part ahead only of poorer Southern and Eastern European countries. It was also well below key non-European economies such as the USA and Japan and indeed even China.

R&D spend in the three Northern English regions ... totalled only £4.42 billion

The ONS figures also illustrate how the regional distribution of R&D spend reflects the variations within the UK explored in earlier chapters, especially England (see chapter 4). Of the £30.6 billion spent on R&D in the UK as a whole in 2014, £16.09 billion – more than half – was in just three regions, London, the South East and East of England. In contrast R&D spend in the three Northern English regions of North West, North East and Yorkshire & Humber, regions where many of the great advances of the industrial revolution took place, totalled only £4.42 billion between them.

This regional distribution reflects the proliferation of high-tech, R&D-focused and internationalised sectors in the areas of the country closest to London's financial markets, Heathrow airport's global transport hub, and pools of scientific expertise in key universities. The advantage is reinforced by the tendency of firms in such sectors to cluster together, whether in university science parks, along the M4 motorway, or in the capital. Older industries with low levels of technological innovation are disproportionately found in the North, often scattered around declining towns with a low skills base. The level of investment in R&D, commonly backed by local banks, in smaller technology-based manufacturing companies in provincial Germany is rarely matched in Britain. While the UK continues to score successes in some cutting-edge sectors, its R&D in less glamorous areas of science and technology has not always been to the fore: thus in the global $81 billion machine tool industry, for instance, Germany ranks second only to China; Britain now barely figures, despite having long been the world leader, its tools once used to make things in every corner of the globe.

Of UK R&D in 2014, 65% was carried out by business, 26% by academic higher education, 7% by government and research councils and 2% by private non-profit organsations. Business was the dominant contributor in all but two regions: London and Scotland, where the higher education sector led, reflecting the strength of their universities. The biggest areas of business R&D (in descending order) were pharmaceuticals, information technology, the motor vehicle industry, aerospace, and telecommunications. These are all areas in which multinational companies, with a global perspective on R&D and appetite to make use of British scientific talent, tend to dominate.

Why a gap exists between scientific invention and further development has long been a matter of speculation. Lack of access to funding can hardly be an adequate explanation given London's pre-eminence in world financial markets, though short-term horizons among investors are sometimes blamed. The UK has lower labour costs than some competitor nations (and, with immigration, a relatively plentiful labour supply) and this has likely been a factor discouraging technological innovation in some industries: the resultant low productivity has been balanced by low wages.

However, explanations may also be found in some distinctive characteristics of British culture. Industry and business, especially manufacturing industry, has long been viewed with a degree of disdain among the political, educational and cultural elite. This phenomenon, discussed since at least the 1950s, has perhaps an echo from the industrial revolution, when the application of science to productive purpose became forever associated with self-made men from the North while more esteemed wealth was that which flowed from land, property and the empire. From Labour leader (and soon to be prime minister) Harold Wilson calling in 1963 for a 'new Britain' to be forged in 'the white heat' of technology to recent chancellor George Osborne urging a 'march of the makers' a few politicians have sought to correct this imbalance, but with only limited results.

The state and science

The 20th century saw an enormous growth in the reach and responsibilities of the state. In two great world conflicts the state committed itself to total war, hugely boosting weapons research. The approach to (and experience of) World War I brought the submarine, the mine, the 'all big gun' battleship, the tank, the development of the aeroplane and the invention of the aircraft carrier. The approach to and experience of the Second World War brought asdic, radar, code-breaking, the jet engine and (partly through British efforts) the atomic bomb. Both wars created a demand for volume chemicals of which one fruit was the formation of the giant scientific innovator Imperial Chemical Industries (ICI) in 1926, the biggest manufacturing company in Britain in its heyday but now broken up. After 1945, the colossal new military and industrial complex in the United States overshadowed British military science. However, ensuing decades demonstrated that scientific energy could be diverted to peaceful and profitable purposes: civil, not military aviation; life science, not chemical warfare.

Government policy-making in science is today assisted by the Government Office for Science, headed by the chief scientific adviser. An independent Council for Science and Technology provides high level advice directly to the prime minister. Its 2015-2016 priorities included supporting national growth and increasing UK productivity by linking science, innovation and industrial enterprise; boosting regional growth by building on existing science and innovation activity; using technology to develop modern and cheaper public services; preventing or addressing emergencies, and mapping national security risks.

Government sponsors science through the Department for Business, Energy and Industrial Strategy (BEIS), the product of a 2016 merger of the Business department with that for Energy and Climate Change. Since 2007, the Business department has committed over £3 billion in capital funding to major science projects and planned a further £6 billion from 2016-2021. Its targets are oceanographic research ships, supercomputers, research institutes and UK participation in international programmes such as the European Space Agency. A government agency, Innovate UK, seeks to help correct Britain's historic failure to convert discoveries to profitable production, supporting business-led innovation. But BEIS also funds pure science, channelling funds through seven research councils and the Higher Education Funding Council for England (HEFCE) spanning the medical and biological sciences, astronomy, physics, chemistry and engineering, social sciences, economics, environmental sciences, arts and humanities. The Medical Research Council alone committed more than £3 billion to research in 2015.

EEC entry in 1973 opened new horizons. The strong UK science base benefited from the EU's practice of directing funding towards excellence rather than a proportional distribution. At 15.4 per cent its share of Horizon 2020 (science) research funding was exceeded only by Germany's: the first four universities by participation in research funding were all British. In 2007-2013, science research funding from EU sources doubled. It now amounts to nearly a tenth of university research funding with a further €1.6 billion committed from EU structural and investment funds up to 2020.

British science has become increasingly international: about half of its research publications now involve cross-border collaboration. It is a leader in Europe's big intergovernmental research organisations. The three biggest – the European Space Agency, the European Southern Observatory and Cern (which runs the Large Hadron Collider) – are all separate legal entities to the EU, so the UK role should outlive Brexit. Nevertheless, many universities have expressed anxiety that withdrawal from the EU will imperil both their funding flow and the UK residence rights of the many EU nationals among their scientific staff. Some British scientists fear the country's 'science superpower' status is at stake. But Scientists for Britain, a pro-Brexit group, has argued that access to Horizon 2020 funding could be maintained and that low national funding of science would be boosted after withdrawal. It has further been argued that the EU over-regulates and that this operates as a restraint on research in clinical trials as well as on stem cell research. Other areas that might prefer a more light-touch regime would be the application of GM crops, vaccines or genomics.

Some British scientists fear the country's 'science superpower' status is at stake

Beyond government

Though the Royal Society has received government grants since the 19th century it remains independent. It was founded in November 1660 – six months after the restoration of the monarchy in the person of Charles II – as a learned society gathering leading polymaths (Christopher Wren, Robert Boyle, John Wilkins) and in 1663 it became 'The Royal Society of London for Improving Natural Knowledge'. The Royal Society was determined to withstand the domination of authority, above all to verify factually all statements by experiment. It emerged in the late 17th century up-surge of innovation and freer inquiry in many areas of the arts, science and

The young Isaac Newton (1643-1727). He was president of the Royal Society from 1703 to 1727

commerce (as also seen in the creation of London's financial institutions) that followed the restoration of a constitutionally restrained monarchy in 1660: political absolutism, the 'divine right of kings', had been ended with the execution of Charles I in 1649; so too the zealous theological fundamentalism of the puritans with the end of the rule of the army.

The Royal Society has played a part in some of the most important discoveries in scientific history and its scientists continue to make outstanding contributions in many research areas. Among its 8,000 fellows are to be found many of the leading scientific lights of the past four centuries, among them Newton, Darwin, Einstein, Dawkins, Hawking and Tim Berners-Lee. It is now one of four independent (but much newer) 'national academies' promoting cultural endeavour: the British Academy (for social science), the Academy of Medical Sciences, and the Royal Academy of Engineering. There are also various other societies with royal charters in specialised scientific areas such as the Royal Society of Medicine (founded in 1805), the Royal Astronomical Society (1820) and the Royal Society of Chemistry (1980).

The Academy of Medical Sciences (founded 1998) represents the diversity of medical science. Its 1,200 elected fellows work in fundamental biological sciences, clinical academic medicine, public and population health, health technology implementation, veterinary science, dentistry, medical and nursing care and other professions allied to medical science. An integral part of the UK's strong biomedical research community, it collaborates with funders, medical research charities, the NHS and the private health sector. What is now the British Science Association (BSA) dates from 1831 when the British Association for the Advancement of Science was founded amid concerns over the faltering impetus behind scientific inquiry. Over time its emphasis shifted: once a forum for the exchange of scientific findings it now works towards disseminating knowledge of the importance of science throughout society. Another famous institution with a similar aim is the Science Museum. It too has lineage: it opened in 1857 as part of the 'South Kensington Museum' inspired by the Great Exhibition.

'Stephenson's Rocket' at the Science Museum: the most famous of all early steam locomotives

Britain's universities stand alongside the Royal Society, engineering and medical science academies and the BSA in pure science. London University's Imperial, King's and University colleges, Glasgow and Bristol are eminent in science as are Loughborough and Imperial in engineering. In addition to Imperial College, which was 8th among world universities in the 2016-2017 THES World University rankings, two stand out: Cambridge and Manchester.

Cambridge University, with 48 Nobel laureates mostly in science, has a history reading like the history of science itself: intellectual home to William Harvey (circulation of the blood), John Flamsteed (astronomy) and Isaac Newton (mathematics and physics) in the 17th century; Charles Babbage (inventor of the 'difference machine', an early computer forerunner), Charles Darwin (natural science), James Clerk Maxwell and J. J. Thomson (physics) as well as opening the Cavendish Laboratory in the 19th. In the 20th century,

> *Cambridge University, with 48 Nobel laureates ... has a history reading like the history of science itself*

Cambridge was the setting for numerous advances in quantum theory and nuclear science, the discovery of DNA, the discovery of pulsars and pioneering work on monoclonal antibodies.

Cambridge scientists work in a university with medieval origins. Manchester in contrast was the world's first modern industrial city and its university reflects its character. It has produced 22 science Nobel laureates. Distinguished scientists on its staff include (in the 19th century) T.H. Huxley, biologist and science educationist; (in the 20th) Ernest Rutherford, pioneer of nuclear physics and Alan Turing, mathematician, computer scientist and codebreaker; and (in the 21st) Andre Geim and Kostya Novoselov who in 2004 isolated graphene for the first time. That same year it merged with the neighbouring Institute of Science and Technology to form Britain's largest university. The university's Jodrell Bank Centre for Astrophysics comprises research activities in astronomy and astrophysics, the world leading facilities of the Jodrell Bank Observatory, the e-MERLIN/VLBI National Facility and hosts the Square Kilometre Array Organisation. Manchester was the European City of Science 2016.

New Zealand-born Ernest Rutherford (1871-1937), the 'father of nuclear physics'

The third great funding source for scientific research is the charity sector, above all in the field of medical research. UK charities invested over £1.3 billion in 2013 – more than one-third of publicly-funded research. Three charities stand out. The Wellcome Trust, created originally to administer the fortune left by pharmaceuticals magnate Henry Wellcome, has a fund of £20.9 billion for research, supporting programmes in many countries as well as the UK and with current plans to disburse around £1 billion per annum. It is reported to be the second-biggest private funder of medical research in the world after the Bill & Melinda Gates Foundation. The biggest science funder among voluntary charities is Cancer Research UK: it spent over £340 million on research in 2014-2015. The British Heart Foundation funds over £100 million of research annually and there is in addition a host of smaller charities that contribute to specific medical research causes.

Life sciences and the digital economy

Industrial development is also soaked in science. In post-industrial times two science-based industries stand out: life sciences and the digital economy.

UK life sciences (sciences concerned with the study of living organisms and, by extension, their application) are among the world's strongest and most productive, claimed to generate a turnover in excess of £50 billion. The sector's 5,000 companies (including non-manufacturing and service companies) employ over 180,000 people. The industry is high-tech, innovative and highly diverse, spanning pharmaceuticals, medical technology (devices and diagnostics) and medical biotechnology, but with applications elsewhere across the economy.

The success of the life sciences sector illustrates the close interaction of universities and industry. London, Oxford and Cambridge are sometimes described as a 'golden triangle' of elite research universities that have key companies working alongside: about half the UK's life sciences jobs are in this golden triangle.

For all this domestic activity, the sector cannot function on a purely national basis. Today, via the Wellcome Sanger Institute, the UK remains a major participant in the Human Genome Project, mapping 30 per cent of the human DNA sequence as part of an international collaboration, the beginning of the 'genetic revolution'.

London, Oxford and Cambridge are sometimes described as a 'golden triangle' Its backing kept the results public, allowing researchers to freely and permanently obtain access to the data. There is also great international exchange of findings and personnel.

However the chain that runs from research to application can be long: famously, while the first observation by Alexander Fleming of the inhibitive impact of penicillin on bacteria in a London hospital laboratory took place in 1928, development was slow. It was not until the galvanising impact of World War II that its mass production began – but in the USA, and for military use; in 1945 it became available for civilian use in the USA and then as a prescription drug in the UK in 1946. The translational research chain may often be shorter today, but Britain still lacks the unique and collaborative research and funding environment of Boston or San Francisco where federal funding and an efficient system for converting research into business propositions thrive. This is one reason why companies emerging from UK science parks frequently end up as subsidiaries of US companies.

Scottish-born Sir Alexander Fleming (1881-1955): he discovered penicillin while working at St Mary's hospital, Paddington

However the British state has also invested impressively in life sciences. The huge £650 million Francis Crick Institute opened in 2016, a unique partnership between the Medical Research Council, Cancer Research UK, the Wellcome Trust, and three of the University of London colleges – University, Imperial and King's. It is a biomedical discovery centre probing the scientific mechanisms of living things, why disease develops and seeking new ways to treat, diagnose and prevent cancer, heart disease, stroke, infections, and neurodegenerative diseases. When fully occupied and operational, the Institute will employ 1,250 scientists, with staff from 70 countries, making it the biggest single biomedical research centre in Europe.

The Francis Crick Institute, London, named after the British co-discoverer of the structure of DNA

Applied research in the life sciences implies the manufacture and development of drugs. Half of the total investment in pharmaceuticals R&D in Europe takes place in the UK and the pharmaceuticals sector is by some margin the biggest UK business spender on R&D. The industry is also one of Britain's leading manufacturing sectors: the value of pharmaceutical exports in 2013 was £21.3 billion, the third greatest of nine major UK industrial sectors.

The UK's two largest pharmaceutical companies are among the most successful in the world. GlaxoSmithKline is the sixth biggest pharma company in the world by sales – the product of numerous mergers and acquisitions dating back to the 19th century. Its R&D is in three primary areas: pharmaceuticals, vaccines and consumer healthcare; it says it invested over £3 billion in these areas in 2015. GlaxoSmithKline has operations worldwide, and its biggest single market is the USA, but its headquarters are in London and it operates important R&D and manufacturing facilities here, with R&D based in Hertfordshire, to the north of London. AstraZeneca, an Anglo-Swedish descendant of ICI, also has global reach and strong partnerships with universities across the UK; it is the 8th biggest pharmaceuticals company in the world by sales. AstraZeneca's former UK research base was at Alderley Park in Cheshire (near Manchester), where many cancer drugs were developed in a 40-year stay before it relocated to Cambridge.

Half of the total investment in pharmaceuticals R&D in Europe takes place in the UK

Digital business is a second key sector and comprises both digital innovation per se and the application of digital technology to older industry. At the dawn of the digital revolution, British inventors were prominent: Clive Sinclair produced an affordable home computer; Tim Berners-Lee invented the worldwide web, the single most important development in science and technology for decades. Adoption of new technology occurs fast. Britons spend £2,000 annually online, more than any other country and

Sir Clive Sinclair: his inventions were an engaging mix of the commercially successful and downright eccentric

one-third (mainly the young) use a mobile phone as a first online resort. 78 per cent of adults went online daily in 2015, well over twice the number nine years earlier; social networking is used by over three-fifths of adults, 80 per cent of them daily. 86 per cent of households in Great Britain have internet access and 95 per cent of British homes and businesses will have access to superfast broadband by the end of 2017. Yet this receptiveness was not enough to sustain a domestic industry: this booming home market for digital products is largely supplied by imports.

Much of the digital technology sector exists in clusters – the equivalent of the science parks which host the country's life sciences. London is the largest centre, followed by Reading & Bracknell (Berkshire) and Bristol & Bath (Gloucestershire/Somerset). Perhaps the best-known digital technology cluster is around a convergence of roads in Shoreditch just beyond the City of London: it is a booming area for start-ups popularly referred to, in semi-ironic reference to the USA's 'Silicon Valley', as 'Silicon Roundabout'.

Scotland also has an area of its central belt dubbed 'Silicon Glen', though its history has been rather different. Computer and peripherals manufacturers began operating there in the earliest days of the industry and by 1996 Silicon Glen was producing 35 per cent of all the PCs built in Europe. Since then, however, much of the computer manufacturing in Silicon Glen has collapsed or relocated in the face of competition from lower-cost countries in Eastern Europe or Asia. In 2002, the value of Scottish computer equipment exports was £5.6 billion, with electronics accounting for 28 per cent of Scotland's exports. By 2014, the export value was down to £1.1 billion or 4 per cent of exports.

Engineering, aerospace and defence

The Royal Academy of Engineering (founded 1976) champions excellence in all fields of engineering. Its first fellows included some of the UK's finest engineers: the jet engine visionary Sir Frank Whittle; design guru Sir Ove Arup; radar pioneer Sir George MacFarlane; bouncing bomb inventor Sir Barnes Wallis; Lord Hinton, who had spearheaded the UK's early lead in the peaceful use of nuclear energy; and Sir Maurice Wilkes, father of the UK computer industry. Others had yet to do their greatest work: Sir Frederick Warner, would lead the first international inspection team into the Chernobyl meltdown ten years later.

In many areas of engineering, Britain's one time eminence has evaporated. Revolutionary designs in shipbuilding came from Britain for centuries, and on the eve of World War I about half the world's shipping was built in UK yards, principally in the North of England, Scotland and Northern Ireland. Now that whole industry has virtually disappeared, what remains being mainly dependent on UK military contracts. Symptomatically, while Britain had the world's first civil nuclear energy programme, opening the first power station for the commercial generation of nuclear energy at Calder Hall (Windscale) in 1956, it is now dependent on French and Chinese expertise to develop new generation nuclear power stations. However, areas of strength do continue: perhaps the best examples of applied engineering in the UK are offered by the aerospace, defence, security and space industries.

the UK has the second largest aerospace industry in the world

With a £31 billion turnover and 3,000 companies employing about 230,000 people, the UK has the second largest aerospace industry in the world, after the USA. The aerospace sector spent £1.4 billion on R&D in 2012 which represented 12% of total R&D spend across manufacturing industry. The major domestic firms are BAE Systems, GKN and Rolls-Royce, but their global rivals tend to have UK operations too. Yet the sector also has Europe's largest number of small and medium sized enterprise companies, specialising in the design and manufacture of large aircraft wings, production of aircraft engines, design and manufacture of helicopters, building landing gear systems, and creating advanced aircraft systems. Rolls-Royce is the world's second largest aircraft engine manufacturer.

Sir Frank Whittle, inventor of the turbo-jet engine

A large maintenance, repair and overhaul sector services military and civil aircraft. It accounts for one-sixth of the global business.

The British aerospace sector pioneered the jet revolution in civil aircraft after World War II, with a series of pathbreaking planes that culminated in the supersonic jetliner Concorde, which first flew in 1969. However engineering skill was not always matched by commercial judgement. Concorde, a prestige project of Anglo-French cooperation designed to take a small number of passengers at twice the speed of sound and great cost, proved not to be the future: instead US manufacturer Boeing, with the 747 jet (which also flew for the first time in 1969, with commercial flights from 1970), took control of the skies with its formula of subsonic speed and large numbers of passengers at lower cost. By the time Concorde finally began commercial flights in 1976 it was already a white elephant. Ultimately Concorde was only ever bought by the national carriers of Britain and France, the countries which built it, and only 14 were ever used for commercial flights.

Defence remains a major part of the UK's aerospace sector. Aircraft development was enormously stimulated by both world wars, World War I beginning just 11 years after the first powered flight by the Wright brothers in the USA. From the outset a close relationship developed between the UK's burgeoning aircraft industry and the country's defence requirements and it has never faltered. In addition to BAE Systems, the world's third biggest defence contractor, a number of other international companies work on defence projects in the UK and the defence industry supports over 32,000 research, design and engineering jobs. According to the Stockholm Institute for Peace Research, so far this century Britain has ranked fifth in the volume of its arms exports, behind the USA, Russia, Germany and France, though in 2015 overtaken for the first time by China.

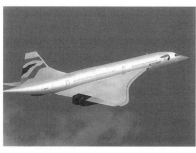

Concorde: an icon of engineering design but a commercial failure

The UK space sector works on exploration of space and

technologies for space-based communication. Galileo, Europe's global navigation satellite system, maintains 30 satellites, positioned in space around the earth. The first four were all built in the UK and the payloads of the next 22 will be manufactured in Guildford (Surrey). The ExoMars rover (to be launched in 2018) will land on Mars in 2019. Airbus Defence and Space is its lead builder and five UK universities will lead the development of its panoramic camera and CCD camera. NovaSAR is a constellation of four satellites designed for low cost missions to help monitor drug trafficking and illegal fishing: its first satellite will be built in the UK by SST.

Appendix: Invention and innovation

In 2013 the Radio Times listed 50 British inventions spanning four centuries. While some doubtless have rival claimants from other countries or were perfected or first brought to a mass market elsewhere, the list at least serves to illustrate one long-standing aspect of British inventiveness: its sheer eclectic diversity, with no field untouched.

The Reflecting Telescope (1668);
the Seed Drill (1701);
the Marine Chronometer (1761);
the Spinning Frame (1768);
the Toothbrush (1770);
Soda Water (1772);
the Hydraulic Press (1795);
the Steam Engine (1801);
Waterproof Material (1823);
the Glider (1804);
the Tension-Spoked Wheel (1808);
the Tin Can (1810);
the Modern Fire Extinguisher (1818);
the Electric Motor (1821);
Cement (1824);
the Passenger Railway (1825);
the Lawnmower (1827);
Photography (1835);
the Electric Telegraph (1837);
the Chocolate Bar (1847);
the Hypodermic Syringe (1853);
Synthetic Dye (1856);
the Bessemer Process (1856);
Linoleum (1860);
the Sewage System (1865);
the Modern Torpedo (1866);

the Light Bulb (1880);
the Steam Turbine (1884);
the Safety Bicycle (1885);
the Pneumatic Tyre (1887);
the Thermos Flask (1892);
the Electric Vacuum Cleaner (1901);
Disc Brakes (1902);
Stainless Steel (1913);
the Military Tank (1914);
Television (1925);
the Catseye (1933);
the Jet Engine (1937);
the Electronic Programmable Computer (1943);
the Hovercraft (1953);
the Automatic Kettle (1955);
Float Glass (1959);
the Hip Replacement (1962);
the Carbon Fibre (1963);
the Collapsible Baby Buggy (1965);
the ATM (1967);
the Wind-Up Radio (1991);
the Worldwide Web (1989);
Graphene (2004);
Steri-Spray (2008).

21.   A green and pleasant land?

> I will not cease from Mental Fight,
> Nor shall my Sword sleep in my hand:
> Till we have built Jerusalem,
> In England's green & pleasant Land.
>
> *William Blake (1808)*

The British countryside has a degree of familiarity to many visitors even before they arrive. There are the land or seascapes – the Scottish Highlands, the Lake District (Cumbria), the Jurassic Coast (South Devon and Dorset), and the Giant's Causeway (in Northern Ireland), the last two UNESCO natural World Heritage sites. Then there is a built environment spanning Stonehenge, the Houses of Parliament and the 13th century (Edwardian) castles of Wales: these are some of the 23 UNESCO-designated World Heritage cultural sites. Visitors to such places make the UK the eighth most popular tourism destination globally.

Why do they come? Many, of course, for London, in Europe rivalled only by Paris as an international destination. But others come to seek out the real Highlands, their imaginations stirred by images of brooding mountains and unfathomable lochs, a rugged landscape purple with heather. Others yet seek out rural England: a Cotswold scene, perhaps, a cluster of thatch-roofed and honey-coloured stone cottages bordering a village green, edged by ancient church and pub; here the natural and built environments seem in harmony. The skylines and cityscapes of London, Edinburgh and Oxford are instantly recognisable. But beyond them lies the built evidence of up to five millennia of human occupation, the more ancient the less easily distinguishable from the natural landscape. Most of England – though less of Wales, Scotland and Ireland – has

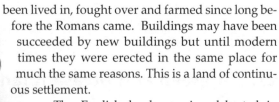

been lived in, fought over and farmed since long before the Romans came. Buildings may have been
succeeded by new buildings but until modern
times they were erected in the same place for
much the same reasons. This is a land of continuous settlement.

The English landscape is celebrated in
countless paintings, poems and novels. Rural
Suffolk may seem almost familiar to the visitor from the paintings of Constable; the English
Lakes courtesy of Wordsworth; the Yorkshire
moors thanks to the Brontës; the heaths and lush

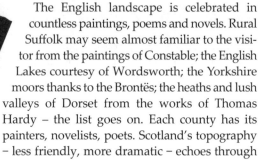

Thomas Hardy (1840-1928): the 'Wessex' of his novels was rooted in real places and landscapes

valleys of Dorset from the works of Thomas
Hardy – the list goes on. Each county has its
painters, novelists, poets. Scotland's topography
– less friendly, more dramatic – echoes through
many locations visited by Scott's Waverley novels or Victorian
painterly tributes to the Highlands. Wales is also rich in natural
drama, endless space and rugged coast, though its literature (in two
languages) is less well-known. Northern Ireland, indeed the whole
island of Ireland, is replete with rural myth and much remains a land
of villages and small towns.

If these places now lived only in memory they might have less
power, but the vistas that entranced Constable and shaped
Wordsworth are in different ways protected and preserved and can
for the most part still be seen. If a 'green and pleasant' England survives it is because planning controls prevent ribbon development beyond town and city. England is a densely populated country but over
a third of its area is protected by being in the green belt, a national
park, or designated an 'area of outstanding natural beauty'.

New towns and the green belt

The UK is highly urbanised. In Scotland (68 people per sq km in
2013), Northern Ireland (135 per sq km) and Wales (149 per sq km)
the overall density of population is not high, but most of the population in those three countries live in often closely packed towns

and conurbations. In England, with a population density of 413 per sq km, over 82 per cent of people live in larger towns and cities, leaving under 9.5 million in rural areas (i.e. outside settlements with above 10,000 residents) – small towns and their fringes, villages, hamlets or in isolation. They might be in remote, sparsely-populated areas, peripheral-urban dwellers or coastal dwellers. From the start of the 20th century the appearance of the countryside has been shaped by two contradictory impulses: the need adequately to house an expanding population and the wish to preserve the countryside as an amenity for urban dwellers.

Historically various philanthropic industrialists had created model towns for their workers. New Lanark in Scotland was built from the 1780s onwards to provide employment in mills and housing and amenities for the workers; its utopian aspirations for a time drew admiring visitors from many countries. It is now a World Heritage site as is Saltaire (near Bradford), laid out in the 1850s by Sir Titus Salt around his textile mill. Later came Bournville, a suburb created from the 1890s on the edge of Birmingham by the Cadbury chocolate-making family.

These were, however, isolated ventures and in essence company towns. Much wider in ambition was the garden cities movement associated with Ebenezer Howard: it sought to incorporate rural crafts in new housing provision, proposing to build small urban centres with 'the free gifts of Nature: fresh air, sunlight, breathing room and playing room'. Letchworth (in Hertfordshire, north of London) became the first such place in 1902 and still bears the imprint of Howard's vision; Welwyn Garden City, also in Hertfordshire followed soon after World War I. While those were the only such complete towns created in Britain before World War II, some of the ideas were reflected less systemat-

Sir Ebenezer Howard (1850-1928), garden city pioneer

ically or ambitiously in the better-quality suburban development of the inter-war years. The suburban delights of what John Betjeman called 'metroland', as promoted by speculative builders, made many a nod to the style of Letchworth.

After World War II, fresh impetus was given to the creation of purpose-built 'new towns' intended to be complete communities, formalised in the New Towns Act of 1946. This was the era of state planning in every area of life and blueprints for a better tomorrow were very much the fashion. The intensive bombing of London had destroyed many homes and one solution was seen to be in the re-housing of people in new towns in a ring around the capital. This resulted in the creation (submerging pre-existing small towns or villages) of Stevenage, Crawley, Hemel Hempstead, Harlow, Hat-field, Basildon and Bracknell. Similar new towns were created in other parts of the UK, such as Washington, Skelmersdale and Pe-terlee in the North, Corby and Telford in the Midlands, East Kil-bride and Cumbernauld in Scotland and Cwmbran in Wales.

By the 1960s ... the new town movement had largely run out of steam

By the 1960s, however, the new town movement had largely run out of steam. State planning was giving way to a new emphasis on individual choice; the new towns were criticised as soulless, lacking both rural charm and the vi-brancy of city life; much of the building had been rushed and the built environment, so enticing in architects' plans, came to look shoddy. In a smaller way, the British new town experience began to resemble the story of Brasilia. The final big new venture was the creation of Milton Keynes from 1967: an ambitious project for a big town created virtually from nothing half-way between London and Birmingham, Oxford and Cambridge and designed on a grid layout for the age of the car but with the residential districts having a semi-rural aspect. Ironically this final project proved also to be perhaps the most successful: Milton Keynes has grown to a place of a quar-ter-million population, with a buoyant economy, yet it is possible to cross it by road and barely see a house such is the landscaping.

While the new towns movement was one response to the pres-sures of a growing population, it was not the main one: that was the outward expansion of towns and cities by the creation of suburbia. Four million new homes were built between the world wars, mostly on green fields, and this stimulated legislation to curb 'ribbon development', urban sprawl along main roads out of towns. In the 1930s planners were already considering surrounding London – a city that had grown by absorbing villages – with a cordon of countryside. A 1947 law required local authorities to control land use and development in detail: essentially, planning permission would be required even though some sectors, such as agriculture, were exempt. By 1955, a national 'green belt' system was in place to contain urban sprawl and it today embraces 13 per cent of England's land area. Some indication of what might have happened without it can be seen on the arterial roads that stretch out of the capital, flanked by endless rows of that peculiar contribution of the British to architecture – the semi-detached house.

Today the green belt's aims are specific: to check spread around large built-up areas, prevent neighbouring towns merging, defend the countryside against encroachment, preserve the special character of historic towns and assist urban regeneration by encouraging the recycling of derelict land. Construction of new buildings is deemed 'inappropriate'. All the principal English cities and conurbations are surrounded by green belt: it encloses some 30 million urban-dwellers inside its boundaries. They benefit from access to nearby countryside, outdoor sport, attractive landscapes and nature conservation, but agriculture and forestry are meant to thrive too.

critics ... wonder why the urban population must be so hemmed in

Yet the green belt has critics who compare England's 10 per cent of developed land to Germany's 13 per cent (despite Germany having a lower density of population) and wonder why the urban population must be so hemmed in by borders defined decades ago. The green belt can in places seem little more than a *cordon sanitaire* of dreary ploughed fields, crisscrossed with arterial roads and electricity pylons, devoid of charm and amenities: many cities, including London, have far more agreeable woodland and parks within their boundaries, readily accessible by foot and public transport to those who seek green spaces.

The country's huge and growing need for new housing may in any case lead to a relaxation of controls as developers (especially in London) run out of brownfield sites to build ever-smaller and more congested housing units. Beyond England, Scotland has ten designated green belt areas. Wales – it is largely a land of open spaces – has but one strip between Newport and Cardiff and Northern Ireland has abandoned the idea.

National parks and areas of outstanding natural beauty

After World War II, the finest landscapes in England and Wales were awarded special legal status to ensure their preservation 'for the nation's benefit'. In 1949 they were designated either as national parks or as areas of outstanding natural beauty (AONBs), depending on their size, scale and aims. There are ten national parks in England (the Norfolk Broads, Dartmoor, Exmoor, the Lake District, the New Forest, Northumberland, the North York Moors, the Peak District, the Yorkshire Dales, and the South Downs), three in Wales (the Brecon Beacons, the Pembrokeshire Coast, and Snowdonia) and two in Scotland (the Cairngorms and Loch Lomond & the Trossachs). The English and Welsh national parks each have their own independent authority, funded by central government to conserve and enhance their natural beauty, wildlife and cultural heritage, and to promote public appreciation of their special qualities. Each must foster the economic and social well-being of its local communities (and protect the interests of navigation in the case of the Broads). These are for the most part, by British standards, unpopulated areas: the Yorkshire Dales national park, newly expanded almost to the borders of the Lake District, is reported to have a population of only 20,000 in its 840 square miles. The Scottish parks (accountable to the Scottish government) have more specific aims: to conserve and enhance the natural and cultural heritage, to promote sustainable use of natural resources, to promote understanding and enjoyment of each area's special qualities, and to promote sustainable economic and social development.

Because of their fragile natural beauty, the primary purpose of the 46 AONBs is to conserve and enhance the natural beauty of the landscape and, additionally, to meet the need for quiet enjoyment of the countryside and to have regard for the interests of those who live and work there. AONBs tend to be smaller than national parks. 33 are wholly in England, four wholly in Wales, one straddles the English/Welsh border and there are eight in Northern Ireland. Together they cover 18 per cent of the countryside and include some (compared to the national parks) relatively highly populated rural areas of southern Britain. Scotland has several distinct designations meeting similar aims. Both national parks and AONBs contain living communities and economic activity: sheep farming in Wales or Scotland illustrates that they conserve a worked environment. These are not the uninhabited wildernesses of American national parks: each kind of protected area may contain not only livestock and crops but also preserved buildings.

Built heritage

Nestling in the English and Welsh landscape are at least 70 abbeys left in ruins by the dissolution of the monasteries (1536-1541) by King Henry VIII and later neglect; dozens more fell victim to the Reformation in Scotland. All three countries, as well as Northern Ireland have hundreds of castles reduced by military obsolescence to disuse. In addition, almost 2,000 privately and charitably owned historic houses and castles still stand, often – though not always – 'listed' buildings (see below). A few are still inhabited by the descendants of the families they were built for.

Around 500, including Highclere (the 'real' Downton Abbey of ITV's class-infected soap) open their doors to visitors. However, the majority of the most historic great buildings are in public hands. Taken

Rievaulx, a wealthy Cistercian abbey in Yorkshire dissolved by Henry VIII

together, this large portfolio of mouldering or well-preserved piles
– including many symbols of brutal conquest or ostentatious wealth
– is now packaged as a statement of the British past. This reinven-
tion is the work of three large national organisations whose astute
marketing shapes national consciousness.

The National Trust (founded 1895) protects and opens to the
public over 350 historic houses, gardens and ancient monuments.
It is Britain's largest voluntary organisation, claiming a prodigious
4.5 million members and 62,000 volunteers. 20 million pay to enter
its properties; an estimated 100 million visit its open air sites. It is
and always was a private and charitable body, greatly
benefiting from the generosity of co-founder and
social reformer Octavia Hill, children's author
Beatrix Potter, and countless others. Though independent of the state the National Trust plays a
quasi-official role in mediating the nation's surviving past, its evolution shaped over time by
legislation. In 1965 it launched the Neptune
Coastline Campaign to protect the coast
against development and preserve it for the na-
tion in perpetuity: 775 miles of the coast in England, Wales and
Northern Ireland are now in National Trust hands.

A typical National Trust property sign

The separate National Trust for
Scotland, established in 1931, has **The National Trust ... is**
vast responsibilities: 190,000 coun- **Britain's largest voluntary**
tryside acres, 46 'Munros' (moun- **organisation**
tains over 3,000-feet high), 394 miles
of mountain footpaths, 10,000 archaeological sites, 35 major gardens, seven national nature reserves, 45 sites of special scientific interest and St Kilda (64 kilometres into the Atlantic), which is
Britain's only dual (natural and cultural) World Heritage site.

English Heritage (with its national counterparts, see below) is
sometimes perceived by the public as a rival to the National Trust.
Indeed, the two organisations long squabbled over many buildings
of historical importance, turf wars reflecting different approaches
to art conservation. Government had managed old castles and
abbeys since 1882, but hesitated to bankroll the maintenance of

One of English Heritage's premier properties: Osborne House, Queen Victoria's retreat on the Isle of Wight, and where she died in 1901

huge roofed buildings stuffed with art. Ultimately, a rough division of labour left country houses with the National Trust while the Ministry of Works (a government department) retained older monuments. English Heritage evolved from this ministry and today excels at popularisation and access, aiming to capture visitors' imaginations through innovative approaches to history. In 2015 the government relieved English Heritage of the national heritage collection and of its building control responsibilities. Freed from these distractions the organisation retains over 400 historic buildings, monuments and sites (66 castles, 58 prehistoric sites and 53 Roman ones, 27 forts and defences and 84 ecclesiastical sites). Over time it has also plugged the stately homes gap in its portfolio, amassing 47 'halls, houses and domestic dwellings', not to mention seven palaces. Collectively, these attract ten million visitors annually.

> *Government ... hesitated to bankroll the maintenance of huge roofed buildings stuffed with art*

English Heritage's former responsibilities passed to two new organisations. Historic England now champions the nation's wider heritage, runs the listing system, deals with planning matters and dispenses grants. Each year it advises on more than 20,000 applications for planning permission or listed building consent. The National Heritage List for England (NHLE) covers buildings ranging from prehistoric monuments to office blocks, battlefields and parks, all of which benefit from legal protection to differing degrees. It is the only official and up-to-date database of all nationally designated heritage assets.

Different arrangements prevail in the minority nations. Cadw (a Welsh word meaning 'to keep' or 'to protect') is the Welsh government's historic environment service. It conserves the country's heritage, helping people understand and care about their history, sustaining its sense of place and cultural identity. Northern Ireland's built past is directly managed by the devolved government. Meanwhile Historic Environment Scotland has fused two state-owned bodies, Historic Scotland and the Royal Commission on the Ancient and Historic Monuments of Scotland. In contrast to arrangements in England, the new organisation combines managing and curating over 300 sites with the scheduling of monuments, listing buildings and handling scheduled consent.

Across the UK, the listing system protects about half a million buildings of special architectural and historic interest. The older they are, the more likely they are to be *the listing system* listed. All pre-1700 buildings in close *protects about half a* to their original condition are listed, as *million buildings* are most of those built in 1700-1840. Eligibility usually starts only after a building is 30 years old. Buildings are placed in a complex grading system that awards them a degree of protection. This ought to free them from demolition and insensitive or unscholarly alterations, though it does not always succeed. In this work the UK's various parastatal bodies depend greatly on the alertness of a range of voluntary organisations: the Victorian Society, the Twentieth-century Society, the Camden Society and so on. Walkers and ramblers are an important source of information in their work, equipped as they often are not only with highly-accurate large-scale maps (see below) but also with Sir Nikolaus Pevsner's monumental 46-volume series (1951-1974) of county-by-county guide books *The Buildings of Eng-*

land (to which volumes on Scotland, Wales and Northern Ireland have been added).

Natural England absorbed the Countryside Agency in 2006 to become government advisor on the natural environment. It assists land managers and farmers, protects wildlife and landscapes, advises on the protection of the marine environment in inshore waters, improves public access to the coastline, manages 140 national nature reserves and their national trails, provides planning advice and wildlife licences

Nikolaus Pevsner (1902-1983): a refugee from Hitler's Germany, he became the supreme chronicler of England's built heritage

through the planning system and manages the restoration of wildlife habitats. Its broad remit extends to 'rights of way', a contentious matter not finally resolved until the early 21st century. There is now widespread access for walking or certain other leisure activities, plus the traditional public rights of way (footpaths or bridleways) plus a right to roam on open access land including mountains, moors, heaths, downs, common land and some land around the coast path. Even access to private land may still be feasible with landowner permission (termed 'permissive access') or if local tradition upholds it. Access brings risks for landowners, so Natural England publishes a Countryside Code for England and Wales.

Natural England believes walking, often with a dog, to be the most popular reason for visiting the natural environment. No-one in England lives much further than about 75 miles from the sea and this shapes a major strategic goal of the organisation: the England coast path – a new national trail giving people the right of access around the entire open coast for the first time. Here and there this includes 'spreading room', land beyond the trail itself but part of the coastal margin and with public right of access. By 2020 it will be complete, with 2,700 miles of stunning walking routes. Walking is a major pastime, made easier by the country being astonishingly well-mapped, thanks to the publicly-owned Ordnance Survey (OS), a product of 18th century Enlightenment inquiry. In England nearly half the population go for a walk at least five times weekly. OS maps – found of various vintages in many homes – coupled with 'Pevsner' provide the necessary detail for walkers, ramblers and cyclists to explore the 'countryside'– a reassuring term for anywhere that isn't urbanised. And since the British Isles lack wildernesses and predators on humans, they are safe.

Village life

Country walkers cannot go far without coming to a village. But villages, indeed country life generally, face many challenges. The 20th century shift from public to private transport mostly cost them their bus services, and few are fortunate enough to retain – or even be near – a train station. Many attractive village dwellings now belong to second-home owners whose intermittent presence brings little local spending power; amenities (cottage hospitals, cinemas, shops, doctors' surgeries) increasingly relocate to bigger towns or out-of-town centres, accessible only by car. Jobs are scarce: the almost one million home workers in rural areas comprise one-fifth of workers living there, almost twice the rate of urban residents.

Many rural communities resent becoming leisure locations for urban-dwellers and struggle to sustain economic viability. There are national initiatives to help them, for example by subsidising uniform provision of high-speed broadband across the country. Some small settlements are fighting back: in 2016, 80 per cent of residents in the attractive Cornish coastal town of St. Ives voted to permit new housing projects only if reserved for full-time residents – a move aimed at the sale of homes to second-home purchasers. However, the drift away of young people from Cornwall owes more to the lack of well-paid full-time employment in a county far from any economic hubs than it does to the arrival of second-homers. Some parts of the country have flourishing villages sustained by incomers who create clusters of small enterprises, contribute to community organisations, run the village shop as a co-operative and send their children to the local school. However, in broad terms, there are wor- *there are worrying signs ... 50 per cent of the rural population is 45 or older* rying signs: 50 per cent of the rural population is 45 or older; it is 40 per cent in urban areas. With continuing movement of younger people to the cities in combination with an ageing population, that divergence is likely to grow wider.

Three buildings are traditionally present in a village: the church, the pub and the school. A 2005 survey identified over 37,000 English churches, long the centre of community life. While many are in cities and large towns, a parish church is the most visible clue to an enduring village settlement. Two-thirds of Church of England parishes (some serving several churches) are in rural areas, their churches often in a poor state of repair and plagued by thieves who even steal lead flashings protecting the roof from water ingress. Medieval churches are commonly built upon the remains of older churches beneath which may be yet older places of worship – even Roman temples. Villages are often built around organised belief, unlike towns which are more likely to reflect the military exigencies of Roman or Saxon times.

About 50,000 pubs survive. Their number has fallen steeply but they still host over 15 million weekly visitors. 'Country pubs' are especially sought after. They may be idealised as centres of village life, as in the Radio 4 soap *The Archers* – broadcast continuously since 1951, the world's longest-running radio soap opera. The inhabitants of Ambridge, its fictional village, appear to spend a great deal of time in 'The Bull', but with other amenities vanished, what else are they to do? To remain competitive some country pubs have reinvented themselves as upmarket dining locations; many have closed. Rural schools were once a birthright of country-reared chil-

dren who might spill out onto the village green. But these, like pubs, have suffered as the population centre of gravity shifted from country to town. Luckier villages have retained their schools for infant or junior children but sec-

'The Old Bull', Inkberrow, Worcestershire, reputedly the inspiration for 'The Bull' in radio soap The Archers

ondary school is likely to be a car drive away. The price of fuel for cars is a major issue for country-dwellers.

Concern about the decline of rural life has lineage. The Women's Institute (WI) was formed in 1915 with twin aims: to revitalise rural communities and encourage women to become more involved in producing food during the First World War. Since then its aims have broadened and the WI is now the UK's largest voluntary women's organisation with some 212,000 members and 6,600 local branches. The WI for decades supported women in an extension of their traditional domestic role, and for that reason attracted satirical attention. But it has become a more campaigning organisation and, along with more formal institutions – church and school – offers a network to which village and small town life owes its enduring vitality.

Farming

The countryside that quite quickly comes into view on a car or rail trip out of any city is intensively farmed: British agricultural (unlike its industrial) productivity is quite high. While Britain's industrial revolution was a global first, it was predicated on an agrarian revolution. But as the first people gathered in cities, they began to lose their connection to the land. Over time food became a commodity, purchased not grown. As cities and towns expanded the rural proportion fell. At times of national crisis such as the two world wars the land was rediscovered. Civilian 'land armies', often of women labourers, raised food output in the face of shortage; neglected gardens were turned over to cultivation. But food shortages have been unknown since the early 1950s when rationing ended. Increasingly food is sourced globally; the strategic need to be self-sufficient has evaporated. Today, only 54 per cent of UK food consumption originates at home. The value of imports is greater than the value of exports in ten of eleven categories of food, feed and drink tabulated by official statistics. The exception is 'Beverages', largely due to exports of Scotch whisky.

Entry to the EEC in 1973 revolutionised British farming. Already intensively mechanised, it now entered a financial regime primarily designed to sustain the multitude of small peasant farmers in some of the founding nations. This Common Agricultural Policy (CAP) notoriously allowed the accumulation of large surpluses of unwanted produce. At first British farming, which had lost traditional outlets in the empire, failed to replace them with European markets. Its high capital/labour ratio should have given it an edge but European farmers had a guaranteed market. Yet the sector has shown great resilience, diversifying (sometimes merging with tourism), learning to promote product provenance and benefiting from a consumer swing towards localism. Under EU law a food name scheme (appellations) specifies regional and traditional foods whose authenticity and origin can be guaranteed: a named food or drink is legally protected against imitation (see chapter 11 for the British list). Southern England has also returned to the vine with 470 growers and 135 wineries. Renewed pride in traditional British food is evident in the media, shops and markets. Popular cooking and food programmes seem to nourish the trend.

Today's agricultural workforce numbers less than one-third of a million, below one per cent of total employment (though its contribution to GNP is greater). While the population of England has increased by 77 per cent since the start of the twentieth century, rural areas too distant from cities to become commuter dormitories often have populations little changed since 1901: the small towns may have grown somewhat, adding jobs in services that have no connection with agriculture, but the villages and hamlets have lost their populations of farmhands, farriers, carters, blacksmiths and other rural trades. Rural depopulation is even starker in parts of Scotland and Wales, countries where the overall increase in population has been much less than in England.

Today's agricultural workforce numbers less than one-third of a million

For many Britons the countryside has become a product to be enjoyed vicariously in an urban setting via accessories purchased on a visit to a National Trust site or food from a city-located 'farmers' market'. A sanitised version of farming bears little resemblance to the real thing which retains its power to shock a population largely ignorant of how agriculture works. Periodically, public controversies erupt that illustrate a considerable gulf between the sensibilities of country and town. The 2005 foot-and-mouth outbreak (an emergency for the one, an inconvenience for the other); successive protests over fuel prices (car dependency is great in rural areas starved of public transport); the badger culls of 2012 onwards (deemed vital by farmers scared of bovine TB but offensive to sentimental townies) and popular resistance to genetically-modified (GM) foods shed a harsh light on meagre urban knowledge of agricultural production methods. Ironically, such knowledge as urban-dwellers have of the realities of agricultural life often comes from *The Archers*, discussed above: originally conceived as a vehicle for providing up-to-date farming advice for the rural population, its audience of 5 million listeners is today mostly in towns and cities.

But nothing illustrates the gulf of understanding better than controversy over fox-hunting. Attempts to ban it, mostly promoted by Labour MPs, stretch back at least to 1949. Animal rights campaigners effectively publicised the horrors of the hunt. Urban-dwellers long had little acquaintance with foxes (though they have now become common in cities), judged them by their noble appearance, and regarded all forms of hunting as upper-class recreation – 'the unspeakable in pursuit of the uneatable', as Oscar Wilde put it. To farmers and many country-dwellers foxes were simply predatory vermin and hunting a jolly way of keeping their numbers down.

A Countryside Alliance sprang up in defence of rural pursuits such as hunting and shooting. It argued that shooting was worth £2 billion annually to the rural economy and supported 74,000 jobs, that 600,000 shot and two million hectares were

Although fox-hunting is banned, many hunts still meet to follow artificial trails for the 'thrill of the chase' and for the English love of dressing up in costumes

actively managed for shooting, bringing conservation benefits and preserving important habitats. But in 2005 it could not stop the Labour government making fox hunting with dogs (and hare-coursing) illegal in England and Wales (it had been banned in Scotland three years earlier). Ranged against the Countryside Alliance was a range of animal welfare organisations including the world's oldest, the Royal Society for Prevention of Cruelty to Animals (RSPCA, founded 1824).

This cleavage of countryside from all towns of significant size may mark an identity conflict more profound than regional difference. It is imperfectly reflected in politics, where once the Ministry of Agriculture, Fisheries and Food (MAFF) acted as a conveyor belt for the farming interest. Today MAFF has been swallowed up by the Department for Environment, Food and Rural Affairs: the farming interest is now muffled by environmental concerns. In the House of Commons, nearly all constituencies with significant tracts of cultivated land ('the shires') have Conservative MPs. While farming retains their support, its social weight nationally seems slight.

the farming interest is now muffled by environmental concerns

In the 2016 EU referendum the farming community might have been expected to rally to the Remain cause: most farmers receive substantial EU subsidies and many depend on migrant labour, especially for the tough work of picking in the fields. A Conservative prime minister (representing a country seat) was the leading Remain campaigner. But the voice of the National Farmers' Union (strongly pro-Europe at the time of the 1975 referendum) this time was muted, sensitive to a rising critical mood among its members, and urged only a qualified Remain vote. It knew that many farmers found EU bureaucracy irksome but it was also apparent that, whatever the logic of economic self-interest, many in farming had come to share with their rural neighbours a generalised dislike of the social effects of EU migration and had found a message that appealed in the attacks on Brussels and the metropolitan elite. The final vote bristled with hostility: nearly all English rural areas – and all outside the South – returned a thumping landslide for Leave. Identity trumped sectional economic interest.

Index

Names mentioned only in passing or in lists are not indexed.

British Council 151
British Empire 134–5, 233–4, 238
British Museum 115, 117, 152, 227–8
British Science Association 306
British-Irish Council 69
British-Irish intergovernmental confer-
    ence 69
Britishness 10–12
Britten, Benjamin 230
broadcasting 80, 119, 152–3, 220–21, 251–
    9, 327
Brown, Gordon 10, 11, 92, 94, 125–6
Brown government 35
Brunel, Isambard Kingdom 46
buses 118
Bush, George W. 143, 154
Butler, R.A. 15
Butskellism 15

cabinet
    collective responsibility 30
    private education 169
Cadw 324
Cambridge 43
Cambridge University 44, 169, 209, 299,
    306–7, 308
Cambridge University Press 222
Cameron, David 30
    2015 election 31
    coalition government 28–9
    EU referendum 32, 126–7, 132
    ideology 16, 20
    mentions 169, 176, 195, 206
    and the press 263
    resignation 32
    and Scottish referendum 92–3
    and Syria 30–31, 145–6
Cameron government 169
Cancer Research UK 307, 309
Canterbury cathedral 188
Cardiff 84, 86, 129
Carson, Sir Edward 58
cathedrals 188–9
Catholic church 70, 71, 102, 190–91, 192
Channel Islands 1, 69
charities 307
Charles I, King 115, 305
Charles II, King 13, 305
Charles III (play) 27
Charles, Prince of Wales 4–5, 6
chemicals industry 303
Chilcot report 153–4, 298

Christianity 44, 52, 72, 185, 187, 195
Christie, Agatha 221, 222
Church of England 186, 187–90, 194
churches 188–9, 191–2, 327
Churchill, Winston 60, 122, 123, 142–3,
    146, 205, 262
cinema 218, 219–20
cities 40, 105
City of London 110, 114–15, 157–60
civil law 281
civil partnerships 196
civil service 33–4
Civil War 44, 46, 50, 52, 106
class 167–71, 235, 245
classical music 230–31
CND (Campaign for Nuclear Disarma-
    ment) 147
Cold War 139, 143, 148–9
Commonwealth 139–42
computers 300
    see also internet
Concorde 313
Conservative Party
    Brighton bombing 63
    coalition government (2010-15) 16,
        24, 28–9
    and Europe 123, 124–5, 126, 128
    finance 26
    history 15
    ideology 15–16, 20
    membership 21
    and Scotland 90, 91, 94–5, 96
    supporters 56
constituencies 22
constitutional reform 34–6
construction industry 161–2
contraception 273
copyright 224
Corbyn, Jeremy 20, 21, 128
Cornwall 45–6
Coronation Street 55, 56
courts 292, 293–5
Cox, Jo 129
creative arts 214–15
cricket 120, 233, 244–6, 250
crime 288–91
criminal law 281
Cromwell, Oliver 42
Crown Prosecution Service (CPS) 282–3
culture 213–33
    Cities of Culture 232
    creative arts 214–15